D1739943

Thomas Allmer's outstanding book is characteristic for the high relevance of critical theories and critical political economy of the Internet today. He elaborates in an impressive and astute manner an ideology and commodity critique of Internet privacy and surveillance as well as social media's political economy by making use of and actualising Marx and Marxist theory for the dialectical critique of twenty-first century digital capitalism. This book is an essential must-read for anyone who cares about the Internet and wants to know why we should (dis)like Facebook.

Professor Christian Fuchs, *author of* Culture and Economy in the
Age of Social Media, Digital Labour and Karl Marx, Social Media:
A Critical Introduction, Internet and Society

In this book, Thomas Allmer has pulled off the difficult trick of combining a comprehensive re-reading of the relevance of the critical tradition to digital times with original research on internet users, to produce a provocative analysis of the contradictory potentials of new media and the forces shaping their deployment. By reconnecting discussion of privacy, connectivity and surveillance with fundamental underlying questions of emancipation and control it moves debate beyond the superficiality of much contemporary commentary to confront the complex entanglements of emerging media with prevailing patterns of inequality and power and the prospects for challenge and change. Anyone concerned with our possible futures needs to read it.

Graham Murdock, *Professor of Culture and Economy,*
Loughborough University, UK

Critical Theory and Social Media

Social media platforms such as Facebook, YouTube, and Twitter are enormously popular: they are continuously ranked among the most frequently accessed websites worldwide. However, there are as yet few studies which combine critical theoretical and empirical research in the context of digital and social media. The aim of this book is to study the constraints and emancipatory potentials of new media and to assess to what extent digital and social media can contribute to strengthen the idea of the communication and network commons, and a commons-based information society.

Based on a critical theory and political economy approach, this book explores:

- the foundational concepts of a critical theory of media, technology, and society;
- users' knowledge, attitudes, and practices towards the antagonistic character and the potentials and risks of social media;
- whether technological and/or social changes are required in order to bring about real social media and human liberation.

Critical Theory and Social Media examines both academic discourse on, and users' responses to, new media, making it a valuable tool for international scholars and students of sociology, media and communication studies, social theory, new media, and information society studies. Its clear and interesting insights into corporate practices of the global new media sector will mean that it appeals to critical social media users around the world.

Thomas Allmer is Lecturer in Social Justice at the University of Edinburgh, Scotland, UK. His research focuses on critical theory and political economy of media and communication.

Routledge advances in sociology

Critical Theory and Social Media

Between emancipation and commodification

Thomas Allmer

Routledge
Taylor & Francis Group

LONDON AND NEW YORK

First published 2015
by Routledge
2 Park Square, Milton Park, Abingdon, Oxfordshire OX14 4RN

and by Routledge
711 Third Avenue, New York, NY 10017

First issued in paperback 2016

Routledge is an imprint of the Taylor & Francis Group, an informa business

© 2015 Thomas Allmer

The right of Thomas Allmer to be identified as author of this work has been asserted by him in accordance with sections 77 and 78 of the Copyright, Designs and Patents Act 1988.

All rights reserved. No part of this book may be reprinted or reproduced or utilized in any form or by any electronic, mechanical, or other means, now known or hereafter invented, including photocopying and recording, or in any information storage or retrieval system, without permission in writing from the publishers.

Trademark notice: Product or corporate names may be trademarks or registered trademarks, and are used only for identification and explanation without intent to infringe.

British Library Cataloguing in Publication Data
A catalogue record for this book is available from the British Library

Library of Congress Cataloging in Publication Data
Allmer, Thomas.
Critical theory and social media : between emancipation and commodification / Thomas Allmer.
  pages cm. – (Critical theory and social media)
  1. Critical theory. 2. Social media. I. Title.
  HM480.A45 2015
  302.23'1–dc23   2014042642

ISBN: 978-1-138-63682-8 (pbk)
ISBN: 978-1-138-80876-8 (hbk)

Typeset in Times New Roman
by Wearset Ltd, Boldon, Tyne and Wear

Contents

Figures

Tables

Introduction

We live in times of global capitalist crisis, widespread precarious labour, and rising inequality between the rich and the poor. According to the last Global Wage Report of the International Labour Organization (2013), economic productivity has increased and has vastly benefited corporate profits at the expense of wages in almost all parts of the world since the 1960s. The enormous increase of profits was achieved by a relative drop in wage rates. This asymmetrical development has even expanded since the housing and financial crisis occurred in 2007. Figures I.1 and I.2 compare the decrease of the wage share to the relative increase of annual profits in the United States.

According to the Annual Macro-Economic Database (AMECO) of the European Commission's Directorate General for Economic and Financial Affairs (2013), productivity has grown from an index value of 56.3 in 1960 to 104,5 in 2013 in the United States. During the same period, the wage share has fallen

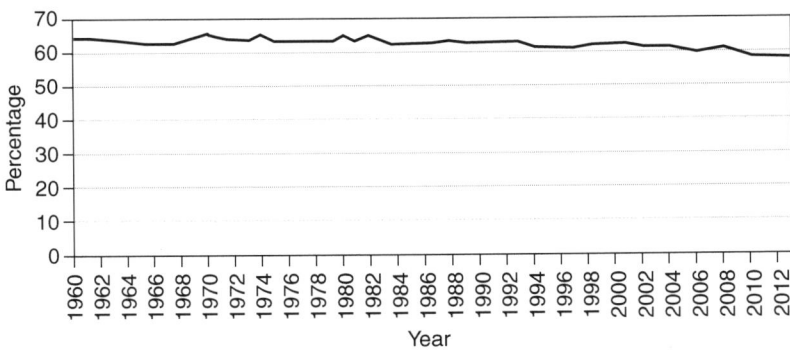

Adjusted wage share, total economy as percentage of gross domestic product (GDP) at current market prices (compensation per employee as percentage of GDP at market prices per person employed)

Figure I.1 The development of the wage share in the United States (source: European Commission's Directorate General for Economic and Financial Affairs (2013)).

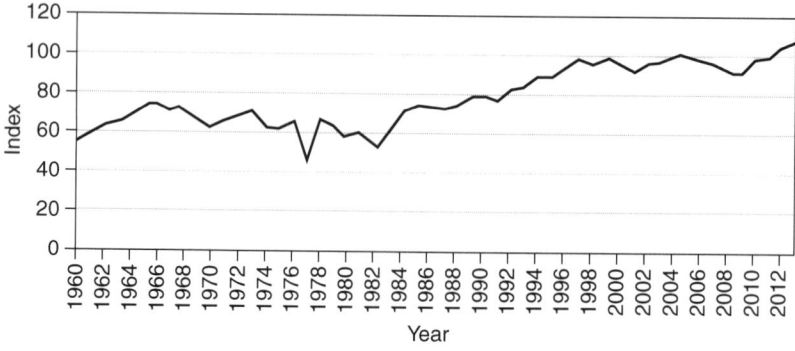

— Net returns on net capital stock, total economy, index unit: 2005 = 10

Figure I.2 The development of profits in the United States (source: European Commission's Directorate General for Economic and Financial Affairs (2013)).

from 65.2 per cent of GDP in 1960 to 58.2 per cent of GDP in 2013 and total annual corporate profits have risen from an index value of 55.2 in 1960 to 106.3 in 2013. In Spain, productivity has increased from an index value of 45,1 in 1960 to 101.8 in 2013. During the same period, the wage share has increased from 61.7 per cent of GDP in 1960 to 52.0 per cent of GDP in 2013 and total annual corporate profits have dropped from an index value of 74.9 in 1960 to 94.7 in 2013 (all data: European Commission's Directorate General for Economic and Financial Affairs 2013, index units: 2005 = 100). Similar calculations can be worked out for other parts of the world.

The Indignados movement in Spain or the Occupy movement may be considered as part of the response to such developments questioning capitalist logics (Harvey 2012, 159; Dean 2012, 207). The Indignados movement has protested against neoliberal cuts, social and economic inequality, rising costs of living and housing, increasing unemployment rates, etc. The movement states in its manifesto that "the will and purpose of the current system is the accumulation of money, not regarding efficiency and the welfare of society. Wasting resources, destroying the planet, creating unemployment and unhappy consumers" (¡Democracia real YA! 2013). The Occupy movement has claimed that large corporations and the global financial system control the world that benefits a minority and undermines democracy. The movements used digital and social media including social networking sites, online video channels, micro-blogging services, online newspapers, Internet chats, online encyclopaedias, and Internet live video streaming platforms for organizing, coordinating, and communicating their protest (see: www.demo-craciarealya.es and http://occupywallst.org).

Facebook (2012) says that its "mission is to give people the power to share and make the world more open and connected". Social media activities such as announcing personal messages on Twitter, uploading or watching videos on

YouTube, writing personal entries on Blogger, and creating profiles and sharing ideas on Facebook enable the collection, analysis, and sale of personal data by commercial web platforms. With the help of legal instruments including privacy policies and terms of use, social networking sites have the right to store, analyse, and sell personal data of their users to third parties for targeted advertising in order to accumulate profit. The co-founder and CEO of Facebook, Mark Zuckerberg, is the thirty-sixth richest person in America with a net worth of US$13.3 billion (Forbes 2013). Figure I.3 shows the development of Facebook's annual revenue from 2008 to 2012.

Facebook's revenue has increased by a factor of 18.7 from US$272 million in 2008 to US$5.1 billion in 2012. At the same time, there was an enormous increase in the number of monthly active users on Facebook, from 360 million in December 2009, 608 million in December 2010, 845 million in December 2011, to 1.1 billion in December 2012. People are considered to be monthly active users if they have used the service at least once in a calendar month. Facebook generates a substantial majority of its revenue from advertising (Securities and Exchange Commission 2013). Critics have highlighted that social media's advertising practices create data protection problems. "Europe-v-Facebook" was founded by a group of Austrian students of law in order to raise awareness about Facebook's privacy policy in terms of personal data abuse and forwarding. The group has reported Facebook for permanently violating the data protection right in the European Union and thereby undermining a fundamental human right. "Europe-v-Facebook's" objectives are to claim data transfer transparency, launch opt-in systems on social platforms, and to create open social networks. Facebook is currently under investigation by the Irish Data Protection Commissioner after receiving 22 complaints by the group in August 2011 (Europe-v-Facebook 2013).

If we look at the global value chains of the ICT industry, one can see that the realm of digital and social media is also related to handcraft and industrial labour

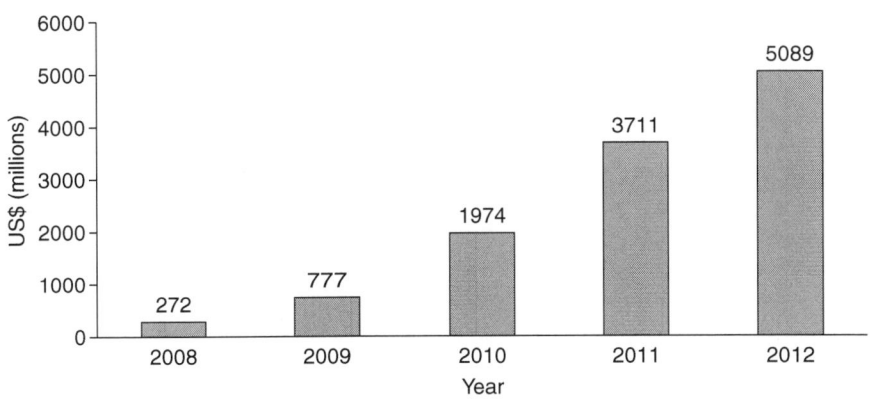

Figure I.3 The development of Facebook's revenue (source: Securities and Exchange Commission (2013)).

that poses global social and ecological problems (Dyer-Witheford 2001, 76; Fuchs 2014). Minerals such as cassiterite, wolframite, coltan, and gold are essential in the manufacture of a variety of electronic devices including mobile phones, tablets, music players, and laptops. The ICT-related minerals are especially extracted in mines in the eastern provinces of the Democratic Republic of the Congo amidst slavish working conditions. The raw materials are mined in conditions of armed conflict and human rights abuses. The profits from the sale of the resources finance continued fighting by the Congolese national army and various armed rebel groups. The control of lucrative mines becomes a focus of the fighting as well. A number of organizations are working to raise awareness of and find solutions for conflict minerals; examples include Conflictminerals. org, Conflict Free Tin Initiative, and Stand Canada (Le Monde diplomatique 2003).

The minerals are shipped to corporations such as Foxconn Electronics and Wintek Corporation in several Asian countries for the production of information and communication technologies that are sold by multinational electronics companies: to name but a few, Apple, Samsung Electronics, LG, Panasonic, Sony, and HP. Different media and corporate watchdog platforms have reported on the unacceptable and inhumane working conditions of the supply chain manufacturers of Apple and Co. (Sandoval 2014, 98–109). For instance, the assembly line workers at Foxconn are forced, through strict disciplinary measures as well as harsh and humiliating management methods, to work 10- to 12-hour shifts six days a week with regular overtime. The workers' wages are insufficient to cover basic living expenses and workers also risk their health by having to use toxic substances without adequate protection equipment. Eighteen workers at different Foxconn campuses attempted to commit suicide due to the unbearable working conditions. Some of them jumped from the top of the factory buildings which resulted in the installation of safety nets to prevent further suicides and more blows to the company's public image. The main reason for the relocation of digital media production to China, Malaysia, Thailand, etc. is to reduce costs. Computer companies are able to accumulate a lot of profit with the sale of the products that are manufactured in Asian factories. For example, Apple is the world's fifteenth biggest company calculated on sales, profits, assets, and market value (Forbes 2013). Its profit (net income) has enormously increased in recent years, from US$6.119 billion in 2008 to US$41.733 billion in 2012 (Securities and Exchange Commission 2012). While the scope is limited, labour right groups and activists as well as corporate watchdog organizations protest against the inhuman treatment of workers in the IT industry. Make IT Fair is a project of a group of European corporate watchdog organizations which organized an international day of action in May 2011 in order to raise public awareness. Although strikes by electronics factory workers are not without risks, several thousand Foxconn workers protested against low wages in the Chinese city of Foshan in 2011 (Sandoval 2014, 107–108).

The previous examples indicate that the display of power and counter-power, domination and spaces of power struggles, and the commons and the commodification of the commons characterize modern society. Contradictions and antagonisms between the haves and the have-nots shape contemporary society. The Indignados and the Occupy movement have faced these contradictions with the help of digital and social media. An asymmetrical economic power relation characterizes social networks, because companies own the platform, the data of their users, and the profits, and they decide on terms of use and privacy policies, while the users do not share ownership rights, do not control corporate social media platforms, have no right to decide on terms of use and privacy policies, and do not benefit from the profit being created out of user data produced for free. Corporate new media accumulate capital by dispossession (Harvey 2003) of personal information and data being produced in social and creative processes. This process may be considered as the accumulation by dispossession on web 2.0 (Jakobsson and Stiernstedt 2010), although the example also shows that Facebook users have tried to exert counter-power against Facebook's powerful and dominating role. Global social and ecological problems arise within new media production that also prompts protests, political actions, and strikes against such developments.

The Internet and social media are fields of conflict in this power struggle. The media are power structures and sites of power struggles, and are able to support both the expansion and the commodification of the commons. New media are tools for exerting power, domination, and counter-power. Based on a critical and dialectical perspective, it is possible to comprehend these contradictions occurring between emancipatory potentials of new and digital media that imply a logic of the commons and processes of commodification and enclosure that tend to jeopardize the commons and incorporate them into the logic of capital.

Questions arising in this context are as follows:

- What is the role of technology and media in capitalism?
- To what extent are media and technology able to support the enlargement of the commons?
- What are the limitations and potentials of new information and communication technologies?
- How is this linked to class relations and to forces and relations of production?
- How far are the productive forces rooted in capitalist interests and does the technological movement of the productive forces refer to opportunities of human liberation in the realm of digital and social media?

The germ form (*Keimform*) of capitalism is the commodity and the germ form of communism is the common (Dyer-Whiteford 2007, 81; Hardt and Negri 2009, 273). A commodity is a good produced for exchange and a common is a good produced by collectivities to be shared with all. The common is the dialectical sublation of private property and public goods. By the common, Hardt and Negri (2009, viii) mean "the common wealth of the material world ... and more significantly those results of social production that are necessary for social interaction and further production, such as knowledges, languages, codes, information, affects, and so forth". That is to say, the commons are material/physical and immaterial/intellectual goods that are both incorporated into alternative projects and partially produced by capital. The capitalist command again and again privatizes economic, political, cultural, natural, and technological commons, and strives to transform them into private property. But today's network, communication, intellectual, cultural, and creative products are easily reproduced and tend towards being common and thereby question the capitalist logic of private property (Gorz 2010). The commons come into friction with capital's hegemony. New information technologies appear as both instruments for the circulation of commodities and means for the circulation of struggles (Dyer-Witheford 1999, 121–122). Digital productive forces advance new forms and strategies of capital accumulation, and undercut the commodity character and point towards new forms of cooperation. Alternative and critical social media projects that strengthen the logic of the commons include diaspora*, N-1, Occuppii, and The-GlobalSquare. Profit-oriented social media platforms transforming the commons into private properties are, to name but a few, Facebook, Google+, Twitter, and YouTube.

Many authors have recently argued that the Internet has been transformed from a system being mainly oriented towards informational elements into a system being more oriented towards enabling communication and cooperation (Beer and Burrows 2007; boyd and Ellison 2007; Fuchs 2010a; Kolbitsch and Maurer 2006; O'Reilly 2005a; Saveri *et al.* 2008). The notions of "web 2.0", "social software", "social media", "participative web", and "social network(ing) sites" (SNS) have emerged in this context. Most approaches see the active involvement of users in the production of content as the main characteristic of web 2.0. There has been an intensification and extension of informational commodities based on knowledge, ideas, communication, relationships, emotional artefacts, cultural content, etc. over the past decades of capitalist production (Fuchs and Sevignani 2013, 257). The emergence of corporate social software may be seen in the context of the need to find new strategies of capital accumulation under post-Fordist conditions following the dot.com crisis around the turn of the millennium. The fact that one can find social media platforms such as Facebook (rank 2), YouTube (rank 3), Twitter (rank 14), and LinkedIn (rank 13) among the most frequently accessed websites worldwide indicates the enormous popularity of these sites (Alexa Internet 2013). Apart from a few exceptions (e.g. Fernback and Papacharissi 2007; Fuchs 2012b; Sandoval 2012), there are no studies combining critical theoretical and empirical research in the context of digital and social media. This is the task for the study at hand.

In the positivist dispute of German sociology about the methodology of the social sciences and the philosophy of science in the 1960s, Habermas (1976b, 131–162; 1976a, 198–225) drew the important epistemological insight that academic knowledge production is always embedded in social contexts and thus not able to be value-free, neutral, and apolitical. Empirical data are not objective observations of reality, and both theoretical considerations and descriptive statements are related to normative attitudes and moral concepts. "I should like to

justify the view that the research process, which is carried out by human subjects, belongs to the objective context which itself constitutes the object of cognition, by virtue of cognitive acts" (Habermas 1976a, 220). Adorno (1976b,
27–32; 1976a, 68–86) argues that traditional social research tends to ignore
objective conditions and relationships of society, because they stem from the
individual subject to social processes. Positivistic and uncritical research limits
itself to empirical facts and to the analysis of the mere appearance, and thereby
celebrates society as it is and neglects complex and transcendental thoughts. The
claim that academia should remain value-free frequently results in an affirmative
and ideological agenda legitimating the status quo and undermines critical and
dialectical thinking. Traditional social research "supports what exists in the over-
zealous attempt to say what exists" and "becomes ideology in the strict sense – a
necessary illusion" (Adorno 1976a, 76).

The study at hand is based on these insights and follows a critical and emancipatory research interest. I suggest a normative and partial approach giving
voice to the voiceless and supporting the oppressed classes of society. A point of
departure for such a critical approach is the work of Karl Marx. Marx's (2000a,
77) notion of critique derives from the humanist insight that "man is the highest
being for man, that is, with the categorical imperative to overthrow all circumstances in which man is humiliated, enslaved, abandoned, and despised". Marxist
critique is opposed to all forms of human exploitation, domination, and oppression. Critical theory studies the dialectics of essence and appearance, considers
social phenomena in the context of societal totality, is characterized by an
interest in human emancipation, and conceives social reality as the historical
result of specific human practices and therefore as changeable (Horkheimer
2002, 188–243; Marcuse 1988, 134–158). Based on Hegel's dialectical philosophy, critical theory defines categories in relation to other things. Categories
emerge in a dual way, and cause, contradict, and negate each other; hence, it is a
negation. Furthermore, raising quantity causes new qualities in dialectical categories at a certain critical point; hence, it is a turnover from quantity to quality.
Finally, dialectical categories sublate each other. New qualities emerge, old ones
are eliminated but are kept in a new form and on a higher level; hence, it is a
negation of negation (Marcuse 1955, 312–322; Bhaskar 2008, 162–190). Dialectical social criticism emphasizes negations in society and supports a negation
of negation for a "future society as a community of free men" (Horkheimer
2002, 217). Critical and dialectical analysis aims to identify the contradictory,
open, and dynamic tendencies of social phenomena that incorporate certain risks
and potentials.

Philosophy is the general scientific reflection about the human existence in
the world. According to Hofkirchner (2013, 47–55), basically three fundamental
questions constitute philosophy and philosophical thinking, namely the question
of the ability to comprehend the world, the question of the composition of the
world, and the question of the reasons to intervene in the world. The epistemological domain is traditionally concerned with the first, the ontological domain
deals with the second, and the praxiological domain of philosophy considers the

third question. Epistemology may be described as the philosophical theory of method, ontology as the philosophical theory of reality, and praxiology as the philosophical theory of praxis. The epistemological perspective includes knowledge and understanding, the ontological perspective comprises the being, and the praxiological perspective involves norms, values, ethics, and aesthetics. But the epistemological, ontological, and praxiological spheres are not independent and exclusive; rather, they are interconnected and mutually shape each other:

> Explicitly taking a human stance, we can reformulate the fundamental questions of philosophy by starting with the praxiological question and subsequently introducing the ontological question and the epistemological question, each one being the presupposition for the question before: (1) How should humans act, or better, what should the world be like? (2) How can humans intervene in the world, or better, how can humans make the world be as it should be? (3) How can humans comprehend the world, or better, how can humans know how to make the world be as it should be?
>
> (Hofkirchner 2013, 48)

Hence, there is an inclusive relationship between the epistemological, ontological, and praxiological level. Praxis builds upon reality and reality builds upon method; or speaking more generally, praxiology builds upon ontology and ontology builds upon epistemology (see Figure I.4).

Critical and Marxian-inspired media and information studies therefore strives for the development of theoretical research methods (epistemology) in order to focus on the analysis of media, information, and communication in the context of domination, asymmetrical power relations, resource control, social struggles, exploitation, and alienation (ontology). Critical media and communication studies aims to overcome social injustices and supports political processes and social transformations towards the "communicative commons" (Murdock 2013, 160) and a commons-based information society (praxiology). This volume is thus structured according to this distinction. Part I strives for the development of theoretical foundations of the relationship between technology and society, productive forces and relations of production, as well as privacy and surveillance (epistemology) in order to focus in Part II on empirical results of social media in

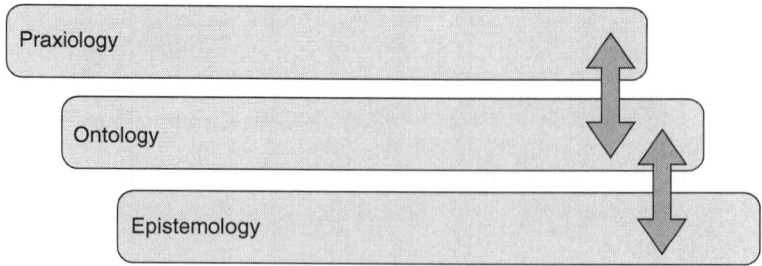

Figure I.4 Praxio-Onto-Epistemology (POE) (based on Hofkirchner (2013, 49)).

the context of advantages and disadvantages as well as emancipation and affirmation (ontology). Part III evaluates the prospects and limitations of the commons and commodification of the commons in the realm of new media and argues for the need for a techno-social revolution in terms of achieving a commons-based information society (praxiology). Parts I, II, and III of this volume are interconnected and shape each other mutually. The recommendation to strengthen the idea of the communication and network commons and a real liberation of society is based on an empirical case study of social media in the context of emancipation and affirmation being grounded in the theoretical foundations of media, technology, and society. Part III builds upon Part II and Part II builds upon Part I.

The work advances a theoretical approach combined with an empirical study, moving from the abstract to the concrete level. The overall aim of the work at hand is to study the objective and subjective aspects of new media and to deal with the limitations and prospects in terms of the expansion of the commons in the realm of digital and social media. The main research questions thus are:

How do the constraints and emancipatory potentials of new media look like and to what extent can digital and social media strengthen the idea of the communication and network commons and a commons-based information society?

For approaching an answer to these main questions, the subsequent specific research questions are required to be addressed in Parts I, II, and III.

Part I: Theoretical foundations

Before turning to new information and communication technologies and the Internet, it is important to come to a more general understanding of media, technology, and society, and to raise more philosophical questions about the prospects and limitations of technology and media in society. This is also linked to the economic question of what the relationship between forces and relations of production looks like. The following research question is thus the subject of Chapter 1:

How can the role of the dialectics of productive forces and relations of production be conceptualized by a critical theory of media, technology, and society?

Chapter 1 provides some foundational concepts of a critical theory of media, technology, and society, continues with the dialectics of productive forces and relations of production, and concludes with describing the means of communication as means of production.

Based on these findings, it becomes possible to conduct a well-founded analysis of new media in terms of theorizing the Internet and bringing up the question of the social aspects of social media. When it comes to the risks of new information and communication technologies, we must look at the other side of the coin as well. There has been an extension and intensification of privacy threats and surveillance risks in economic, political, and cultural contexts over recent years being also based on the employment of various surveillance technologies. The Internet and new media are one of these technologies. Before moving on to the empirical analysis, the work at hand must thus be theoretically situated in the context of the state of the art in the fields of the web, privacy, and surveillance. The question guiding this analysis therefore is:

Which theoretical foundations are needed for studying the Internet, privacy, and surveillance critically?

The aim of **Chapters 2, 3, and 4** is to clarify how the web, privacy, and surveillance are defined in the academic literature, what the different concepts have in common, what distinguishes them from one another, and which advantages and disadvantages such definitions have in order to clarify if there is a gap in the existing literature. Based on a critical theory and political economy approach, I argue that the existing literature is insufficient for studying the Internet, privacy, and surveillance. In contrast, a critical theory avoids pitfalls of the existing literature and strives for the development of theoretical and empirical research methods in order to focus on the web, privacy, and surveillance in the context of domination, asymmetrical power relations, resource control, social struggles, and exploitation.

Part I may be considered as an epistemological approach, because it provides the theoretical research methods for this study.

Part II: Case study

The economic and political logic shaping the strategies of profit-oriented social media platforms produces an antagonism between communicative opportunities and privacy and surveillance threats. This points out the antagonistic structure of communication technologies in capitalism. The overall aim of Part II is to study users' knowledge, attitudes, and practices towards this antagonistic character and the potentials and risks of social media. Part II may be considered as a case study of the critical theory and dialectics of media, technology, and society. I will analyze which advantages and disadvantages students consider in the context of social networking sites. The results are based on a survey conducted in Austria (N=3558). Social networking site users are primarily young and educated people. Thus, for example, 45 per cent of the users of MySpace are aged 18 to 34, 42 per cent of the users of Facebook are aged 18 to 34, and 53 per cent of Facebook users have attended college or graduate school (all data: Quantcast 2013). We may thus assume that young people are early adopters of new technologies. It is therefore important to consider their usage behaviour because they may anticipate future trends. Due to their education standards, students tend to be very sensitive towards new issues confronting society. Given that students are early adopters and sensitive citizens, it is important to analyse their use of social media. The main research question for the empirical study is:

Which major advantages and disadvantages of social networking platforms do Austrian students see?

In **Chapter 5**, a discussion of some of the most cited studies should give a representative overview of typical empirical research approaches that assess privacy on social networking sites. I will demonstrate that there is a predominance of traditional and uncritical research in the context of privacy on web 2.0. This research does not reflect structural power asymmetries in capitalism. Some critical theoretical studies about surveillance on digital and new media are thus examined. I will highlight the need for a critical empirical study of privacy and surveillance on social media. The task of **Chapter 6** is to address what students consider to be the main potentials and risks of social media. In doing so, the general characteristics of the respondents as well as perceived advantages and disadvantages of social networking sites will be outlined.

Part II may be considered as an ontological approach, because it focuses on the analysis of digital media and the concrete use of social media.

Part III: Techno-social revolution

Part III unites the theoretical foundations and the empirical case study, and asks what the results of the empirical study mean and how they may be interpreted with the help of a dialectical and critical theory of social media. In addition, Part III raises the question of whether technological and/or social changes are required in order to bring about real social media and to change the information society for the better. Thus the specific research question is:

How can the dialectics of social media be conceptualized by critical theory and what are its political implications?

Based on certain foundational concepts of a critical theory of media, technology, and society and the dialectics of productive forces and relations of production discussed in Chapter 1, **Chapter 7** contains a theoretical interpretation of the empirical results. This chapter deals with the dialectics of technological design and assessment and the (dis)advantages of social media. It also treats the dialectical relationship of productive forces and relations of production of social media. **Chapter 8** summarizes the results of this work and draws some political conclusions. It evaluates the prospects and limitations of the objective and subjective characteristics in the realm of digital and social media in terms of achieving a commons-based information society.

Part III may be considered as a praxiological approach, because it discusses political implications and argues for the need for political interventions.

In summary, the media are power structures and sites of power struggles, and are able to support both the commons and the commodification of the commons. New information technologies appear as both instruments for the circulation of commodities and means for the circulation of struggles. Based on a critical and dialectical approach, it is possible to comprehend contradictions occurring between emancipatory potentials of new and digital media that imply a logic of the commons and processes of commodification and enclosure that tend to jeopardize the commons and incorporate them into the logic of capital. The overall aim of the work at hand is to study the constraints and emancipatory potentials of new media, and to assess to what extent digital and social media can contribute to strengthening the idea of the communication and network commons and a commons-based information society. I follow a critical and emancipatory research interest and suggest a normative and partial approach. This book is based on a theoretical approach combined with an empirical study, advancing from the abstract to the concrete level.[1]

Note

1 The research presented in this publication was conducted in the project "Social Networking Sites in the Surveillance Society", funded by the Austrian Science Fund (FWF): Project No. P 22445-G17. Project coordination: Professor Christian Fuchs. For a summary of the main arguments of this book, see Allmer (2014).

Part I
Theoretical foundations

1   Critical theory and dialectics

Introduction

Feenberg (2002, 5) distinguishes between instrumental and substantive theories of technology. "The former treats technology as subservient to values established in other social spheres (e.g. politics or culture), while the latter attributes an autonomous cultural force to technology that overrides all traditional or competing values" (Feenberg 2002, 5). Instrumental theories consider technologies as neutral tools that serve the purposes of their users. Such tools are useful in any social context – "A hammer is a hammer". In this view, technology is designed in a vacuum isolated from political ideologies. Instrumental notions give priority to the rational character of technology. Technology is comprehended as pure instrumentality being employed to achieve efficiency. This strictly functional approach is the dominant view of modern governments (Feenberg 2002, 5–6). In contrast, substantive theories deny the neutrality of technology and focus on the negative technological consequences for humanity and nature. Technology has become a whole way of life and is substantive to modern society. This view argues that technology and machinery are "overtaking" us and that there is no escape other than a retreat and return to tradition and simplicity. This apocalyptic vision often claims absurd, quasi-magical powers of technology and is best known through the writings of Ellul and Heidegger (Feenberg 2002, 6–8):

> Despite their differences, instrumental and substantive theories share a 'take it or leave it' attitude toward technology. On the one hand, if technology is a mere instrumentality, indifferent to values, then its design is not at issue in political debate, only the range and efficiency of its application. On the other hand, if technology is the vehicle for a culture of domination, then we are condemned either to pursue its advance toward dystopia or to regress to a more primitive way of life. In neither case can we change it: in both theories, *technology is destiny*. Reason, in its technological form, is beyond human intervention or repair.
>
> (Feenberg 2002, 8)

This chapter is inspired by these important findings and argues for the need for a third approach, a critical and dialectical theory of technology that understands the technological developments and dynamics as progressive and regressive, and entails a moment of techno-social change (Marcuse 1998, 2001; Bloch 1986; Feenberg 2002; Dyer-Witheford 1999; Fuchs 2008). I thus present some foundational concepts of a critical theory of media, technology, and society in the second section, continue with the dialectics of productive forces and relations of production in the third section, and conclude the chapter by describing the means of communication as means of production.

Foundational concepts of a critical theory of media, technology, and society

A medium establishes and organizes a relation between two entities that generate information (Fuchs and Hofkirchner 2003, 209). Media enable and constrain information processes. Information is a subjective and objective process of cognition, communication, and cooperation. On an individual level, a subjective and cognitive structure characterizes system A (cognitive information process). On an intermediate level, occurring interaction between system A and system B provides an objective relation of communication (communicative information process). This communication process results in new information in system B (A to B) and may also be the other way round (B to A). It is determined that the information of system A has an effect on system B, but it is not exactly predestined what this effect looks like. On an integrational level, system A and system B are able to produce new combined information due to synergetic effects, which cannot be found on the individual or intermediate level (cooperative information process). Media exist in physical, biological, and social systems. Generally speaking, media provide objective relations of information between systems, but subjective effects play a major role. The existence of a medium is compulsory, but not a sufficient precondition for the self-organization of complex systems. Specifically speaking, societal media establish objective human relations and operate between living social actors where subjective interpretations and meanings are decisive. The existence of a societal medium is a compulsory precondition for communication, but understandings, responses, and constitutions of communication actors' sense and meaning are not determined but relatively autonomous (Hofkirchner 2013, 184–196).

Material and ideal aspects characterize media (see Figure 1.1). For instance, computer-mediated communication such as the Internet incorporates both technological transmissions as well as content being produced by human actors.

Societal media are artefacts such as instruments, means, natural resources, property, power, and definitions mediating human relations and actions. That is to say, societal media are technologies that produce and organize information of interpersonal relations; hence, societal media are information technologies. Medium is a more abstract term than technology, because media exist in all

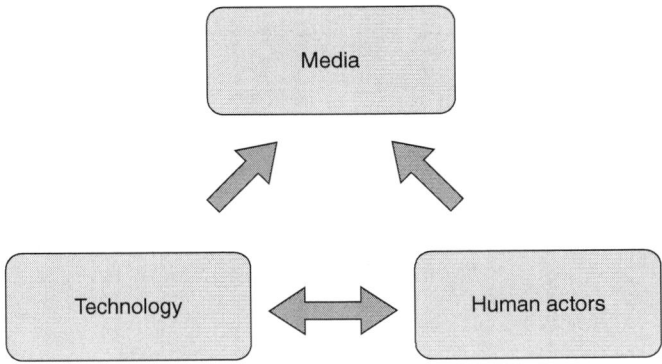

Figure 1.1 Media, technology, and humans.

self-organizing (physical, biological, and social) systems and technology is a certain characteristic of the social system (Fuchs and Hofkirchner 2003, 195–233).

Originally, in the same meaning as "tekton", which means builder or carpenter, the word "techne" had been constituted and become a philosophical concept in ancient Greek, before the term "technology" became generalized and familiar in modern societies (Kurrer 1990, 536). Technology may be understood as a purposeful unity of objects, means, methods, abilities, processes, and knowledge that are necessary in order to fulfil individual or social needs (Fuchs 2008, 47; Kurrer 1990, 535). That is to say, technology is a totality of objective and subjective factors and only objective aspects of technology are media (Fuchs and Hofkirchner 2003, 227). Technology is comprehended as a multifaceted unity in which the proper technics as certain methods adopt a subordinated position and are of secondary importance (Marcuse 1998, 41).

Technology mediates the relationship between human beings and nature (see Figure 1.2).

"Technology reveals the active relation of man to nature, the direct process of the production of his life, and thereby it also lays bare the process of the production of the social relations of his life, and of the mental conceptions that flow from those relations" (Marx 1976, 493, fn.4). Technology regulates the metabolism between the individual or a group of individuals (society) and nature (Hofkirchner 2002). Human actors make use of technology in order to adapt nature to society and to fulfil human needs. "Society ... projects and undertakes the technological transformation of nature" (Marcuse 1972, 119) and "as technics expand their role in the reproduction of society, they establish an intermediate universe between Subject (methodical, transforming theory and practice) and Object (nature as the stuff, material of transformation)" (Marcuse 2001, 45). In the material and organic composition of capital, hence the relationship between means of production (natural and technological means of production) or

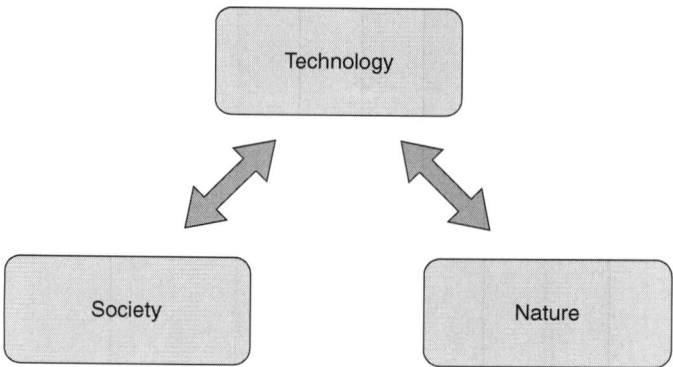

Figure 1.2 Technology, society, and nature.

constant capital (circulating and fixed capital) and labour power or variable capital; that is, through the means of production/labour power or c/v (Marx 1976, 762), we can identify the relationship between nature (constant circulating capital), technology (constant fixed capital), and human beings (variable capital) as well. In order to avoid the impression that society and technology act on the same level, it must be said that society is an upstream process and technology only exists because of society. The possibility that technology can also mediate the relationship between human actors and human knowledge/culture is treated in Chapter 7.

There is a mutual shaping of society and technology. Society constructs and shapes technology (design) on the one hand, and technology impacts upon and transforms society (assessment) on the other (see Figure 1.3).

The mutual relationship of society and technology is a dynamic process with

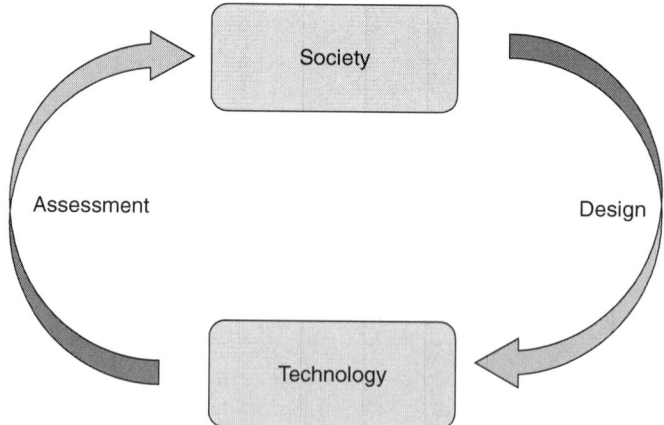

Figure 1.3 Mutual shaping of society and technology.

shaping effects onto each other (Fuchs 2008, 2–3; Feenberg 2002, 48). Human beings are able to design and control the employment of technology and technology reacts upon society. Technology is therefore a subsystem of society.

Based on Giddens, Bourdieu, and Habermas, Fuchs (2008, 62) differentiates between the economic (disposition of resources), political (decision on regularities), and cultural (definition of rules) system as the core elements of society (see also Hofkirchner 2013, 241).

> In order to survive, humans in *society* have to appropriate and change nature (*ecology*) with the help of *technologies* so that they can produce resources that they distribute and consume (*economy*), which enables them to make collective decisions (*polity*), form values, and acquire skills (*culture*).
>
> (Fuchs 2008, 62, emphasis added)

In reference to the notion of the mutual relationship of society and technology, we may therefore argue that economic, political, and cultural processes shape technology and technology has in return an impact upon the economic, political, and cultural system. This includes that technological developments and the technological movement of the productive forces are not solely an economic process due to political and cultural impacts (Fuchs 2002, 323–324). Examples include the following:

- Governments and political groups previously regulated the sector of telecommunications to a certain degree.
- Privacy laws and data protection regulations constrain commercial web platforms to implement new technologies such as Google Street View and Facebook Beacon:
  - Google Street View is a technology that providing panoramic views from positions along many streets around the world. Privacy advocates have pointed out that Google Street View shows people engaging in visible activities in which they do not wish to be seen publicly (e.g. men leaving strip clubs, protesters at an abortion clinic, and sunbathers in bikinis). The concerns have led to temporary stoppages of Street View in some countries.
  - Beacon was part of Facebook's advertisement system for the purpose of allowing targeted advertisements, which sent data from external websites to Facebook. After a class action lawsuit, Facebook had to shut down the service in September 2009.

The dynamics of technological progress additionally follow specific social norms and values. Cultural aspects also play an important role in the establishment of new technologies and technological innovations. For example:

- The open source community is an open access and open knowledge culture with cooperative production forms having developed the Linux operating system. It may be interpreted as a cultural expression of the discontent with proprietary commodities and the idea of the free distribution of digital knowledge.

Technology is in capitalism medium and result of economic, political, and cultural processes, and is mutually mediated with antagonisms in economy, politics, and culture. Technology is the medium and outcome of these contradictions. Although the development of technology as a social process is the result of processes of negotiation and conflicts of interests between individuals, economic actors such as large corporations play a dominant role in this process, because available resources decide power dimensions extensively and intensively. One may argue that there is an asymmetrical relationship between economic, political, and cultural actors in the process of the technological movement of the productive forces with a predominant and powerful position of the economy. This insight goes hand in hand with Marxist notions about the dialectical relationship of base (nature, technology, and economy) and superstructure (polity and culture) (Williams 2005a; Hall 1986; Bhaskar 1998, 71–73; Holz 2005, 534; Fuchs 2008, 70) (see Figure 1.4).

The base is a necessary but not a sufficient condition of the superstructure and a complex and nonlinear reflection of the superstructure that trigger each other. Both the material base enables and constrains superstructural practices and the superstructure reacts upon basic structures. The dialectics of determination and indetermination shapes the relationship of base and superstructure. In addition, the superstructure is no mechanic effect or epiphenomenon of basic structures; the base is not an external force that mechanically determines superstructural actions. The superstructure may neither be deduced from nor reduced to the material base. A dialectical view on base and superstructure denies both economic reductionism and theoretical idealism. Polity and culture are simultan-

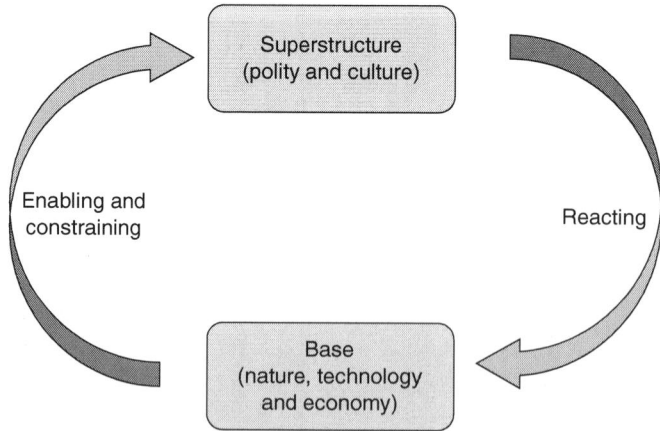

Figure 1.4 Dialectical relationship of base and superstructure.

eously shaped by economic structures and open and interconnected practices having "relative indeterminacy" (Hall 1986, 43) and "relative autonomy" (Bhaskar 1998, 71).

> We have to revalue "determination" towards the setting of limits and the exertion of pressure, and away from a predicted, prefigured and controlled content. We have to revalue "superstructure" towards a related range of cultural practices, and away from a reflected, reproduced or specifically dependent content. And, crucially, we have to revalue "the base" away from the notion of a fixed economic or technological abstraction, and towards the specific activities of men in real social and economic relationships, containing fundamental contradictions and variations and therefore always in a state of dynamic process.
>
> (Williams 2005a, 34)

In addition, there is an interplay of technological structure and technological agents. The technological structure enables and constrains human activity and thinking on the one hand and is the outcome of productive and reproductive processes on the other (Fuchs 2008, 123). That is to say, technology mediates human actions and technology is devised, constructed, maintained, and modified by agents. Technology is therefore inherently a social system with relative autonomy. This dialectical thinking allows for taking into account the possibilities of social design on the one hand and the self-reinforcing tendencies of technology on the other. At the same time, technology is embedded in society and has relative autonomy. A dialectical view on technology bears in mind the genesis of technology; that is, the social design of technology, and the assessment of technology; that is, technological effects on society (see Figure 1.3). Applying such a view to capitalist society could mean that asymmetrical social relationships of power and domination are embedded in the conception, construction, maintenance, and modification of technics and that technological effects depend on how technologies are used. "Technology as such cannot be isolated from the use to which it is put; the technological society is a system of domination which operates already in the concept and construction of techniques" (Marcuse 1972, 14).

Technology is the expression and form of social relations, corresponds to a certain historical period (Leisewitz 1990, 935), is not neutral (Feenberg 2002, 14), and is biased (Feenberg 2002, 63). Marx indicated that capitalist forms of machinery and technology incorporate elements of domination: "By machinery ... domination of former over living labour preserves not only social – expressed in the relation between capitalist and worker – but so to say technological realization" (Marx 1982, 2059, my translation).[1] Social purposes and values of capital shape technology in its design and development (Feenberg 2002, 15, 48). The technological design must be rooted in capitalist interests and social forces. Capitalist interests generate a conception of technology being incompatible with a full development of the sociosphere (Feenberg 2002, 49) and the ecosphere.

Technology is not designed in a vacuum isolated from the social context. Rather, the social context forms the technological product and the corresponding labour. The dynamics of technological development are embedded in social relations and are thus not neutral dynamics.

> In advanced industrial society, the technical apparatus of production and distribution functions, not as a sum total of mere instruments which can be isolated from the social and political context without losing their identity, but rather as an apparatus which determines a priori the product as well as the individual and social operations of servicing and extending it, that is to say, determines the socially needed demands, occupations, skills, attitudes – and thus the forms of social control and social cohesion.
>
> (Marcuse 2001, 42; see also Marcuse 1972, 13)

Capitalist technology in its foundational form is also a technology of power and domination. The repressive elements of technology in capitalist societies are not solely due to its applications, but technology is inherently a means of power and domination (Marcuse 1972, 129, 130, 131, 137, 198). Capitalist interests not only shape the employment and purpose but also the design of technology. Not just the ends, but also the means of production must be transformed (Feenberg 2001, 140).

> The technology which the industrial societies have inherited and developed, and which rules our lives, is in its very roots a technology of domination ... I suggested that it is a gross oversimplification if the repressive elements of industrial society are attributed only to a specific use of technology, to a specific application of scientific reason. In a sense, the application was pre-formed by the method: there was a pre-established harmony and affinity between the idea and its realization.
>
> (Marcuse 2001, 57)

Technology is a form of organization and maintenance of social relations and a means of control and domination. In the course of the development of technology a new rationality has been established in society, which plays an important role in the development of machinery and mass production (Marcuse 1998, 42). The objectives of capitalist technology – that is, value creation – had been defined before the actual conception and construction of technology took place. Technological control is internal to their very structure (Feenberg 2002, 51, 66, 76, 82) and therefore a transformation and redesign of technology is necessary in order to establish an alternative society.

For instance, the production of nuclear energy may be seen as an expression of power relations in capitalist societies. Nuclear energy is a typical energy source of Fordist mass production, which emerged in the capitalist centres after the Second World War. Besides fossil fuels, nuclear energy is a profitable form of energy, and fits into and supports the logic of capital accumulation. Due to their complexity, nuclear power plants tend to cascade failures and become uncontrollable, which could end in unpredictable catastrophic accidents and unavoidable nuclear disasters (Perrow 1999). Such high-risk technologies are destructive and inhumane forces having the potential for mass annihilation, and they have the capacity to endanger the survival of the socio- and the ecosphere, as the nuclear catastrophe of Fukushima showed in 2011. Technology no longer mediates the relationship between society and nature in this case; instead, it rather extinguishes society and nature. Nuclear power stations are designed and constructed as high-risk technologies being embedded in the capitalist relations of production, where profit has priority over human lives and nature. Adopting and employing nuclear power plants in socialism could also result in a global nuclear disaster, because the risks and threats do not primarily arise from the application but from the conception and construction of complex technological high-risk systems. The traditional idea of simply taking technology in an unchanged way over from capitalism to socialism was emphasized in orthodox Marxism (Fuchs 2005, 125). Orthodox Marxism ignores Marx's critical remarks on technology and believes that productive forces need solely to be liberated from capitalist characteristics of the relations of production (Feenberg 2002, 45; Dyer-Witheford 1999, 70). In this context, Stalin states that "machines ... are as indifferent to classes as is language and may, like it, equally serve a capitalist system and a socialist system" (Stalin 2000). Taking Stalin and orthodox Marxism seriously would mean employing nuclear power plants in socialism, applying inhumane and "destructive forces" (Marx and Engels 1998, 464), and risking the mass annihilation of social and ecological life. Neither nationalization nor socialization is able to change instrumentality and rationality that is inherent to capitalist technology. In order to avoid misunderstandings, the above example does not mean that technology exists independently of social relations and is able to exercise power and domination by itself. Technology is only able to strengthen those asymmetrical social relationships being exercised by human actors. But it shows that control, power, and domination may already be embedded in the capitalist design of technologies.

At the same time, technology cannot be isolated from its application. For instance, employing automation in the capitalist mode of production reinforces competitive relationships between human beings and machinery, the redundancy of the human labour force, unemployment, poverty, alienation, exploitation, and the intensification of labour. Instead, employing technology in the automated process of production in a commons-based society could primarily help to intervene to reduce necessary labour time to a minimum in order to have time for the full development of the individual, to increase the wealth of society, and could contribute to a real liberation of human beings. Modern technology has made possible the satisfaction of needs and the reduction of toil. Marcuse (1969, 12) thus asks:

> Is it still necessary to state that not technology, not technique, not the machine are the engines of repression, but the presence, in them, of the masters who determine their number, their life span, their power, their place

in life, and the need for them? Is it still necessary to repeat that science and technology are the great vehicles of liberation, and that it is only their use and restriction in the repressive society which makes them into vehicles of domination?

Technological development incorporates alternative potentials and possibilities, and we do not have to "reinvent the wheel" in order to establish a real liberation of society being based on technological innovations. Marcuse (1969, 12) claims in this context that:

> not the automobile is repressive, not the television set is repressive, not the household gadgets are repressive, but the automobile, the television, the gadgets which, produced in accordance with the requirements of profitable exchange, have become part and parcel of the people's own existence, own "actualization".

If we take a look at new information and communication technologies including the Internet and the corresponding struggles between competition and cooperation and the commons and the commodification of the commons, one can see that the capitalist process of production has driven the productive forces forward to an extent also showing possibilities of transforming society. Technology incorporates potentials. The dynamic interaction between technological essence and appearance is the source of tensions that move technological development in one direction or another and could reveal technological potentials (Feenberg 2003, 48). Real technological potentials could be brought to fruition having "not yet" been realized (Bloch 1986). In the appearance of capitalist technology (being-for-itself) are also technological potentials (being-in-itself) and it is important to uncover and reveal those hidden and suppressed potentials for a real liberation of human beings.

In summary, power and domination are embedded in the conception, construction, maintenance, and modification of technology, and at the same time technological effects depend on the application and employment of technology (see Figure 1.5).

The dialectical view of technology as the expression of social relations in a certain historical period, as well as depending on how technologies are used, may likewise be found in Marcuse's writings. He claims that although the dynamics of technological progress take place within a social context, certain technological developments may be used for different purposes:

> The technological a priori is a political a priori inasmuch as the transformation of nature involves that of man, and inasmuch as the "man-made creations" issue from and re-enter a societal ensemble. One may still insist that the machinery of the technological universe is "as such" indifferent towards political ends – it can revolutionize or retard a society. An electronic computer can serve equally a capitalist or socialist administration; a cyclotron can be an equally efficient tool for a war party or a peace party.
>
> (Marcuse 1972, 126)

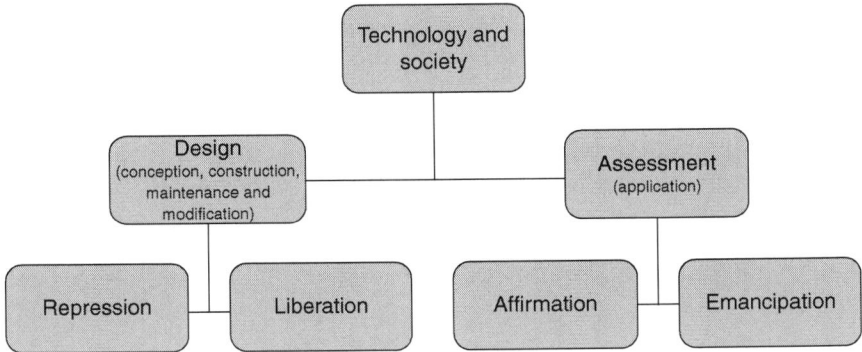

Figure 1.5 Different possibilities of technological and social design and assessment.

A dialectical view sees the development of technology as progressive and regressive, liberating and repressive, as potential and risk (Fuchs 2005, 120). It indicates different possibilities of technological dynamics between resignation and utopia (Feenberg 2002, 13, 15). This view is neither techno-deterministic nor socio-constructivist; neither is it techno-optimistic nor techno-pessimistic (Dyer-Witheford 1999, 71), and it takes into consideration the design and assessment of technology. The differentiation of technological/social design and assessment also raises the question of whether technological and/or social changes are needed in order to strengthen the idea of a real liberation and will be discussed in the concluding chapter.

The dialectics of society and technology (social design of technology and technological effects on society) is related to the dialectics of productive forces and relations of production. Society constructs and shapes technology and technology impacts upon and transforms society. The relations of production as economic structure enable and constrain the development of the productive forces and are at the same time the result of the corresponding productive forces. That is to say, society and relations of production are social structures enabling and constraining technology and productive forces in turn reacting upon society and relations of production. Just as technology is not neutrally developed and constructed (design) and could be applied differently to another society (assessment), so productive forces mature the contradiction and antagonism of the capitalist form of production (design) and simultaneously ripen "the elements for forming a new society and the forces tending towards the overthrow of the old one" (Marx 1976, 635) (assessment). The dialectics of society and technology takes place on the economic, political, and cultural level whereas the dialectics of forces and relations of production is an economic phenomenon. The dialectics of society and technology is thus more abstract. The productive forces are a system of living labour force and technological and natural means of production. The dialectics of forces and relations of production is thus more encompassing.

The dialectics of productive forces and relations of production

The mode of production is based on productive forces, which include labour power, means of production, objects and instruments of labour and relations of production such as property relations and interactions (see Figure 1.6 for a formal overview and Table 1.1 for a citation-based explanation of the concepts).

The productive forces are a system of living labour forces and facts and factors of the process of production that cause and influence labour (Leisewitz 1990, 939). There is a relationship between labouring human actors (subject) and means of production (object) changing historically which is based on a concrete formation of society such as capitalism. On the one hand, subjective productive forces are the unity of the physical and spiritual labour forces of an individual (Marx 1997b); that is, physical ability, qualifications, knowledge, abilities, experiences, etc. On the other hand, objective productive forces are factors of the process of labour and production that are not related to an individual; that is, objects (natural means of production) and instruments (technical means of production) of labour including oil, silicon, technology, science, cooperation, division of labour, and methods of organization. By and large,

> labour is … a process between man and nature, a process by which man, through his own actions, mediates, regulates and controls the metabolism between himself and nature…. In the labour process, therefore, man's activity, via the instruments of labour, effects an alteration in the object of labour which was intended from the outset. The process is extinguished in the product.
>
> (Marx 1976, 283, 287)

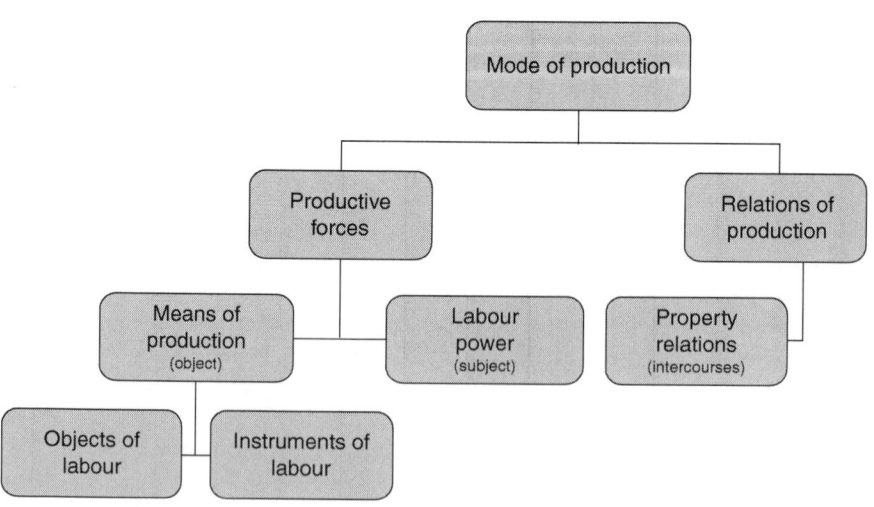

Figure 1.6 Mode of production.

Table 1.1 Conceptions and explanations of the mode of production

Conception	Explanation
Productive forces	"The simple elements of the labour process are (1) purposeful activity, that is work itself, (2) the object on which that work is performed, and (3) the instruments of that work" (Marx 1976, 284). "Originally … the labour process … sorted itself out into certain qualitatively different parts, material of labour [objects of labour] … means of labour [instruments of labour] and living labour [labour power]" (Marx 1973).
Labour power/labour force/ variable capital (v)	"We mean by labour-power, or labour-capacity, the aggregate of those mental and physical capabilities existing in the physical form, the living personality, of a human being, capabilities which he sets in motion whenever he produces a use-value of any kind" (Marx 1976, 270); that is, the unity of physical and spiritual forces (physical ability, qualification, knowledge, abilities, experience, etc.). "He sets in motion the natural forces which belong to his own body, his arms, legs, head and hands, in order to appropriate the materials of nature in a form adapted to his own needs" (Marx 1976, 283).
Means of production/constant capital (c)	"If we look at the whole process from the point of view of its result, the product, it is plain that both the instruments and the object of labour are means of production" (Marx 1976, 287).
Objects of labour/natural means of production/ circulating capital (c_{cir})	"The land … in its original state in which it supplies man with necessaries or means of subsistence ready to hand is available without any effort on his part as the universal material for human labour" (Marx 1976, 284). This includes natural forces, raw materials, principal substances, and accessories such as fishes, timber, ore, coal for a steam-engine, oil for a wheel, hay for draft horses, chlorine for unbleached linen, dye for wool, or silicon for a central processing unit (CPU) in a PC.
Instruments of labour/ technological means of production/fixed capital (c_{fix})	"An instrument of labour is a thing, or a complex of things, which the worker interposes between himself and the object of his labour and which serves as a conductor, directing his activity onto that object. He makes use of the mechanical, physical and chemical properties of some substances in order to set them to work on other substances as instruments of his power, and in accordance with his purposes" (Marx 1976, 285). This includes technical tools and instruments of production such as hammer, machines, workshops, canals, and roads, as well as – and more in the direction appropriate to contemporary capitalism – technology, science, cooperation, division of labour, level of socialization of labour, and methods of organization. "The development of fixed capital indicates to what degree general social knowledge has become a direct force of production, and to what degree, hence, the conditions of the process of social life itself have come under the control of the general intellect and been transformed in accordance with it" (Marx 1976, 284).
Relations of production	"In the social production of their life, men enter into definite relations that are indispensable and independent of their will, relations of production which correspond to a definite stage of development of their material productive forces" (Marx 1951, 328). "The relations [of production] in which productive forces are developed, are anything but eternal laws, but that they correspond to a definite development of men and of their productive forces" (Marx 2000b, 227).
Property relations	"The existing relations of production, or – what is but a legal expression for the same thing … the property relations" (Marx 1951, 329). The property relations determine who produces and who owns property.
Intercourses (Verkehrsformen)	"The form of intercourse determined by the existing productive forces at all previous historical stages, and in its turn determining these, is civil [bourgeois] society.… This conception of history thus relies on expounding the real process of production – starting from the material production of life itself – and comprehending the form of intercourse connected with and created by this mode of production, i.e., civil [bourgeois] society in its various stages, as the basis of all history" (Marx and Engels 1998, 57, 61). In the "German Ideology", Marx and Engels speak of social relationships as forms of intercourses. Marx later replaced this term by the one of relations of production.

The labour force is the productive and creative power of capital and therefore the central aspect of the productive forces. The objects and instruments of labour operate not as autonomous productive forces, but are only efficient as productive forces in combination with living labour force. The productive forces cannot be reduced to one particular element of the system of productive forces (Leisewitz 1990, 931–932). The process of production takes place within certain social relationships/structures. The relations of production constitute social relations between human beings, which act as agents or as social groups in economic processes. Relations of production have a specific historical form such as the relationship between wage labour and capital in capitalist societies. The relationship of wage labour and capital is a certain form of property relation in capitalism being based on exploitation and specifies who produces and who owns property (Krysmanski 1990, 895).

The mode of production is based on a dialectical relationship of productive forces and relations of production. The economic structure enables and constrains the development of the productive forces, which form the relations of production. The relations of production are both means and the outcome of the productive forces (see Figure 1.7).

The competition of capital as coercive law of capitalist production forces individual capitalists and society to produce more in less time – otherwise there exists the possibility to get extinguished as individual an capitalist. The directing motives of the individual capitalist's operations and the inner nature of capital are to increase the productivity of labour by technological movement of the productive forces. The relations of production and relations of competition drive the development of the productive forces forward. The capitalist process of production means permanent further development. In a short period of time the bourgeois society has developed more productive forces than all former societies put together. On the other hand, the "capitalist mode of production comes up against

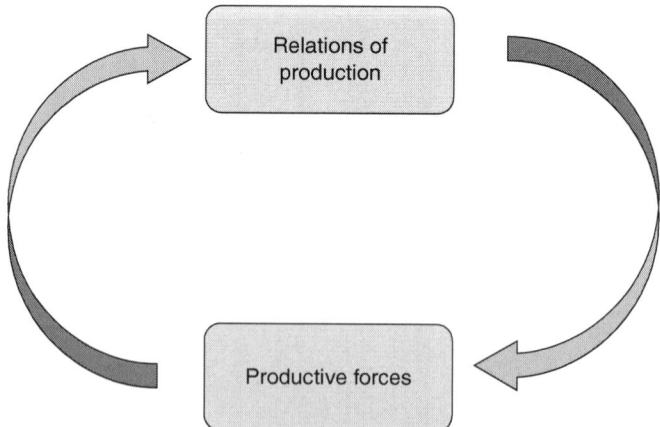

Figure 1.7 Dialectical relationship of productive forces and relations of production.

a barrier to the development of the productive forces" (Marx 1991, 350). The relations of production become an obstacle in the development of the productive forces and instead new relations are put into action and are correspondent to the new productive forces, as long as it becomes a new obstacle (Marx and Engels 1998, 101).

> At a certain stage of their development, the material productive forces of society come in conflict with the existing relations of production ... within which they have been at work hitherto. From forms of development of the productive forces these relations turn into their fetters.... No social order ever perishes before all the productive forces for which there is room in it have developed; and new, higher relations of production never appear before the material conditions of their existence have matured in the womb of the old society itself.
>
> (Marx 1951, 329)

Due to new productive forces and to the change in obtaining a livelihood, people also change their social relationships and those mutated relations of production again form the development of the productive forces. Hence, the dialectical relationship of productive forces and relations of production is the driving force of social development.

In capitalist societies, the characteristics and development of the productive forces have to be analysed in the context of the valorization process and the production of exchange value:

> Some light is already thrown for us on the essence of the present-day "productive forces" by the fact that in the present state of affairs productive force consists not only in, for instance, making man's labour more efficient or natural and social forces more effective, but just as much in making labour cheaper or more unproductive for the worker. Hence productive force is from the outset determined by exchange value.
>
> (Marx 1997a)

A theoretical consideration of the productive forces in capitalism without reflecting value creation is scientifically untenable (Leisewitz 1990, 922), because value forms the productive forces. In the following, I will show that the developments of the productive forces do not take place in a vacuum and are thus not neutral dynamics. Rather, value creation and capital accumulation form the dynamic development of the productive forces. The technological movement of the productive forces is rooted in capitalist interests and social forces. Just as technology is not neutrally developed and constructed (design of technology), so productive forces mature the contradiction and antagonism of the capitalist form of production (design of productive forces). Machinery and technology as productive forces are the medium and outcome of capitalist development. Technology is a powerful means of raising productivity and therefore a medium of capitalist development. Due to the economic force of capital accumulation, the capitalist process of production strives to produce surplus value by reducing necessary labour and expanding surplus labour by employing technology. The existing organization of capitalist society and the vital need for constantly raising the productivity of labour drives this society towards technological innovations. Technology is thus also an outcome of capitalist development.

> The mass of means of production with which he [the worker] functions in this way increases with the productivity of his labour. But those means of production play a double role. The increase of some is a *consequence*, that of the others is a *condition*, of the increasing productivity of labour.
>
> (Marx 1976, 773, emphasis added)

I will successively address the differentiation of use value and exchange value, process of production, concrete and abstract labour, labour process and valorization process, constant and variable capital, rate of surplus value, the production of absolute and relative surplus value, and machinery and technology and I will conclude with the dynamic development of the productive forces in capitalist societies.

Marx analyses the process of producing capital in Volume One of *Capital*. The process starts with commodities and money, and continues with labour-produced surplus value and methods for producing absolute and relative surplus value. By analysing a single commodity and the corresponding labour, Marx differentiates between use value and (exchange) value as well as concrete and abstract labour, and continues with the value form. The use value reveals different qualities of products. A use value exists, if usefulness occurs and human needs can be fulfilled. The usefulness emerges out of the material nature of things. In the first instance, the use value is independent from the exchange value, because a thing or a product is able to have a use value without having an exchange value. For example, if I use a chair only for sitting on without exchanging it, the chair has only use value for me. But the specific characteristic of the capitalist mode of production is that a use value is only a means to an end in order to produce an exchange value of a commodity. The use values "are also the material bearers [*Träger*] of ... exchange-value" (Marx 1976, 126). The use value is therefore the condition of the exchange value.

Contrary to the use value, the exchange value is not a natural but a social form; that is, an exchange value is only realized through social exchange and marks a quantitative relationship. If a thing is not only a use value but also an exchange value, it evolves to a commodity. This indicates that a commodity is not realized in the process of production, but only in exchange. For example, if I exchange one PC for two printers, the exchange value of this PC is two printers. The exchange value therefore emerges in relation to other commodities. Every single commodity is characterized by many different exchange values.

It may be possible to exchange one PC – instead of two printers – for four hard drives. If 1 PC = 2 printers = 4 hard drives, different commodities are equated. The different commodities must contain a common element making them reducible: "In the same way the exchange values of commodities must be reduced to a common element, of which they represent a greater or a lesser quantity" (Marx 1976, 127). Based on Smith, Marx states that the amount of the socially (and not individually) average necessary labour time for producing the commodity is the common quality of the different commodities. This means that 1 PC = 2 printers = 4 hard drives is only valid if the same amount of labour time is used for the production of one PC as for the production of two printers and four hard drives. The commodities "can no longer be distinguished, but are all together reduced to the same kind of labour, human labour in the abstract" (Marx 1976, 128). The human labour time as the value creating substance therefore forms the value of a commodity. The exchange value expresses this commodity value in the form of money. The socially average necessary labour time is an inconstant variable and depends on certain conditions. Examples include that through the application of machines and technology more commodities can be produced in less time and the magnitude of value decreases. On the other hand, if the productive force of labour drops caused by a poor harvest, the magnitude of value increases:

> In general, the greater the productivity of labour, the less the labour-time required to produce an article, the less the mass of labour crystallized in that article, and the less its value. Inversely, the less the productivity of labour, the greater the labour-time necessary to produce an article, and the greater its value.
>
> (Marx 1976, 131)

In understanding the process of production, it is helpful to analyse how Marx described the circuit of capital. For Marx, the circuit of capital contains three stages, namely the stage of money capital (sphere of circulation), the stage of productive capital (sphere of production), and the stage of commodity capital (sphere of circulation).

The first stage of the circuit of capital starts with a certain amount of money (M), which at this stage is money capital. With this money, the capitalist purchases two different commodities (C), namely labour power (L) and means of production (mp; objects and instruments of labour). This act may be expressed as follows:

$$M - C \begin{cases} L \\ mp \end{cases}$$

Money is transformed into commodities and the capitalist appears as a buyer. It is a transformation of money capital into commodity capital. With labour power and the means of production, the capitalist is able to start the process of production (Marx 1992, 118).

The second stage of the circuit of capital is a productive process. The capitalist consumes the purchased commodities in order to produce a new commodity (C') with an increased value because of surplus labour. P indicates the process of production. The dots signify that the sphere of circulation is interrupted by the sphere of production. This act may be expressed as follows:

$$C \left\{ \begin{array}{c} L \\ \overline{mp} \end{array} \right. ...P...C'$$

With a commodity of greater value than its single elements of production, the capitalist is able to sell the commodity on the market (Marx 1992, 118–121).

In the third stage of the circuit of capital, the capitalist sells the commodity on the market and transforms the commodity into money. The capitalist ends up with a greater amount of money (M') than what he owned at the beginning. This act may be expressed as follows:

$$C' - M'$$

The capitalist turns back to the market as a seller. It is a transformation of commodity capital into money capital (Marx 1992, 121–131).

> We have seen how the circulation process, after its first phase ... has elapsed, is interrupted by P, in which the commodities bought on the market, L and mp, are consumed as material and value components of the productive capital; the product of this consumption is a new commodity, M', altered both materially and in value. The interrupted circulation process, $M-C$, must be supplemented by $C - M''$.
>
> (Marx 1992, 131–132)

Finally, the circuit as a whole may be expressed as follows:

$$M - C \left\{ \begin{array}{c} L \\ \overline{mp} \end{array} \right. ...P...C' - M'$$

The first and the last stage take place in the sphere of circulation, whereas the second stage takes place in the sphere of production. Surplus value is produced only in the sphere of production. The sphere of circulation represents a transformation of money capital into commodity capital and a transformation of commodity capital into money capital (Marx 1992, 131–143).

> Here capital appears as a value that passes through a sequence of connected and mutually determined transformations, a series of metamorphoses that form so many phases or stages of a total process. Two of these phases belong to the circulation sphere, one to the sphere of production. In each of these phases the capital value is to be found in a different form, corresponding to a different and special function. Within this movement the value advanced not only maintains itself, but it grows, increases its magnitude. Finally, in the concluding stage, it returns to the same form in which it appeared at the outset of the total process. This total process is therefore a circuit.
>
> (Marx 1992, 132–133)

The circuit of capital indicates the dialectical relationship of the productive forces and the relations of production:

Relations of
production

$$M - C \left\{ \begin{matrix} L \\ mp \end{matrix} \right| ...P...C' - M'$$

Productive forces

As already mentioned, the productive forces are a system of living labour forces and facts and factors of the process of production that cause and influence labour. The labour power is the unity of physical and spiritual labour forces of an individual; that is, physical ability, qualification, knowledge, abilities, experiences, etc. The means of production are factors of the process of labour and production not being related to an individual; that is, objects (natural means of production) and instruments (technical means of production) of labour such as oil, silicon, technology, science, cooperation, division of labour, and methods of organization. In reference to the above circuit, labour power and means of production express the productive forces producing a commodity. The capitalist relations of production constitute the relationship between wage labour and capital, and are a certain form of property relation specifying who produces and who owns property. The circuit starts with the capitalist who is able to purchase and apply labour power and means of production in the process of production in order to produce a commodity and to sell it on the market, and ends with a greater amount of money for the capitalist. That is to say, labour power produces the commodity and the capitalist owns the commodity and gets the profit, and expresses the relationship between wage labour and capital. The property relations between possession and non-possession enable the existence of labour power as a productive force in the process of production, because this process requires an actor who has a certain amount of money. It requires an individual who is free in the double sense of being free to dispose of its labour power and being free of the means of production ("double free worker"). At the same time, the productive forces produce and reproduce the relation of production. The relations of production are therefore the means and outcome of the productive forces.

Just as commodities entail a dual character, namely use value and value, so labour embodied in commodities entails a dual character, namely concrete and abstract labour. Labour contained in commodities has a twofold nature. "This point is crucial to an understanding of political economy" (Marx 1976, 132).

All work represents concrete labour, but certain labour represents both concrete and abstract labour, inasmuch as only labour embodied in commodities involves abstract labour. Hence, work contained in products not being exchanged involves only concrete labour. Various concrete labours produce qualitatively different use values. For instance, a programmer produces a computer program and a web designer produces a website. Watching someone working means watching someone carrying out concrete labour. Concrete labour produces use values, and is visible, quantifiable, and existential for human life.

Nevertheless, concrete labour does not form the value of a commodity. Different commodities must consist of a common element in order to be able to realize exchange, namely a certain amount of human labour power. Only labour embodied in exchanged commodities creates value. If the values of different commodities are qualitatively equal, the works having produced the values of the different commodities also contain qualitatively the same human labour. "They are merely two different forms of the expenditure of human labour-power" (Marx 1976, 134) and the commodities "can no longer be distinguished, but are all together reduced to the same kind of labour, human labour in the abstract" (Marx 1976, 128). By means of putting the values of different commodities on the same level, we abstract from concrete labour. Labour is creating value only as a result of the abstraction from the concrete form of labour; that is, an abstraction of labour occurs mediated by exchange. Abstract labour is invisible and not quantifiable.

Marx differentiates further between labour process and valorization process. This distinction must be seen in the context of the distinction between use value and value of commodities and the distinction between concrete and abstract labour. This means that "just as the commodity itself is a unity formed of use-value and value, so the process of production must be a unity, composed of the labour process and the process of creating value [*Wertbildungsprozess*]" (Marx 1976, 293). The labour process characterizes the qualitative part and creates use value in the process of production, whereas the valorization process characterizes the quantitative part and creates value. "The production process ... considered as the unity of the labour process and the process of valorization, it is the capitalist process of production" (Marx 1976, 304).

The labour process is a human activity where, with the help of the instruments of labour, an alteration of material is effected. Marx (1976, 284) understands the labour process as a relationship of human activity with its physical and intellectual capabilities on the one hand and the means of production with its instruments and objects of labour on the other hand.

As already mentioned, the valorization process characterizes the quantitative part in the process of production and involves the value of labour power as well as the value of means of production. Just as with value creation and abstract labour, so the valorization process characterizes the specific capitalist structure in the process of production.

> The same elements of capital which, from the point of view of the labour process, can be distinguished respectively as the objective and subjective factors, as means of production and labour-power, can be distinguished, from the point of view of the valorization process, as constant and variable capital.
>
> (Marx 1976, 314)

The means of production such as objects and instruments of labour are the constant capital (c) and the labour force is the variable capital (v). The reason for this distinction is based on the different functions of means of production and labour power in the process of production.

> That part of capital, therefore, which is turned into means of production, i.e. the raw material, the auxiliary material and the instruments of labour, does not undergo any quantitative alteration of value in the process of production. For this reason, I call it the constant part of capital, or more briefly, constant capital. On the other hand, that part of capital which is turned into labour-power does undergo an alteration of value in the process of production. It both reproduces the equivalent of its own value and produces an excess, a surplus-value, which may itself vary, and be more or less according to circumstances. This part of capital is continually being transformed from a constant into a variable magnitude. I therefore call it the variable part of capital, or more briefly, variable capital.
>
> (Marx 1976, 317)

According to Marx, the distinction of constant and variable capital is based on the assumption that constant capital does not undergo an alteration of value in the process of production, whereas variable capital does. But what does the magnitude of value in the process of production mean?

As already mentioned, the process of production is a unity composed of the labour process and the valorization process. The labour process creates use value and the valorization process creates value. The means of production undergo an alteration of use value in the labour process. From the point of view of the labour process, the human labour force produces out of various means of production (e.g. control unit, arithmetic logic unit, memory, system bus, and input/output as means of labour) a product with a changed use value (e.g. a PC). A PC's use value is different to the use values of control unit, arithmetic logic unit, memory, system bus, and input/output as single elements. From the point of view of the valorization process, the means of production do not undergo an alteration of the magnitude of value. The means of production transfer the value to the new product. Control unit, arithmetic logic unit, memory, system bus, and input/ output have the same value as they have as single elements. Most importantly, the value of human labour power has changed due to the fact that an alteration of value in the process of production has taken place through human activity. "The property therefore which labour-power in action, living labour ... is a gift of nature which costs the worker nothing, but is very advantageous to the capitalist" (Marx 1976, 315). This means that only living labour force as variable capital is able to create value and surplus value in the process of production. The productive forces of labour are the ability of labour power to produce surplus value.

The rate of surplus value indicates the valorization of variable capital and expresses the degree of exploitation of labour power. The rate of surplus value is, from the point of view of the valorization process, a ratio of surplus value to variable capital respectively, from the point of view of the labour process, a ratio of surplus labour to necessary labour. "Surplus value is in the same ratio to variable capital as surplus labour is to necessary labour. In other words, the rate of surplus value, s/v=surplus labour/necessary labour" (Marx 1976, 326). For example, a man works eight hours a day, whereas necessary labour and surplus labour are each performed for four hours. The necessary labour is the work being necessary for the reproduction of the worker (cost of living). The surplus labour is the second period of the labour process that is no longer necessary labour and creates no value for the worker but surplus value. The ratio of these two variables, s/v=4/4 multiplied by 100 (in order to be able to express it in per cent), results in a rate of surplus value respectively of a degree of exploitation of 100 per cent.

In the capitalist mode of production, entrepreneurs consume purchased labour power as variable capital (v) and purchased means of production as constant capital (c) in order to produce commodities. Due to the coercive laws of the capitalist process of production, the overall aim of capitalists is to produce as much surplus value as possible in order to accumulate profit. There are two different possibilities for doing so: the production of absolute surplus value through the extension of the working day, and the production of relative surplus value through the intensification of the working day and increased productivity.

> I call that surplus-value which is produced by the lengthening of the working day, absolute surplus-value. In contrast to this, I call that surplus-value which arises from the curtailment of the necessary labour-time, and from the corresponding alteration in the respective lengths of the two components of the working day, relative surplus-value.
>
> (Marx 1976, 432)

Elsewhere, Marx (1976) explains the difference between the two forms of the production of surplus value on the basis of extensity and intensity:

> Our analysis of absolute surplus-value dealt primarily with the extensive magnitude of labour, its duration, while its intensity was treated as a given factor. We have now to consider the inversion [*Umschlag*] of extensive magnitude into intensive magnitude, or magnitude of degree.

The production of absolute surplus value is achieved by the prolongation of the working day. The working day consists of definite necessary labour time and indefinite surplus labour time. The length of the working day is therefore simultaneously definite and indefinite and to a certain extent variable. Marx introduces a minimum and maximum limit of the working day. "We have a minimum limit, i.e. the part of the day in which the worker must necessarily work for his own maintenance" (Marx 1976, 341). Generally speaking, the minimum limit is the sum of necessary labour time and surplus labour time, whereas surplus labour time is equal to zero. Marx rejects this possibility, because the production of surplus value is essential for the capitalist mode of production and surplus labour must be greater than zero in reality. The maximal limit results from the length of a day of 24 hours and certain physical barriers including eating, cleaning, relaxing, sleeping, and moral barriers involving the fulfilment of spiritual and social needs. The working day is thus to a certain extent variable and its length marks the historical result of the struggles between the class of the capitalists and the working class.

> There is here therefore an antinomy, of right against right, both equally bearing the seal of the law of exchange. Between equal rights, force decides. Hence, in the history of capitalist production, the establishment of a norm for the working day presents itself as a struggle over the limits of that day, a struggle between collective capital, i.e. the class of capitalists, and collective labour, i.e. the working class.
>
> (Marx 1976, 344)

Due to the fact that the production of absolute surplus value and the extension of the working day are finite through physical and moral barriers, it seems in the context of capital accumulation to be more efficient in producing relative surplus value. This may be done through changing the ratio of necessary to surplus labour by driving the development of the productive forces of labour forward. That is, the value of labour power decreases and surplus value increases simultaneously. Increasing the productive forces of labour means to rationalize the mode of production in order to produce more in less time.

> The objective of the development of the productivity of labour within the context of capitalist production is the shortening of that part of the working day in which the worker must work for himself, and, the lengthening, thereby, of the other part of the day; in which he is free to work for nothing for the capitalist.
>
> (Marx 1976, 438)

Besides cooperation and the division of labour, Marx highlights the application of machinery and technology as important aspects of the production of relative surplus value and moving the development of the productive forces of labour forward. Hence, the development and technological movements of the productive forces are a dynamic process.

On the one hand, the development of machinery and the technical movement of the productive forces appear as historical *necessities* in the capitalist mode of production:

> Once adopted into the production process of capital, the means of labour passes through different metamorphoses, whose culmination is the machine, or rather, an automatic system of machinery (system of machinery: the automatic

one is merely its most complete, most adequate form, and alone transforms machinery into a system).... The development of the means of labour into machinery is not an accidental moment of capital, but is rather the historical reshaping of the traditional, inherited means of labour into a form adequate to capital.... Machinery appears, then, as the most adequate form of fixed capital, and fixed capital, in so far as capital's relations with itself are concerned, appears as the most adequate form of capital as such.

(Marx 1997b)

On the other hand, machinery (nowadays we speak of technology) is for Marx a *means* of production in societies in general and a means for the production of surplus value in capitalist societies in particular. Employing technology transforms the process of production into a technological process. Technology is part of the fixed constant capital and plays an important role in the production of surplus value, because it is 'the most powerful means of raising the productivity of labour" (Marx 1976, 526) by reducing necessary labour and expanding surplus labour. Through technological innovation it is possible to produce more surplus value in less time and therefore to intensify labour:

It imposes on the worker an increased expenditure of labour within a time which remains constant, a heightened tension of labour-power, and a closer filling-up of the pores of the working day ... compression of a greater mass of labour into a given period.

(Marx 1976, 534)

The development of contemporary high-tech capitalism indicates the importance of employing technology in the process of production. Machinery does not create value, but acts as a supporting means for human labour producing surplus value. "Machinery, like every other component of constant capital, creates no new value, but yields up its own value to the product it serves to beget" (Marx 1976, 509).

In summary, it has become clear that value forms the productive forces. The analysis has shown that the development of the productive forces is from the outset determined by exchange value, abstract labour, valorization process, capital, and the production of relative surplus value.

The productive forces mature the contradiction and antagonism of the capitalist form of production and simultaneously ripen "the elements for forming a new society and the forces tending towards the overthrow of the old one" (Marx 1976, 635). Within different relations of production, technology and machinery could be employed for shortening labour time, lightening the load of labour, and for supporting wealth and freedom.

Since Machinery in itself shortens the hours of labour, but when employed by capital it lengthens them; since in itself it lightens labour, but when employed by capital it heightens its intensity; since in itself it is a victory of man over the forces of nature but in the hands of capital it makes man the slave of those forces; since in itself it increases the wealth of the producers, in the hands of capital it makes them into paupers.

(Marx 1976, 568–569)

This means that "the productive forces developing in the womb of bourgeois society create the material conditions for the solution of that antagonism" (Marx 1951, 329). The technological movement of the productive forces points to the degree of development of wealth generally (Marx 1997b). One may therefore conclude that

it is one of the civilizing aspects of capital that it extorts this surplus labour in a manner and in conditions that are more advantageous to social relations and to the creation of elements for a new and higher formation than was the case under the earlier forms of slavery, serfdom, etc.

(Marx 1991, 958)

The technological movement of the productive forces refers to opportunities of human liberation. The technological forces of the advanced industrial society incorporate Utopian opportunities on a global level, which could abolish poverty and scarcity in the near future.

Although the technological movement of the productive forces is shaped by value creation in capitalist societies, the development of the productive forces indicates opportunities of the commons within different relations of production (see Figure 1.8).

This differentiation raises the question of whether changes of productive forces and/or relations of production are needed in order to point towards a radically transformative concept, and will be discussed in the concluding chapter.

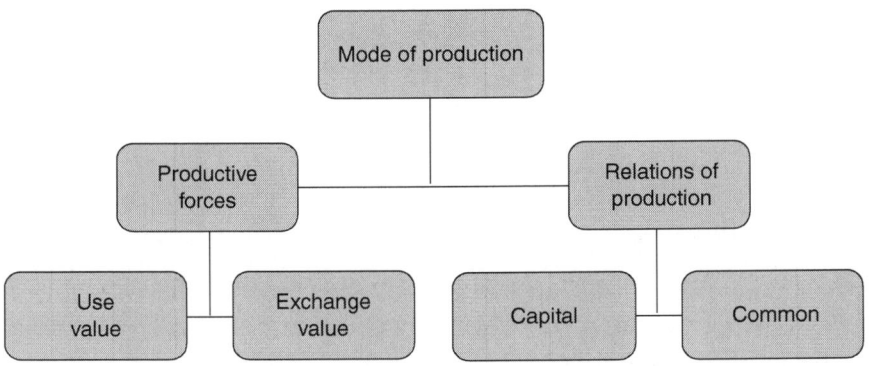

Figure 1.8 Different possibilities of productive forces and relations of production.

Conclusion: means of communication as means of production

This chapter has provided some foundational concepts of a critical theory of media, technology, and society in the second section. The subsequent arguments summarize the main results:

- Media enable and constrain information processes. Information is a subjective and objective process of cognition, communication, and cooperation.
- Societal media incorporate technological and human aspects.
- Media are artefacts such as instruments, means, natural resources, property, power, and definitions mediating human relations and actions. That is to say, media are technologies that produce and organize information of interpersonal relations; hence, media are information technologies.
- Technology may be understood as a purposeful unity of objects, means, methods, abilities, processes, and knowledge that are necessary in order to fulfil individual or social needs. Technology is a totality of objective and subjective factors and only objective aspects of technology are media.
- Technology mediates the relationship between humans and nature/culture.
- There is a mutual shaping of society and technology. Society constructs and shapes technology (design) on the one hand, and technology impacts upon and transforms society (assessment) on the other.
- There is an interplay of technological structure and technological agents. The technological structure enables and constrains human activity and thinking on the one hand and is the outcome of productive and reproductive processes on the other.
- Technology mediates human actions, and technology is devised, constructed, maintained, and modified by agents.
- A dialectical view on technology bears in mind the genesis of technology, that is, the social design of technology; and the assessment of technology, that is, technological effects on society.
- Applying such a view to capitalist society could mean that asymmetrical social relationships of power and domination are embedded in the conception, construction, maintenance, and modification of technics and that technological effects depend on the application and employment of technology.
- A dialectical view sees the development of technology as progressive and regressive, liberating and repressive, as potential and risk. It indicates different possibilities of technological dynamics between resignation and Utopia. This view is neither techno-deterministic nor socio-constructivist, neither techno-optimistic nor techno-pessimistic, and takes into consideration the design and assessment of technology.
- The dialectics of society and technology is related to the dialectics of forces and relations of production.

Therefore, the dialectics of productive forces and relations of production was presented in the third section. The following points sum up the most important outcomes:

- The productive forces are a system of living labour forces and facts and factors of the process of production that cause and influence labour. The relations of production constitute social relations between human beings, which act as agents or as social groups in economic processes. Relations of production have a specific historical form such as the relationship between wage labour and capital in capitalist societies.
- The mode of production is based on a dialectical relationship of productive forces and relations of production. The economic structure enables and constrains the development of the productive forces, which form the relations of production.
- Value creation and capital accumulation form the dynamic development of the productive forces. The productive forces are rooted in capitalist interests and social forces.
- But the technological movement of the productive forces also refers to opportunities of human liberation. The technological forces of the advanced industrial society incorporate Utopian opportunities on a global level, which could abolish poverty and scarcity in the near future.
- Productive forces are the medium and outcome of capitalist development.

Just as productive forces and technology are the medium and outcome of capitalist development, so are means of communication. Means and technologies of communication are powerful ways of raising productivity. Media and communication technologies are technologies of rationalization, support intra-organizational corporate communication, drive the globalization of capitalism forward, advance commodity sales, reduce the circulation and turnover time of capital, and are means for the spatial centralization of capital (Fuchs 2011b, 141–151). "Machinery and the revolution in the means of transport and communication provide the weapons for the conquest of foreign markets" (Marx 1976, 579). Means of communication are thus a medium of capitalist development. The economic force of capital accumulation and the dynamic movement of the productive forces have brought technological innovations including transportation and communication systems. "The whole earth has been girded by telegraph cables" (Marx 1991, 164). Means of communication are thus also an outcome of capitalist development.

Media, information technologies, and means of communication are means of production, since information and communication are intrinsic to the process of production (Williams 2005b, 50). The means of communication have a specific productive history, because there are "relative homologies" (Williams 2005b, 50) between means of communication and productive forces and relationships. Traditional and orthodox Marxism has ignored the role of means of communication in the process of production and communication has been analysed as a second-order process. Therefore, it requires an especially sharp contemporary correction, since the means of communication as means of social production, and in relation to this the production of the means of communication themselves, have taken on a quite new significance, within the generally extended communicative character of modern societies and between modern societies. This can be seen, very strikingly, within the totality of modern 'economic' and 'industrial' production, where, in the transport, printing and electronic industries 'communicative production' has reached a qualitatively different place in its relations to – more strictly its proportion of – production in general.

(Williams 2005b, 53)

Today, we can add that means of communication and communication technologies have also reached a qualitatively different place in the commodification of the Internet and social media.

I will argue throughout this study that information and social knowledge may also serve as objects of labour and direct forces of production in informational capitalism in general and in social media in particular. In the last decades of capitalist production, there has been an intensification and extension of informational commodities that are based on ideas, creativity, communication, social relationships, emotional artefacts, experiences, user-generated content, etc. These characteristics may be considered as superstructural practices being generated in social, communicative, and cultural relationships now transforming into economic structures. It is the culturalization of the material base in contemporary capitalist societies. Based on autonomist Marxism, I will also claim throughout this volume that capital tends to subsume the whole of society into the production process and the logic of the factory is extended to society. Corporate social media move towards the total commodification of social life, human communication, experiences, feelings, and creativity on the Net. The whole of social life becomes subsumed under capital on the Internet. These tendencies may be considered as basic phenomena now transforming into social and cultural experiences. It is the economization of superstructural practices in modern capitalist societies (see Figure 1.9).

One may thus argue that the production and consumption of information and communication technologies and social media are both part of the base as technological means of production (media) and part of the superstructure as (social) means of communication. Although this tendency does not undermine the distinction between base and superstructure entirely, it "indicates that the traditional distinction between the economic, the political, the social, and the cultural become increasingly blurred" (Hardt and Negri 2004, 109).

Based on these findings, it becomes possible to conduct a well-founded analysis of new media in terms of theorizing the Internet and bringing up the question of what is social about social media. Chapter 2 provides theoretical foundations of critical Internet and social media studies.

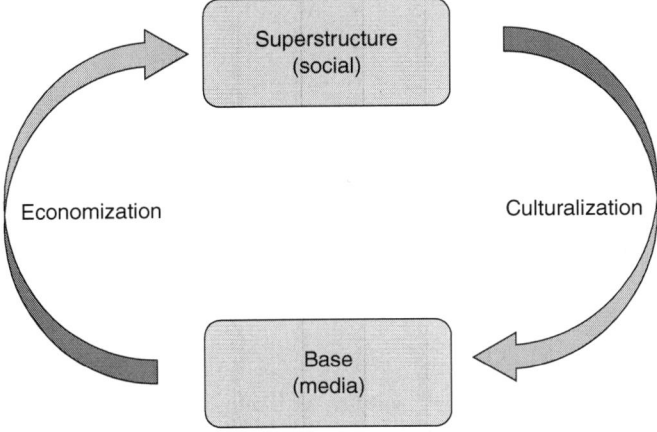

Figure 1.9 Dialectical relationship of social (superstructure) media (base).

Note

1 "Mit der Maschine ... erhält die Herrschaft der vergangenen Arbeit über die lebendige nicht nur soziale – in der Beziehung von Kapitalist und Arbeiter ausgedrückte – sondern sozusagen technologische Wahrheit."

2 Critical Internet and social media studies

Introduction

The beginning of the Internet goes back to ARPANET in 1969, a computer network founded by ARPA (Advanced Research Projects Agency) and financially supported by the Defence Department of the United States. Although the idea of the Internet had to a certain extent been based on military aims, its primarily task was to mobilize research resources at universities and to share information among research groups. The key technological developments that led to the Internet were built around government institutions, universities, and student hacker communities (Castells 2001, 22). The origin of the Internet is not purely explicable out of economic terms, because in the beginning it was not permitted to be used for business purposes (Feenberg 2012, 11). The Internet was more a cultural creation of certain US university campuses of the 1960s and 1970s, where people enjoyed relatively free spaces and individual freedom. Community networks extended the system far beyond its original scope to an open, decentralized, and cooperative project. The Internet "was created on the basis of state support, open usage, and cooperative self-organization. A proliferation of autonomous activity transformed a military-industrial network into a system that in many ways realizes radical dreams of a democratic communication system" (Dyer-Witheford 1999, 122). Many Internet-based applications have emerged since that time (e.g. LISTSERV, MUD, e-mail, and Netserv), but probably the best-known and most influential Internet-based application is the World Wide Web (WWW). It was developed by Tim Berners-Lee at CERN in 1990 and is based on the Hypertext Markup Language (HTML). Not least, the user-friendliness of the WWW contributed to the popularization of the Internet in the 1990s (for the history of the Internet see Abbate 1999; Naughton 2001; Murphy 2002). Since the early 1990s commercial online activities have been permitted, and by the mid-1990s the Internet had been privatized and commodified (Feenberg 2012, 11).

Many authors have recently argued that the Internet has been transformed from a system being mainly oriented towards informational elements into a system more oriented towards enabling communication and cooperation (Beer and Burrows 2007; boyd and Ellison 2007; Fuchs 2010a; Kolbitsch and Maurer

2006; O'Reilly 2005a; Saveri *et al.* 2008). The notions of "web 2.0", "social software", "social media", "participative web", and "social network(ing) sites" (SNS) have emerged in this context. SNS such as Google+, Facebook, diaspora*, and Kaioo are Internet-based communication platforms allowing people to create profiles and share ideas, announce personal messages, upload or watch videos, and write personal entries. Most approaches see the active involvement of users in the production of content as the main characteristic of web 2.0.

In an interview, Berners-Lee, the originator of the World Wide Web, criticizes the concept of web 2.0 as a myth:

> Web 1.0 was all about connecting people. It was an interactive space, and I think Web 2.0 is, of course, a piece of jargon, nobody even knows what it means. If Web 2.0 for you is blogs and wikis, then that is people to people. But that was what the Web was supposed to be all along. And in fact, you know, this Web 2.0, quote, it means using the standards which have been produced by all these people working on Web 1.0. It means using the document object model, it means for HTML and SVG, and so on. It's using HTTP, so it's building stuff using the Web standards, plus JavaScript, of course. So Web 2.0, for some people, it means moving some of the thinking client side so making it more immediate, but the idea of the Web as interaction between people is really what the Web is. That was what it was designed to be as a collaborative space where people can interact.
>
> (Laningham 2006)

Notions such as participatory culture, web 2.0 as radically new services, economic democracy, and consumer participation are used in an inflationary way in academic and public discourse. In particular, business advocates and cultural theorists, including Jenkins (2006), Bruns (2008), Benkler (2006), Shirky (2008), and Tapscott and Williams (2006) claim that user-generated content platforms have advanced a more participatory and democratic society. According to Fuchs, web 2.0 is in contrast not a participatory techno-social system, but predominantly a capitalist structure benefiting the few at the expense of the many. "'Web 2.0' and 'social media', conceived as participatory culture and participatory economy, are ideological categories that serve the interests of the dominant class. They ignore power structures that shape the Internet" (Fuchs 2012c, 728). Web 2.0 is not a democratic area of equal participants, but rather a space of capital accumulation. From the standpoint of participatory democracy theory, the notion of participatory web 2.0 may thus be considered as an ideology (Fuchs 2011b, 255).

I agree it should be questioned if the term "web 2.0" best describes the technological infrastructure and the notion of participatory web as a business strategic ideology, but it cannot be rejected that there have been some technological and social transformations on the Internet in resent years. Fuchs (2010a, 769–770) compared the top 20 websites used in the United States in 1998 and 2008 according to whether they are technologically more oriented towards cognitive tasks or more focused on enabling communication and cooperation. He found that the number of websites being solely oriented in informational elements has decreased and the technological foundations for communication and cooperation have increased. In addition, Fuchs (2010a, 771) also assessed if subjective usage patterns have changed and concludes that community functions have been rising during the past few years. Web 2.0 is an ideology and reality at the same time. The use of terms such as "web 2.0" implies more technological transformations, whereas others including "participative web" focus more on social changes of the current web. From my point of view, the concept of "social media" best describes the current developments, because it indicates social and technological transformations. For practical reasons, I will use the different terms that have arisen in this context interchangeably and as synonyms.

There is much public talk about the transformations and the social and communicative aspects on the web. The following collected news clips indicate this development:

- "Hoax Won't Deter Tweeting. Companies to Push on with Social-Media Disclosure; Banks Expanding Access" (*Wall Street Journal*, 25 April 2013).
- "Hackers caused panic with 'Obama injured' tweet. Hackers spooked markets after breaking into the Associated Press's Twitter account and falsely reporting President Barack Obama had been injured after two blasts at the White House" (*The Sowetan*, 24 April 2013).
- "Social media helping locate quake victims in China" (*The Times of India*, 21 April 2013).

These examples indicate how important the topic of social media and SNS has become for the public and for our daily lives. In addition, the fact that one can find web 2.0 platforms including Google (rank 1), Facebook (rank 2), YouTube (rank 3), Wikipedia (rank 6), Twitter (rank 13), LinkedIn (rank 14), Bing (rank 16), WordPress (rank 23), Ask (rank 38), and Craigslist (rank 45) (Alexa Internet 2013) on the most frequently accessed websites worldwide points out the enormous popularity of these sites. Nevertheless, what is actually meant by terms such as web 2.0, social software/media, and SNS? Although there is much public talk and rising popularity, it seems there is no definite answer, but rather, ambiguous concepts of what characterizes these phenomena. Beer and Burrows (2007) argue that a sociological consideration of web 2.0 is needed and "there has been little systematic research into the activities that are generating this new web content". This chapter offers such a systematic analysis of the web.

The overall aim of this chapter is to clarify how the web is defined in the academic literature, what the different concepts have in common, what distinguish them from one another, and which advantages and disadvantages such definitions have in order to clarify if there is a gap in the existing literature. The next section contains a systematic discussion of the state of the art of different notions of the web by establishing a typology and discussing commonalities and differences. The third section concludes with a critical theory of the Internet.

Foundations of Internet and social media studies

Several authors have already provided classifications of the web: Saveri and colleagues (2008, 19), for instance, distinguish between eight different technologies of the web, namely self-organizing mesh networks, community computing grids, peer production networks, social mobile computing, group-forming networks, social software, social accounting systems, and knowledge collectives. Kollock and Smith (1999, 4–8) discern six online communications systems: (1) e-mail and discussion lists, (2) Usenet and BBSs, (3) text chat, (4) MUDs, (5) World Wide Web sites, and (6) graphical worlds. Kaplan and Haenlein (2010, 62–64) provide six different types of social media: collaborative projects, blogs, content communities, social networking sites, virtual game worlds, and virtual social worlds. According to Schmidt (2006, 34), social software facilitates three specific processes, namely information management (collaborative bookmarking services), identity management (blogs), and relationship management (social networking sites). Beer and Burrows (2007) focus on four types of web 2.0 applications: wikis, folksonomies, mashups, and social networking sites. Mandiberg (2012, 2) differentiates between the concepts of user-generated content, convergence culture, people formerly known as the audience, participatory media, peer production, and web 2.0. These typologies of different web technologies are arbitrary and stated without a theoretical criterion for a certain typology. There are no theoretical foundations given for the categories and the suggested definitions. A theoretical criterion is missing that is used for discerning different web types. A theoretically founded typology of defining the web is important in order to undertake a theoretical analysis of the web in modern society. Providing such an analysis is a meta-theoretical task.

In order to establish a systematic typology of the web, it is important to make use of social theory. According to Hofkirchner (2002, 24; 2010, 18; 2013, 184), information and knowledge processes occur in the form of human cognition, communication, and cooperation. Cognition, communication, and cooperation describe different system dimensions of social information and knowledge processes. On the cognitive level, individuals produce contents of consciousness and ideas. Cognition refers to the elements of social systems (individual dimension). On the communicative level, individuals produce common understanding. Communication refers to the interaction of individuals as elements of social systems (interactional dimension). On the cooperative level, individuals collectively produce sense as common action. Cooperation refers to the social system itself being organized by the interaction of its elements (integrational dimension). Hofkirchner and his working group summarize the idea of knowledge as a threefold dynamic process of cognition, communication, and cooperation as follows:

> By cognition we want to refer to the understanding that a person, based on his/her subjective systemic knowledge, connects to another person by using certain mediating systems. When it comes to feedback, persons enter an

objective mutual relationship, i.e. communication. Communicating knowledge from one system to another causes structural changes in the receiving system. From communication processes shared or jointly produced reality and resources can emerge, i.e. co-operation.

(Raffl *et al.* 2008, 605–606)

Regardless of whether someone agrees with Hofkirchner's approach or not, this treatment indicates that information systems including the Internet in general and the World Wide Web in particular occur either in the form of cognition, communication, or cooperation, or in combined forms.

These findings allow for distinguishing cognitive, communicative, and cooperative notions of defining the web that may be used for constructing a typology of the existing literature (Fuchs 2010a; Fuchs *et al.* 2010; Raffl *et al.* 2008):

- Cognitive notions understand the web primarily as a hypertextual tool for thoughts, ideas, and the consumption of information (individual level; examples: websites, online newspapers).
- In comparison, communicative notions see the web as an interactive medium for human interaction and communication (interactional level; examples: e-mail, chat, blogs, social networking sites).
- Finally, cooperative notions define the web as a collaborative platform that helps develop social relationships in order to support "collective intelligence" (Lévy 1997), collective activities, and common goals (integrational level; examples: wikis, shared workspace systems, graphical worlds).

Cognitive, communicative, and cooperative notions of the web will be outlined below. The following three subsections are therefore structured according to this distinction. The task of these subsections is to give a representative but still eclectic overview of different definitions of the web.

Cognitive theories of the Internet and social media

In "Where the Action Is", Dourish (2001, 56) provides a cognitive definition of the Web when he mentions that

> human–computer interaction can be thought of as a form of mediated communication between the end user and the system designer, who must structure the system so that it can be understood by the user, and so that the user can be led through a sequence of actions to achieve some end result.

He further states:

> This implies that even the most isolated and individual interaction with a computer system is still fundamentally a social activity. The communication between designer and user takes place against a backdrop of commonly held

social understandings. Even the metaphors around which user interfaces are constructed ("private" files versus "public" ones, "dialog" boxes, electronic "mail", documents, wizards, and "publishing" a web page) rely on a set of social expectations for their interpretation and use.

(Dourish 2001, 56)

Dourish's analysis may be interpreted as a cognitive notion of the Web, because he mentions the consumption of information as an individual action.

Communicative theories of the Internet and social media

For boyd (2007, 17), social software is about

a movement, not simply a category of technologies. It's about recognizing that the era of e-commerce centered business models is over; we've moved on to web software that is all about letting people interact with people and data in a fluid way. It's about recognizing that the web can be more than a broadcast channel; collections of user-generated content can have value. No matter what, it is indeed about the *new* but the new has nothing to do with technology; it has to do with attitude.

In addition, boyd and Ellison (2007, 211) define social network sites as:

web-based services that allow individuals to (1) construct a public or semi-public profile within a bounded system, (2) articulate a list of other users with whom they share a connection, and (3) view and traverse their list of connections and those made by others within the system.

Similarly, Shirky (2003) understands social software primarily as "software that supports group communications" and further states that

we now have communications tools that are flexible enough to match our social capabilities ... these communications tools have been given many names, all variations on a theme: "social software," "social media," "social computing," and so on.

(Shirky 2008, 20)

Benkler (2006, 373) defines social software as "software whose design characteristic is that it treats genuine social phenomena as different from one-to-one or one-to-many communications". For Kennedy (2004, 249), "social software supports a conversational interaction between two individuals or a group".

boyd, Shirky, Benkler, and Kennedy may be classified into communicative notions of the Web, because they mainly understand the Web as a medium for human interaction and communication. In the next subsection, cooperative notions of the web will be discussed.

Cooperative theories of the Internet and social media

As already mentioned, cooperative notions define the Web as a collaborative platform that supports human cooperation. In answering the question, what is web 2.0, O'Reilly (2005a) lists seven core principles of web 2.0: (1) web as platform; (2) harnessing collective intelligence; (3) data is the next Intel Inside; (4) end of the software release cycle; (5) lightweight programming models; (6) software above the level of a single device; (7) rich user experiences (see also O'Reilly and Battelle 2009). O'Reilly (2005b) also provides a more compact definition of web 2.0:

> Web 2.0 is the network as platform, spanning all connected devices; Web 2.0 applications are those that make the most of the intrinsic advantages of that platform: delivering software as a continually-updated service that gets better the more people use it, consuming and remixing data from multiple sources, including individual users, while providing their own data and services in a form that allows remixing by others, creating network effects through an "architecture of participation," and going beyond the page metaphor of Web 1.0 to deliver rich user experiences.

Kolbitsch and Maurer (2006) argue that the Web has been transformed into more community-based services in recent years. This transformation is characterized by the emergence of web communities including blogs, wikis, file sharing and social networks, bookmarking services and podcasting groups. For Kolbitsch and Maurer (2006, 205), these new services feature both openness and user participation, and "support individuals in making their knowledge explicit and help collective intelligence unfold". Likewise, Gillmor (2006, 26) mentions the cooperative elements of the Web in the sense that in "the read-write web" (forums, weblogs, wiki, peer-to-peer) collective knowledge would be more than individual knowledge: "In no sphere is the whole more intelligent than the sum of its parts than in digital networks."

Tapscott and Williams (2006, 19) state that "we're all participating in the rise of a global, ubiquitous platform for computation and collaboration" that is globally and openly organized and supports peering and sharing. These new services on the Web include "platforms for collaboration" (Tapscott and Williams 2006, 18), "platforms for participation" (Tapscott and Williams 2006, 183), "platforms for web services and communities" (Tapscott and Williams 2006, 188), as well as "platforms for grassroots action" (Tapscott and Williams 2006, 199).

For Saveri and colleagues (2008, 17), "social software is a set of tools that enable group-forming networks to emerge quickly. It includes media and applications that empower individual efforts, link individuals together into larger aggregates, interconnect groups, and provide metadata about network dynamics". In addition, social software develops local trust-building mechanisms and surrogates, makes social networks visible, and supports social norms. In addition, social software concretizes personal relationships into social capital, shapes cooperation, provides feedback on group status, provides group memory, and is a vehicle for establishing multiple personal brands (Saveri *et al.* 2008, 19). Bruns (2008, 3) understands social software and the concept of web 2.0 as spaces for human collaboration and environments for produsage. Produsage is a "seemingly endless string of users acting incrementally as content producers by gradually extending and improving the information present in the information commons" (Bruns 2008, 21). In this context, "produsers take on a hybrid user/produser role which inextricably interweaves both forms of participation" (Bruns 2008, 21).

A more formal definition of social media is provided by Kaplan and Haenlein (2010, 61): "Social media is a group of Internet-based applications that build on the ideological and technological foundations of Web 2.0, and that allow the creation and exchange of User Generated Content." Web 2.0 are platforms, where "content and applications are no longer created and published by individuals, but instead are continuously modified by all users in a participatory and collaborative fashion" (Kaplan and Haenlein 2010, 61). User-generated content consists of "various forms of media content that are publicly available and created by end-users" (Kaplan and Haenlein 2010, 61).

The Organisation for Economic Cooperation and Development (OECD) (2007, 17) argues that the participative web (web 2.0, wikis, and social networking) "is based on intelligent web services and new Internet-based software applications that enable users to collaborate and contribute to developing, extending, rating, commenting on and distributing digital content and developing and customising Internet applications". The OECD (2007, 17) mentions further elements of the participative web:

> New web software tools enable commercial and non-commercial service providers to draw on an ever-widening array of content sources and what is often called the 'collective intelligence' of Internet users, to use information on the web in the form of data, metadata and user resources, and to create links between them. A further characteristic of the participative web is the communication between users and between separate software applications via open web standards and interfaces.

For a cooperative understanding of the web, see also Dijck (2009).

In summary, cooperative notions define the Web as a collaborative platform that helps develop social relationships in order to support collective intelligence, collective activities, and common goals.

Towards a critical theory of the Internet and social media

The overall aim of the previous section was to clarify how the Web is defined in the academic literature. In doing so, the section contained a systematic discussion of the state of the art of different notions of the Web by establishing a typology and discussing commonalties and differences. Table 2.1 summarizes the results.

Table 2.1 Foundations of Internet and social media theory

Cognitive theories of the Web	Communicative theories of the Web	Cooperative theories of the Web
Cognitive theories understand the Web primarily as a hyper-textual tool for thoughts, ideas, and the consumption of information (individual level)	Communicative theories see the Web as an interactive medium for human interaction and communication (interactional level)	Cooperative theories define the Web as a collaborative platform that helps develop social relationships in order to support collective intelligence, collective activities, and common goals (integrational level)
Dourish (2001)	boyd (2007), Shirky (2003, 2008), Benkler (2006), Kennedy (2004)	O'Reilly (2005a, 2005b), Kolbitsch and Maurer (2006), Tapscott and Williams (2006), Gillmor (2006), Saveri *et al.* (2008), Bruns (2008), OECD (2007), Kaplan and Haenlein (2010), Dijck (2009)

Cognitive notions understand the Web primarily as a hypertextual tool for thoughts, ideas, and the consumption of information; for instance, they are represented by Dourish. In contrast, communicative notions see the Web as an interactive medium for human interaction and communication; for example, representatives are boyd, Shirky, and Benkler. Finally, cooperative notions define the Web as a collaborative platform that helps develop social relationships in order to support collective intelligence, collective activities, and common goals; for instance, they are represented by Saveri and colleagues, Bruns, and the OECD.

Although cognitive, communicative, as well as cooperative notions emphasize important features of the Web, they tend to focus on only one dimension of the information process and overlook the fact that cognition, communication, and cooperation are not mutually exclusive. Rather, there is a relationship between cognition, communication, and cooperation:

> Cognition is the necessary condition for communication and communication the necessary condition for cooperation. In addition, we assume that if one level serves the function of a necessary condition for the next higher level, then the lower level might be influenced, shaped, adjusted according to this function by the higher level. Communication emerges from cognition, cooperation emerges from communication: This means that a subset of cognition processes forms communication processes and that a subset of communication processes are cooperation processes. Communication processes are cognition processes with specific, additional qualities. Cooperation processes are communication processes with specific, additional qualities.
>
> (Fuchs *et al.* 2010, 52)

In this way, cognition, communication, and cooperation are connected and mutually conditioned. Therefore, it makes sense to understand the Internet as a threefold techno-social system of human cognition, communication, and cooperation (Hofkirchner 2007, 495; Raffl *et al.* 2008, 605; Fuchs *et al.* 2010).

The Internet is a techno-social system. It is a network of networks and consists of a technological infrastructure (technological subsystem; network of computer networks) and human actors (social subsystem; network of social networks). The technical structure enables and constrains human activities and is itself produced and reproduced by human agents. The technical structure is a medium and outcome of human agency. The technological infrastructure is a materialized outcome of social action, and social actions (cognition, communication, and cooperation) are based on this infrastructure:

> In a top-down process the existing technological structure that stores objective human knowledge enables human activity, that is, there is the subjectification of objective knowledge in human brains when one consumes knowledge that is represented in the Internet or communicates or cooperates with other human beings via the Internet. In this sense the technological structure mediates human activities and results in emergent aspects of thinking and action. In a bottom-up-process, human beings act, communicate, or cooperate in such a way that the knowledge stored by the technological structure changes, is actualized, and extended. Here objective knowledge emerges from the cooperation of human actors; the actors coordinate their communication in such a way that parts of their subjective knowledge are synergetically shared and coordinated in such a way that new embedded and objectified knowledge emerges that is stored in the technological structure. This double process of bottom-up emergence of objective knowledge and top-down emergence of subjective knowledge constitutes the basic productive loop that is characteristic for the self-organization of the Internet system.
>
> (Fuchs 2008, 122–123)

It is a mutual shaping of technology on the one hand and society on the other hand, in which technologies and human beings are connected in a complex way, produce and reproduce each other, and have relative autonomy.

Further authors have also contributed to an integrative understanding of the Web: For example, for Klobas (2006, 1),

> social software is software that facilitates social interaction, collaboration and information exchange, and may even foster communities, based on the activities of groups of users. In its broadest sense, Social Software includes any software tool that brings people together and "supports group interaction".

The Web may be seen as a threefold knowledge system of human cognition, communication, and cooperation. The Internet in the form of cognition may be called web 1.0, in the form of communication web 2.0, and in the form of cooperation web 3.0. Web 1.0 is a tool for thought and includes the consumption of information, web 2.0 is a medium for human communication, and web 3.0 technologies support human cooperation (Fuchs *et al.* 2010, 50). Whereas web 1.0 is primarily a hypertextual web and web 2.0 is mainly an interactive web, web 3.0 may be defined as a collaborative web that helps develop social relationships in order to support "collective intelligence" (Lévy 1997), collective activities, and common goals for a real cooperative social structure. Nevertheless, a cooperative web 3.0 is not yet realized and is only possible in an overall cooperative society (Hofkirchner 2007, 497).

Conclusion: ideology and commodity critique

When it comes to the risks of new information and communication technologies, we must look at the other side of the coin as well. There has been an extension and intensification of privacy threats and surveillance risks in economic, political, and cultural contexts in recent years being also based on the employment of various surveillance technologies. The Internet and new media are one of these technologies. Before moving on to the empirical analysis, the work at hand must thus be theoretically situated in the context of the state of the art in the fields of privacy and surveillance.

It is often claimed that a critique of political economy, which is rooted in economic theory, focuses more on commodity critique and a critical theory, which is rooted in social theory and philosophy, more on ideology critique (Fuchs 2012c, 696). In this context, Murdock and Golding (1997, 3–4, emphasis added) make the important point that "the obvious starting point for a critical political economy of mass communication is the recognition that the mass media are first and foremost industrial and commercial organizations which produce and distribute *commodities*". Murdock and Golding (1997, 4–5, emphasis added) also include the ideological level in their analysis by saying that "it is this second *ideological* dimension of mass media production which gives it its importance and centrality and which requires an approach in terms not only of economics but also of politics". Due to the fact that ideology and commodification are interconnected core elements of capitalist society, a Marx-inspired contribution to media, technology, information, and communication should focus on the role of media in the context of commodity and ideology; or, speaking more generally, in the context of base and superstructure as outlined in Chapter 1:

- The notion of ideology has been defined in various different ways and has been discussed in traditional theory that prefers to understand it as a neutral and general philosophical term (Schopenhauer, Mannheim) and Marxist theory that tends to define it in a normative and critical way (Marx, Gramsci, Althusser, Lukács, Frankfurt School) (Eagleton 1991). While some theorists focus on epistemological characteristics by criticizing ideologies in liberal thoughts and academia, others analyse from an ontological perspective ideological deceptions in social processes. Sevignani (2009) points out that some philosophers are more interested in the question of how ideologies are created and generated (Gramsci, Laclau, Mouffe), whereas others address the content of ideology and ideological consciousness (Lukács, Frankfurt School). It thus makes sense to differentiate between the analysis of ideology production and consumption. Based on a critical theory, one may argue that the distinction between the objective truth and falseness is essential for the concept of ideology. If there is a contradiction between reality and how an individual or a group of individuals views reality, ideological deception occurs. Ideology is the contradiction between truth and falsity and the confrontation of the spiritual with its realization (Eagleton 1991; Herkommer 2004). Ideological values such as liberty and equality are, on an objective level right, as they contribute to the realization of social aims and, on a subjective level wrong, as contemporary society is not able to fulfil these goals. Ideological values and norms can objectively be true, but subjectively wrong (Sandoval 2014, 79). Ideologies reflect the specific social and material life context of individuals and thus have a material basis. But ideologies are also class-specific interests, where certain groups want to define reality in order to make others see reality the same way (Herkommer 2004). Hence, ideologies are created through human experiences and through the ruling class in capitalist society. Because ideologies conceal and legitimize asymmetrical relations of power and domination and have a stabilizing effect on the status quo, a critique of ideology is of central importance from the perspective of a critical theory.

- The existence of commodities is a special characteristic of capitalist societies. In reference to Chapter 1, if an object entails not only a use value, but also an exchange value, it evolves into a commodity. The process of commodity production involves capitalists that exploit labour power for producing commodities in order to generate surplus value and accumulate capital (M–M′). A critique of commodity is crucial, because the process of commodity production presupposes the existence of proprietors and private property, and is the source of exploitation, social inequality, domination, and oppression.

Ideology and commodity are interrelated aspects of capitalism. Ideologies are a reflection of real-life processes and are based on material foundations. Hence, commodities form ideologies. Values refer to an ideology, including liberalism, freedom, and privacy, and enable the development and progress of modern capitalist societies and processes of commodity production and capital accumulation. Ideologies therefore form commodities in return. Ideological deceptions and processes of commodification shape each other mutually.

I will argue in Chapter 3 that privacy is a modern concept of liberal democracy and is used in order to justify liberty from public intervention and that the debate about privacy advances the idea of possessive and self-protective individualism. The notion of privacy is an ideology of modern society. I will demonstrate in

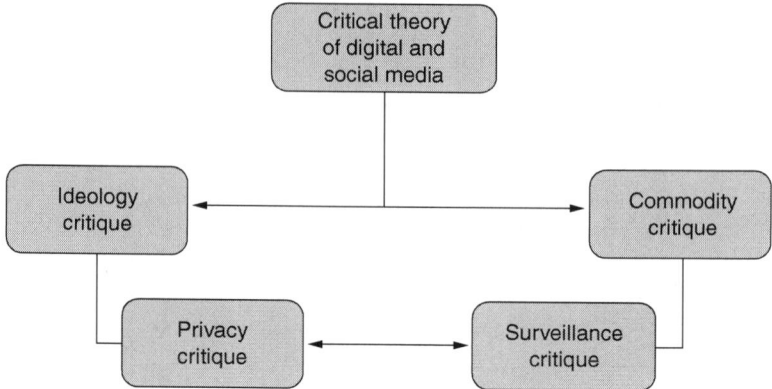

Figure 2.1 Privacy and surveillance critique as ideology and commodity critique.

Chapter 4 that surveillance is an important aspect for guaranteeing the production of surplus value and for accumulating profit in the spheres of production, circulation, and consumption. Surveillance actions are crucial in the process of commodity production in capitalism. Hence, Chapter 3 may be considered as ideology critique and Chapter 4 as commodity critique (see Figure 2.1).

Privacy and surveillance are interrelated characteristics shaping each other. There is a contradiction between privacy and surveillance in modern society, as I will outline in subsequent chapters.

3 Critical (Internet) privacy studies

Ideology critique

Introduction

There is much public talk about privacy in general and Internet privacy in particular. The following collected news clips indicate this development:

- "Google Faces More Inquiries in Europe Over Privacy Policy. Instead of facing one European investigation into its privacy policy, Google now has to contend with at least six of them" (*New York Times*, 2 April 2013).
- "I don't Likes – Facebook boss Zuckerberg's sister's anger over photo: Web nerd's sister is tripped up by the social network's complicated privacy settings" (*Sun*, 27 December 2012).
- "Guidelines help China to take step forward in data privacy" (*South China Morning Post*, 17 April 2013).

The media and the public often alert us to the fact that privacy seems to be under attack and vanishing, caused in particular by the emergence of new information and communication technologies such as the Internet. For instance, web 2.0 activities enable the collection, analysis, and sale of personal data by commercial web platforms. These examples point out how important the topic of privacy has become for the media and for our daily lives. Nevertheless, what is actually meant by the term 'privacy'? Although there is much public talk about privacy, it seems that there is no definite answer; rather, ambiguous concepts exist of what (online) privacy is and what indeed privacy in peril is.

The overall aim of this chapter is to clarify how (Internet) privacy is defined in the academic literature, what the different concepts of privacy have in common, what distinguishes them from one another, and what advantages and disadvantages such definitions have in order to clarify if there is a gap in the existing literature. In doing so, the second section provides a systematic overview of the state of the art of privacy studies by establishing a typology of existing (online) privacy definitions. Based on a critical theory approach, in the third section I argue that the existing literature is insufficient for studying privacy. In contrast, a critical theory of (Internet) privacy avoids pitfalls of the existing literature and strives for the development of theoretical and empirical research methods in order to focus on privacy in the context of domination, asymmetrical power relations, resource control, social struggles, and exploitation.

Foundations of (Internet) privacy studies

Several privacy studies scholars have provided classifications of privacy definitions. Schoeman (1984, 2–3), for instance, distinguishes between three groups of privacy approaches, namely privacy as a claim or entitlement, privacy as the measure of control an individual has over oneself, and privacy as a state or condition of limited access to a person. Solove (2002, 1099–1123) discerns six conceptions of privacy: privacy as (1) the right to be let alone; (2) limited access to the self; (3) secrecy; (4) control over personal information; (5) personhood (this includes individuality, dignity, autonomy, and antitotalitarianism); and (6) intimacy. Solove (2006, 489) additionally develops a taxonomy of privacy and lists four basic groups: information collection, information processing, information dissemination, and invasion. According to Tavani (2011, 137), there are three different views of privacy: accessibility privacy, decisional privacy, and informational privacy. Gormley (1992, 1337–1338) sees four different cluster definitions in the privacy literature, namely privacy as (1) an expression of one's personality or personhood; (2) autonomy; (3) the ability to regulate information about oneself; and (4) a multidimensional approach. These typologies of different privacy approaches are arbitrary and stated without a theoretical criterion for a certain typology. There are no theoretical foundations given for the categories and the suggested definitions. A theoretical criterion is missing, being used for discerning different privacy approaches. A theoretically founded typology of defining privacy is important in order to undertake a theoretical analysis of (online) privacy in modern society. Providing such an analysis is a meta-theoretical task.

"Privacy is a social relation" (Lyon 1994, 184) and therefore a social phenomenon. In order to establish a typology of (Internet) privacy definitions, it makes sense to make use of social theory. Social theories may be classified according to how they deal with the relationship of social structures and social actors (Giddens 1981, 64; Bourdieu 1977, 4; Fuchs 2008, 40). Individualistic and subjectivistic theorists such as Weber, Mead, and Habermas argue that society is constituted by social actors. Structuralistic and functionalistic theorists involving Durkheim, Merton, Parsons, and Luhmann highlight the constraints of social structure (institutionalized relationships) on the individual. Subjective social theories underestimate the constraining effects of social structures and objective social theories do not consider agencies in an appropriate way (Giddens 1981, 15–17; Bourdieu 1977, 3–4). Therefore, it is crucial to elaborate an integrative approach in order to solve the foundational problem of sociology of how social structures and actors are related (Giddens 1981, 64). An integrative approach considers the relationship of society (object) and individual (subject) as mutual in order to bridge the gap between subjective and objective social theories. Integrative (object/subject) approaches "escape from the ritual either/or choice between objectivism and subjectivism in which the social sciences have so far allowed themselves to be trapped" (Bourdieu 1977, 4). Regardless of whether someone agrees with this approach or not, this treatment indicates that social theories deal either with objects or/and with subjects.

These findings allow distinguishing objective, subjective, and integrative (objective/subjective) approaches of defining privacy (on the Net) that may be used for constructing a typology of the existing (Internet) privacy literature.

Objective definitions of privacy (on the Internet) understand privacy as a specific social structure, a moral or legal right, which is used to enable someone's ability to limit or restrict others from access to persons or information (restricted access definition of privacy). Objective definitions of privacy make one or more of the following assumptions:

- Privacy is a (moral and/or legal) right (rights-based conception of privacy).
- Privacy includes the freedom from unwarranted intrusion (non-intrusion).
- Privacy should be protected; for example, by law or certain "zones".
- Restrictions of privacy are violations.
- Privacy should be defined in a normative way.
- Full privacy can only be reached if there is no contact with other social actors.

To a certain extent, objective definitions of (Internet) privacy suggest that the more access to people or information is limited or restricted by a social structure such as the law, the more privacy people have.

In comparison, subjective approaches of defining (online) privacy focus on the individual and understand privacy as control over information about oneself (limited control definition of privacy). Subjective theories understand privacy primarily as self-determination and focus on individual behaviour. Subjective definitions of (Internet) privacy make one or more of the following assumptions:

- Privacy is a personal interest (interest-based conception of privacy).
- Privacy includes the freedom from external interference in one's personal choices, decisions, and plans (non-interference).
- The degree of personal choice indicates how much privacy an individual has.
- Restrictions of privacy are losses.
- Privacy should be defined in a descriptive way.
- Full privacy is reached as long as the individual is able to choose which personalities should be disclosed.

Subjective definitions of (Internet) privacy suggest that the more the individual has control over his or her information, the more privacy he or she enjoys. Subjective theories understand privacy primarily as self-determination and focus on individual behaviour.

Finally, integrative approaches of defining (online) privacy try to combine subjective and objective notions into one concept. Integrative definitions not only understand privacy as a worth-protecting right, they also treat individual control as an important aspect (restricted access/limited control definition of privacy).

Objective, subjective, and integrative (subjective/objective) approaches of privacy in general and Internet privacy in particular will be outlined below. The following three subsections are therefore structured according to this distinction. The task of this section is to give a representative but still eclectic overview of different (online) privacy theories.

Objective theories of (Internet) privacy

Objective theories of privacy

Warren and Brandeis have provided a very influential objective approach of privacy. When numerous photographers and newspapers had been in existence for more than 100 years, Warren and Brandeis (1890) published their seminal paper on privacy in the *Harvard Law Review*. Warren and Brandeis recognized an invasion of individual privacy, because photographers and newspapers collect data on personal lives. For the two authors, privacy is a legal right:

> If we are correct in this conclusion, the existing law affords a principle which may be invoked to protect the privacy of the individual from invasion either by the too enterprising press, the photographer, or the possessor of any other modern device for recording or reproducing scenes or sounds.
>
> (Warren and Brandeis 1890, 206)

The authors see the aim of a law to protect privacy in order to guarantee the "right to an inviolate personality" (Warren and Brandeis 1890, 206) and the "right to be left alone" (Warren and Brandeis 1890, 206). Warren and Brandeis' notion may be classified into objective approaches of defining privacy, because they have developed a rights-based conception of privacy.

Prosser (1960) has analysed the American law in the context of privacy since the Warren and Brandeis article. He concludes that there are four distinct kinds of invasion of four different interests by the law of privacy. These four torts are described as follows: (1) intrusion upon the plaintiff's seclusion or solitude, or into his private affairs; (2) public disclosure of embarrassing private facts about the plaintiff; (3) publicity which places the plaintiff in a false light in the public eye; (4) appropriating the defendant's name or likeness (Prosser 1960, 389).

Based on these findings, Prosser (1960, 392–394) states that Warren and Brandeis' concept of privacy focuses on the disclosure of private data and therefore overlooks the other three kinds of invasions. Prosser criticizes Warren and Brandeis' legal claim and tries to widen the concept of privacy. Nevertheless, his understanding of privacy is still in the context of law and torts.

Scanlon (1975) claims a right to privacy. He argues that law and conventions should offer zones and territories in order to "be able to be free from … intrusions"

(Scanlon 1975, 315). In addition, he states that "our conventions of privacy are motivated by our interests in being free from specific offensive observations and, more generally, in having a well-defined zone within which we need not be on the alert against possible observations" (Scanlon 1975, 320).

In addition, Gavison provides an objective approach of privacy: For Gavison (1980), privacy is not an individual issue based on choice. Rather, privacy is understood as a "condition of life" (Gavison 1980, 425), which should be protected by law. In addition, her concept identifies losses of privacy (Gavison 1980, 424). "The legal system should make an explicit commitment to privacy as a value that should be considered in reaching legal results" (Gavison 1980, 424). For Gavison (1980, 428), privacy is "a limitation of others' access to an individual". She further expresses "that an individual enjoys perfect privacy when he is completely inaccessible to others" (Gavison 1980, 428). In Gavison's understanding it is therefore impossible to achieve full privacy.

In her feminist approach, Allen (1988, 4) states: "the definition of privacy adopted here is very similar to definitions advanced by other restricted-access theorists". Objective definitions of privacy understand privacy as a specific social structure, a moral or legal right, which is used to enable someone's ability to limit or restrict others from access to persons or information (restricted access definition of privacy). For Allen (1988, 3), privacy "denotes a degree of inaccessibility of persons, their mental states, and information about them to the senses and surveillance devices of others".

Some objective concepts make the assumption that privacy includes the freedom from unwarranted intrusion and should be protected. Bok (1983) discusses the relationship between privacy and secrecy. For Bok (1983, 10), "privacy is the condition of being protected from unwanted access by others". This includes access to personal information. Schoeman (1992, 22) defines privacy as "protecting individuals from the overreaching control of others". He further states that "a person has privacy to the extent that others have limited access to information about him, limited access to the intimacies of his life, or limited access to his thoughts or his body" (Schoeman 1984, 3). Schoeman (1984, 3) prefers this form of defining privacy, because it leaves open the question of whether privacy is a desirable state and the possibility to discuss issues concerning abortion, birth control, and social freedom.

In Parent's (1983a, 1983b) view, there is a violation of privacy when others gain personal information about an individual: "A person's privacy is diminished exactly to the degree that others possess this kind of knowledge about him" (Parent 1983a, 269). For Parent (1983b, 306), privacy may be defined "as the condition of not having undocumented personal information about oneself known by others". It may be argued that Parent also suggests an objective approach to privacy, because these concepts tend to view restrictions of privacy as violations.

Objective theories of internet privacy

Camp and Floridi have provided important objective approaches to privacy in the context of new technologies such as the Internet. Camp (1999) wants to know whether Internet users are able to protect their privacy online and offers answers to this question from the American legal tradition. The American legal tradition focuses on a right to privacy, rather than on a European claim for a need for data protection:

> The American tradition of concern for privacy varies from the European approach. The European Community and Canada have principles of data protection, whereas the American tradition revolves around privacy. American considerations are based on common law tradition and a constitutional right, rather than on the more practical approach implied by data protection.
>
> (Camp 1999, 252)

For Floridi (1999, 53), "privacy is nothing less than the defence of the personal integrity of a packet of information" and informational privacy "a form of aggression towards one's personal identity" (Floridi 2005, 194). He considers the protection of personal identity as a "fundamental and inalienable right" (Floridi 2005, 195) and a right to informational privacy as "a right to personal immunity from unknown, undesired or unintentional changes in one's own identity as an informational entity" (Floridi 2005, 195). Camp's and Floridi's notion may be classified into objective approaches to defining privacy, because they have developed a rights-based conception of privacy.

In summary, objective definitions understand (Internet) privacy as a specific social structure, a moral or legal right, which is used to enable someone's ability to limit or restrict others from access to persons or information (restricted access definition of privacy). Objective definitions of (online) privacy assume that privacy is a right, and/or privacy includes the freedom from unwarranted intrusion, and/or privacy should be protected, and/or restrictions of privacy are violations, and/or privacy should be defined in a normative way, and/or full privacy can only be reached if there is no contact with other social actors. We will now move on to subjective approaches of studying (online) privacy.

Subjective theories of (Internet) privacy

Subjective theories of privacy

Subjective approaches to defining privacy focus on the individual and understand privacy as control over information about oneself. Westin provides a seminal individualistic notion of privacy. Westin (1967, 7; see also 2003, 431) defines privacy as the "claim of individuals, groups, or institutions to determine for themselves when, how, and to what extent information about them is communicated to others". Similarly, Froomkin (2000, 1463) uses informational privacy "as shorthand for the ability to control the acquisition or release of information about oneself". He argues that the easiest way to control personal information and databases is not to share it and to keep information to oneself (Froomkin 2000, 1463–1464). For Froomkin (2000, 1466), privacy "encompasses ideas of bodily and social autonomy, of self-determination, and of the ability to create zones of intimacy and inclusion that define and shape our relationships with each other". Miller (1971, 25) defines privacy as "the individual's ability to control the circulation of information relating to him". Gerety (1977) mentions the importance of finding definitions of privacy. He states:

> Privacy will be defined here as an autonomy or control over the intimacies of personal identity. Autonomy, identity, and intimacy are all necessary (and together normally sufficient) for the proper invocation of the concept of privacy. This definition is frankly normative. Its acceptance or rejection carries with it a set of at least preliminary conclusions about rights and wrongs.
>
> (Gerety 1977, 236)

Shils (1966, 282) says:

> privacy exists where the persons whose actions engender or become the objects of information retain possession of that information, and any flow outward of that information from the persons to whom it refers (and who share it where more than one person is involved) occurs on the initiative of its possessors. This includes that other individuals are not able to possess the information, other individuals do not observe the action, nor do they receive information from records or other individuals.... Privacy in one of its aspects may therefore be defined as the existence of a boundary through which information does not flow from the persons who possess it to others.
>
> (Shils 1966, 282)

For Shils (1966, 282), a violation of privacy is characterized by "the acquisition or transmission of information without the voluntary consent or initiative of those whose actions and words generate the information". As mentioned above, subjective concepts of privacy understand privacy as control over individual-specific information by the individual him/herself. Therefore, when Shils states that privacy occurs on the initiative of its possessors, it becomes clear that his notion may be seen in the context of subjective approaches of privacy.

In addition, Fried (1968; see also Fried 1990) suggests an individualistic approach to privacy. He argues that privacy is necessarily related to individual development in order to form personal relationships involving respect, love, friendship, and trust. For Fried (1968, 477), privacy is an essential condition for interpersonal relationships and central for individuals in order to have a moral and social personality.

> It is my thesis that privacy is not just one possible means among others to insure some other value, but that it is necessarily related to ends and relations of the most fundamental sort: respect, love, friendship and trust. Privacy is not merely a good technique for furthering these fundamental relations; rather without privacy they are simply inconceivable.
>
> (Fried 1968, 477)

Privacy is therefore not just a "defensive right" for Fried (1968, 490); rather, it is an aspect of social order for intimate relations by which individuals control access to their information. "Privacy is not simply an absence of information about us in the minds of others; rather it is the control we have over information about ourselves.... Privacy, thus, is control over knowledge about oneself" (Fried 1968, 482–483).

Similar to Fried, Gerstein (1970, 1978) studies privacy in the context of intimate relationships and focuses on the individual. He analyses the connection between privacy and intimacy, arguing that intimacy is impossible without privacy. He understands privacy as a condition for intimacy. For Gerstein (1970, 90), privacy is "a special sort of information, a sort of information which it is particularly important for the individual to be able to control". In addition, Gerstein (1970, 89) highlights "the right of privacy not as an absolute rule but as a principle which would establish privacy as a value of great significance, not to be interfered with lightly by governmental authority".

Likewise, Rachels (1975) tries to answer the question of why privacy is important to us. He stresses that privacy is necessary in order to maintain different forms of social relationships. Therefore, he wants to give

> an account of the value of privacy based on the idea that there is a close connection between our ability to control who has access to us and to information about us, and our ability to create and maintain different sorts of social relationships with different people.
>
> (Rachels 1975, 326)

Because Rachels advances the idea that privacy has to do with the individual ability to control, his notion may be classified as a subjective definition of privacy.

Murphy (1964) discusses theoretically and empirically the functions of social distance mechanisms such as privacy. Similar to Fried, Gerstein, and Rachels, for Murphy (1964, 1257), privacy is crucial for establishing social interactions and maintaining social relationships. In Murphy's view (1964, 1257), privacy is as important in personal relationships as it is in a person's public role, because of the ambivalence of individuals in intimate relationships.

> An area of privacy, then, is maintained by all, and reserve and restraint are common, though not constant, factors in all social relationships. Society could not perdure if people knew too much of one another, and one may

also ask ... if the individual could endure as a social person under the burden of complete self-awareness.

(Murphy 1964, 1257)

Privacy is for Murphy a personal interest needed to establish social interactions and to maintain social relationships. In my point of view, Murphy's notion of privacy may be understood as a subjective approach, because he tends to argue for an interest-based conception of privacy.

Posner (1981) tries to elaborate an economic theory of privacy. He discusses different definitions of privacy and concludes: "The first meaning of privacy set out above – privacy as concealment of information – seems the most interesting from an economic standpoint" (Posner 1981, 405). Posner (1978, 19) further clarifies that he understands privacy as the withholding and concealment of information in a personal context. In addition, Posner's view may be classified as subjective understanding of privacy, because one requires control over information about oneself in order to guarantee the stated withholding and concealment of information.

DeCew (1986) discusses numerous definitions of privacy in the existing literature and suggests an interest-based conception of privacy:

> Since the literature on privacy uses rights terminology I must accommodate that. But because I am making no claim about a theory of rights, whenever possible I shall refer to privacy as an interest (which can be invaded), by which I mean something it would be a good thing to have, leaving open how extensively it ought to be protected.

(DeCew 1986, 147)

In addition, when DeCew (1986, 170) argues for a broad conception of privacy, she considers privacy as "information control and control over decision-making".

Subjective theories of Internet privacy

Subjective approaches to defining Internet privacy focus on the individual and understand privacy as control over information about oneself. In the context of information privacy on the Internet, Clarke (1999, 60) states that "privacy is often thought of as a moral right or a legal right. But it's often more useful to perceive privacy as the interest that individuals have in sustaining a personal space, free from interference by other people and organizations." For Clarke (1998, 62), information technologies such as the Internet have dramatically increased the surveillance threats to personal data and personal identity. He further claims that "the individual must be able to exercise a substantial degree of control over that data and its use" (Clarke 1998, 62). Agre (1997) studies privacy in the context of new information and communication technologies. He argues that the pervasive spread of computer networks has made it much easier to merge databases. Databases of personal information have thereby intensified and extensified on a global level (Agre 1997, 3). Following Clarke, for Agre (1997, 7), information privacy may be understood as control over personal information and as "control over an aspect of the identity one projects to the world". This concept of defining privacy in the context of new technologies such as the Internet is considered as advantageous for several reasons: "It goes well beyond the static conception of privacy as a right to seclusion or secrecy, it explains why people wish to control personal information, and it promises detailed guidance about what kinds of control they might wish to have" (Agre 1997, 7–8). Because Clarke and Agre advance the idea that individuals require control over information about themselves, their notions may be classified as subjective definitions of Internet privacy.

In *Database Nation*, Garfinkel (2000, 4) understands "privacy in the 21st century" in the context of self-possession, autonomy, and integrity. Privacy is

> the right of people to control what details about their lives stay inside their own houses and what leaks to the outside.... It's about the woman who's afraid to use the Internet to organize her community against a proposed toxic dump – afraid because the dump's investors are sure to dig through her past if she becomes too much of a nuisance.... It's about good, upstanding citizens who are now refusing to enter public service because they don't want a bloodthirsty press rummaging through their old school reports, computerized medical records, and email.
>
> (Garfinkel 2000, 4)

As mentioned above, subjective concepts of Internet privacy understand privacy as control over individual-specific information by the individual him/herself. Therefore, when Garfinkel states that online privacy occurs on the initiative of its possessors (a woman who's afraid to use the Internet, citizens who refuse to enter public service), it becomes clear that his notion may be seen in the context of subjective approaches to Internet privacy.

Similar to Clarke, Agre, and Garfinkel, Solove focuses on individual behaviour and understands online privacy as self-determination and control over information about oneself:

> Privacy involves the ability to avoid the powerlessness of having others control information that can affect whether an individual gets a job, becomes licensed to practice in a profession, or obtains a critical loan. It involves the ability to avoid the collection and circulation of such powerful information in one's life without having any say in the process, without knowing who has what information, what purposes or motives those entities have, or what will be done with that information in the future. Privacy involves the power to refuse to be treated with bureaucratic indifference when one complains about errors or when one wants certain data expunged. It is not merely the collection of data that is the problem – it is our complete lack of control

over the ways it is used or may be used in the future.... What people want when they demand privacy with regard to their personal information is the ability to ensure that the information about them will be used only for the purposes they desire.

(Solove 2004, 43, 51)

In summary, subjective definitions of (Internet) privacy assume that privacy is a personal interest, and/or privacy includes the freedom from external interference in one's personal choices, decisions, and plans, and/or the degree of personal choice indicates how much privacy an individual has, and/or restrictions of privacy are losses, and/or privacy should be defined in a descriptive way, and/or full privacy is reached as long as the individual is able to choose which personalities should be disclosed. In the following subsection, integrative approaches of studying (online) privacy (a combination of subjective and objective approaches) are addressed.

Integrative theories of (Internet) privacy

Integrative theories of privacy

Reiman (1976) argues that privacy is essential to the development of personhood and therefore necessary to the creation of human beings. He understands the notion of privacy on the one hand as a right and on the other hand as an interest. For Reiman (1976, 32), privacy is "an important interest in simply being able to restrict information about, and observation of, myself regardless of what may be done with that information or the results of that observation". In contrast, for Reiman (1976, 44), privacy is also

a right which protects my capacity to enter into intimate relations, not because it protects my reserve of generally withheld information, but because it enables me to make the commitment that underlies caring as my commitment uniquely conveyed by my thoughts and witnessed by my actions.

Therefore, it may be argued that Reiman's approach is a combination of objective and subjective notions of privacy. In his paper "Privacy, Intimacy, and Personhood", Reiman (1976, 38) concludes that he is looking for a

fundamental interest, connected to personhood, which provides a basis for a right to privacy to which all human beings are entitled (even those in solitary confinement) and which does not go so far as to claim a right never to be observed (even on crowded streets).

Moor (1997, 31) combines objective and subjective notions in his "control/ restricted access conception of privacy". For Moor (1997, 30–32), the term 'privacy' should be used "to designate a situation in which people are protected from intrusion or observation by natural or physical circumstances" on the one hand and to "give individuals as much personal choice as possible" on the other hand. Moor (1997, 32) further argues that it is important to study privacy in terms of a control/restricted access theory of privacy, "because this conception encourages informed consent as much as possible and fosters the development of practical, fine grained, and sensitive policies for protecting privacy when it is not".

Tavani (2007, 2008) criticizes both objective and subjective notions of privacy. Based on Moor's concept of privacy, Tavani (2008, 144) mentions in his restricted access/limited control theory (RALC) "the importance of setting up zones that enable individuals to limit or restrict others from accessing their personal information" on the one hand and identifies "the important role that individual control plays in privacy theory" on the other hand. Tavani's notion not only understands privacy as a legal right which should be protected; it also treats individual control as an important aspect. In Tavani's (2007, 19) understanding, the restricted access/limited control theory,

> in differentiating normative from descriptive aspects of privacy, enabled us to distinguish between the condition of privacy and a right to privacy and between a loss of privacy (in a descriptive sense) and a violation or invasion of privacy (in a normative sense).

Integrative theories of Internet privacy

Many authors have advanced an integrative approach to Internet privacy by combining rights-based ideas with individual control conceptions. For example, Ess (2009, 58) argues that

> at least in those contexts and spaces where I can legitimately expect privacy, I should also be able to control the information about my behaviors in those spaces. That is, if I have a right to accessibility privacy – a sense that others cannot legitimately intrude upon me and perhaps others in certain contexts – then it would seem that I have a right to informational privacy as well.

Lessig (2006) claims that with the rise of the Internet there are new challenges for privacy and new privacy threats have emerged. He understands Internet privacy as a right and as individual control: "Individuals should be able to control information about themselves. We should be eager to help them protect that information by giving them the structures and the rights to do so" (Lessig 2006, 231). Miller and Weckert (2000, 256) assume that

> the notion of privacy has both a descriptive and a normative dimension. On the one hand privacy consists of not being interfered with, or having some power to exclude, and on the other privacy is held to be a moral right, or at

least an important good.... Naturally the normative and the descriptive dimensions interconnect.

In addition, Introna (1997, 264) underlines that "to claim privacy is to claim the right to limit access or control access to my personal or private domain" and that "to claim privacy is to claim the right to a (personal) domain of immunity against the judgments of others". Spinello (2003, 143) argues that informational privacy "concerns the collection, use, and dissemination of information about individuals. The right to informational privacy is the right to control the disclosure of and access to one's personal information." Because Introna as well as Spinello connect restricted access with limited control definitions of privacy, it may be argued that their approaches provide a combination of objective and subjective notions of privacy.

Nissenbaum (2010) links adequate privacy protection with norms of specific contexts. Her framework requires that the processes of controlling and accessing information are appropriate to a particular context (Nissenbaum 2010, 147). She understands privacy as contextual integrity. Contextual integrity is a decision heuristic focusing on changes of information processes in certain contexts such as education, health care, and psychoanalysis (Nissenbaum 2010, 169–176). The idea of contextual integrity is neither solely a subjective nor exclusively an objective approach to defining privacy in the information age:

> The framework of contextual integrity reveals why we do not need to choose between them; instead, it recognizes a place for each. The idea that privacy implies a limitation of access by others overlaps, generally, with the idea of an informational norm.... Control, too, remains important in the framework of contextual integrity.
>
> (Nissenbaum 2010, 147–148)

Privacy control may change the degree of access in specific social contexts.

In summary, integrative definitions of (Internet) privacy try to combine subjective and objective notions into one concept. Integrative definitions consider both privacy as a right that should be protected and as a form of individual control. The next section provides a discussion of the pitfalls of the existing privacy theories and argues for the need of a critical theory of (Internet) privacy.

Towards a critical theory of (Internet) privacy

The task of the previous section was to clarify how (online) privacy is defined in the academic literature, what the different concepts of privacy have in common, and what distinguishes them from one another. In doing so, the section contained a systematic overview of the state of the art of how to define privacy by establishing a typology of the existing literature. Table 3.1 summarizes the results.

Objective definitions of (Internet) privacy understand privacy as a specific social structure, a moral or legal right, which is used to enable someone's ability

Table 3.1 Foundations of (Internet) privacy theory

Objective theories of (Internet) privacy	Subjective theories of (Internet) privacy	Integrative theories of (Internet) privacy
Objective approaches to defining (Internet) privacy understand privacy as a specific social structure, a moral or legal right used to enable someone's ability to limit or restrict others from access to persons or information (restricted access definition of privacy)	Subjective approaches to defining (Internet) privacy focus on the individual and understand privacy as control over information about oneself (limited control definition of privacy)	Integrative approaches to defining (Internet) privacy try to combine subjective and objective notions into one concept. Integrative approaches consider both privacy as a right that should be protected and as individual control of personal information (restricted access/limited control definition of privacy).
Warren and Brandeis (1890), Gavison (1980), Allen (1988), Bok (1983), Parent (1983a; 1983b), Prosser (1960), Schoeman (1984; 1992), Scanlon (1975), Camp (1999), Floridi (1999)	Westin (1967; 2003), Shils (1966), Fried (1968; 1990), Gerstein (1970; 1978), Froomkin (2000), Miller (1971), Rachels (1975), Murphy (1964), Posner (1978; 1981), Gerety (1977), DeCew (1986), Clarke (1999, 60), Agre (1997), Garfinkel (2000), Solove (2004)	Reiman (1976), Moor (1997), Tavani (2007; 2008), Ess (2009), Lessig (2006), Miller and Weckert (2000), Introna (1997), Spinello (2003), Nissenbaum (2010)

to limit or restrict others from access to persons or information; for instance, they are represented by Warren and Brandeis, Parent, Camp, and Floridi. In contrast, subjective definitions of (Internet) privacy focus on the individual and understand privacy as control over information about oneself; for example, representatives are Westin, DeCew, Clarke, and Solove. Finally, integrative approaches to studying (Internet) privacy try to combine subjective and objective notions into one concept; for instance, they are represented by Reiman, Moor, Tavani, Ess, and, Nissenbaum.

To a certain extent, objective definitions suggest that the more access to persons or information is limited or restricted by a social structure such as the law, the more privacy people have. In other words, these approaches state that the more an individual's information can be kept secret, the more privacy is fulfilled. For instance, in Gavison's (1980, 428) understanding, "an individual enjoys perfect privacy when he is completely inaccessible to others". She further explains that "in perfect privacy no one has any information about X, no one pays any attention to X" (1980, 428). On the Internet, especially web 2.0 activities such as creating profiles, sharing ideas, announcing personal messages, uploading or watching videos, and writing personal entries on social networking sites are based on information, sharing, and attention. Regardless of whether individuals are able to decide which personal information is available on the Internet and regardless of whether individuals are able to choose for whom this information is available, for representatives of an objective approach including Gavison, these forms of information sharing are always restrictions of privacy and therefore should be avoided. For example, I want to upload some photos on my profile on a non-profit and non-commercial social networking platform (e.g. diaspora*) in order to share them with my friends, have fun, and deepen our friendship. Furthermore, in this example I decide which photos should be shared, I choose with whom, and what my friends are able to do with these photos. In an objective understanding, this is still a restriction and violation of privacy, which should be questioned and struggled against, because the more my information is kept secret, the more privacy is attained. Therefore, these approaches tend to underestimate the individual role of control and choice, which is also required for enjoying privacy (Tavani 2007, 142). These approaches do not take into account that individuals can limit or restrict their access, because individuals are able to control the flow of personal information to a certain extent (Moor 1997, 31; Fried 1968, 482). In addition, individuals should be able to control the flow of personal information themselves, because "different people may be given different levels of access for different kinds of information at different times" (Moor 1997, 31).

Subjective definitions suggest that the more the individual has control over his or her information, the more privacy he or she enjoys. This includes if a person is not able to control his or her information anymore, but some other person or organization may do so, privacy is restricted. While social media allow people to make new friends, share information, videos, music, or images, discuss with others, and stay in touch with friends, relatives, and other contacts, they also provide a vast amount of personal(ly) (identifiable) information. If I want to share information on commercial social networking sites, I do not have control over my information anymore, because web platforms are allowed to use my information as well in order to generate profit. Representatives of a subjective approach such as Froomkin (2000, 1463) state that "the most effective way of controlling information about oneself is not to share it in the first place". Therefore, in a subjective understanding, the only opportunity to keep control over one's information and to enjoy privacy is not to use such web platforms. This view ignores the fact that this may cause new problems, because it could result in less fun, fewer social contacts, less satisfaction, a deepening of information inequality, and social exclusion (Fuchs 2009a, 13). My point of view is that one opportunity for users having control over their personal information on such platforms is to foster international data protection regulations in order to hinder the collection, analysis, and sale of personal data by commercial web platforms. Subjective privacy definitions tend to underestimate the constraining effects of social structures, which restrict individual control over information (Tavani 2007, 9; 2008, 143). These approaches do not take into account that having full control over one's personal information cannot be achieved in modern society (Moor 1997, 31) and enclosing information may create new problems.

On the one hand, integrative concepts recognize the constraining effects of social structures, which restrict the individual's control over information. On the other hand, they also consider the individual's role of control and choice, which is also required for having privacy. Integrative notions take into account that having full control over personal information cannot be achieved, but individuals can limit or restrict their access because they are able to control the flow of personal information to a certain extent. In short, integrative approaches of studying privacy try to avoid objective and subjective pitfalls.

Nevertheless, many authors have advanced critiques of the concept of privacy in general (Gouldner 1976, 103; Lyon 1994, 179–198; 2001, 20–23; 2007b, 174–176; Gilliom 2001, 121–125; Etzioni 1999, 183–215; Bennett and Raab 2006, 14–17; Ogura 2006, 277–280; Fuchs 2010d, 174–175; Neocleous 2002, 85–110). Privacy is a modern concept of liberal democracy and is used in order to justify liberty from public intervention (Lyon 1994, 185). In the liberal understanding of privacy, the sovereign individual should have freedom to pursue his or her own interests without interference and those interests are primarily interpreted as property interests and private ownership rights (Fuchs 2010d, 174; Lyon 1994, 186–188). Therefore, the concept of privacy fits neatly into the concept of private property (Fuchs 2010d, 174; Lyon 1994, 186; Ogura 2006, 278). The debate on privacy advances the idea of possessive and self-protective individualism (Gouldner 1976, 103; Lyon 2001, 21). Possessive individualism means that the individual is proprietor of his or her own person, capabilities, potentialities, and capacities (Macpherson 1990, 3). In the understanding of possessive individualism, the nature of human being is that everyone is the owner of him- or herself and that the individual is not part of a larger social whole. The human essence is considered as being the proprietorship of him- or herself, and the overall aim of society in liberal democracy is considered as being the protection of this property (Macpherson 1990, 3). In addition, individuals are seen as being related as proprietors and therefore society is considered as consisting of relations of proprietors. The actual outcome of such an understanding in reality is a competitive and possessive market society (Macpherson 1990, 271). The idea of possessive individualism may be summarized with the following propositions:

1   What makes a man human is freedom from dependence on the wills of others.
2   Freedom from dependence on others means freedom from any relations with others except those relations which the individual enters voluntarily with a view to his own interest.
3   The individual is essentially the proprietor of his own person and capacities, for which he owes nothing to society....
4   Although the individual cannot alienate the whole of his property in his own person, he may alienate his capacity to labour.
5   Human society consists of a series of market relations....
6   Since freedom from the wills of others is what makes a man human, each

individual's freedom can rightfully be limited only by such obligations and rules as are necessary to secure the same freedom for others.

7   Political society is a human contrivance for the protection of the individual's property in his person and goods, and (therefore) for the maintenance of orderly relations of exchange between individuals regarded as proprietors of themselves.

(Macpherson 1990, 263–264)

(Internet) privacy concepts advance the idea of possessive individualism in order to define the private individual embedded in a system of a competitive market society (Gouldner 1976; Lyon 2007b, 174). In a market society, the commodification of privacy is important in order to enable targeted advertising to be used for accumulating profit. Hence, economic actors undertake surveillance in order to threaten privacy. Privacy as ideological value enables surveillance actions and commodity production. There is a contradiction between privacy on the one hand and surveillance on the other hand in modern society (Fuchs 2010d, 175). The privacy ideal of integrative definitions thus comes into conflict with surveillance actions. These privacy concepts claim privacy as a crucial value within a society not being able to fulfil this value. One can imagine a commons-based society, where no substantial surveillance actions take place. In such a society, privacy as an important value would no longer be necessary in this traditional way. It may thus be said that surveillance actions as commodity production enable privacy as an ideological value. Privacy is needed in modern society only because of surveillance.

Conclusion: capitalist privacy threats vs. corporate privacy protection

To sum up, objective definitions of (Internet) privacy tend to underestimate the individual role of control and choice. In contrast, subjective approaches to defining (Internet) privacy tend to underestimate the constraining effects of social structures. Although integrative approaches to studying (Internet) privacy try to avoid objective and subjective pitfalls, these concepts do not recognize the contradiction between privacy and surveillance in modern society and do not give answers to this foundational problem. The existing approaches to privacy seem not to be fruitful for studying privacy. Therefore, the following treatment aims to contribute to a critical theory of (online) privacy:

*   Similar to integrative approaches, a critical theory of (Internet) privacy is interested in combining subjective and objective notions, but does not want to advance the ideas of liberal democracy, private ownership, and possessive individualism.
*   A critical theory of privacy (on the Net) strives for the development of theoretical and empirical research methods in order to focus on privacy in the context of domination, asymmetrical power relations, resource control, social struggles, and exploitation.

- It asks who can obtain privacy and who benefits from the contradiction between privacy and surveillance in modern society. It critically analyses (1) the threats of privacy as important aspects for guaranteeing the production of surplus value and for accumulating profit; and (2) privacy protection of income inequality, property interests, as well as power and ownership structures.
- A critical theory of (Internet) privacy wants to overcome (1) privacy threats as well as (2) entrepreneurial privacy protection and privacy protection for other powerful actors in society in order to establish political processes and social transformations towards a participatory society.

For instance, a critical theory of (online) privacy makes an effort in the individual role of control and choice as well as in the constraining effects of social structures on web 2.0 platforms and social networking sites including Facebook, Google+, Twitter, MySpace, and YouTube. (1) Furthermore, it investigates the principle of web 2.0 platforms; that is, the massive provision and storage of personal(ly) (identifiable) data being systematically evaluated, marketed, and used for targeted advertising. Web 2.0 applications and social software sites collect personal behaviours, preferences, and interests with the help of systematic and automated computer processes and sell these data to advertising agencies in order to guarantee the production of surplus value and to accumulate profit. A critical theory of (Internet) privacy wants to deepen the knowledge of such privacy threats by its user. (2) In addition, to whom personal information is sold by commercial web platforms and how much these corporations such as Twitter earn through targeted advertising and the sale of data is not known to the public, because such transactions are treated as an aspect of a corporation's privacy. One may assume that Twitter's business model is very successful and the company earns a lot of money with the sale of user data, because it was reported that Twitter made more than US$250 million of revenue just in the first quarter of 2014 (Investor 2014). A critical theory of privacy (on the Net) strives to analyse such cases and wants to make them more public in order to deepen the knowledge of social inequality and property interests. A critical theory of (Internet) privacy wants to put (1) privacy threats and (2) ownership structures of such commercial platforms into the larger context of societal problems in public discourse in order to establish political processes and social transformations towards a participatory society. Chapter 4 provides foundations of critical (Internet) surveillance studies.

4 Critical (Internet) surveillance studies

Commodity critique

Introduction

Surveillance has notably increased in the last decades of modern society. Surveillance studies scholars like Lyon (1994) or Norris and Armstrong (1999) stress that we live in a surveillance society. Although there are many other features in contemporary society such as information, neoliberalism, globalization, capital, etc., surveillance is a crucial phenomenon. In order to get a first impression of surveillance, an illustrative example may be given.

According to the American Management Association and the ePolicy Institute (2008), which undertake an annual quantitative survey about electronic monitoring and surveillance with approximately 300 US companies, "more than one fourth of employers have fired workers for misusing e-mail and nearly one third have fired employees for misusing the Internet". More than 40 per cent of the companies monitor the e-mail traffic of their workers, and 66 per cent of corporations monitor Internet connections. In addition, most companies use software to block non-work-related websites such as sexual or pornographic sites, game sites, social networking sites, entertainment sites, shopping sites, and sport sites. The American Management Association and the ePolicy Institute (2008) also stress that companies "tracking content, keystrokes, and time spent at the keyboard ... store and review computer files ... monitor the blogosphere to see what is being written about the company, and ... monitor social networking sites".

The overall aim of this chapter is to clarify how we can theorize and systemize such Internet phenomena. Surveillance studies scholars like Lyon (1994, 119–158; 2001, 40–44) emphasize that economic surveillance such as monitoring consumers or the workplace are central aspects of surveillance societies. Although corporate surveillance is not the only phenomenon in contemporary surveillance societies, the approach being advanced in this chapter recognizes the importance of the role of the economy. But which theory can be used to create a typology in order to systemize surveillance in the modern economy? What are the characteristics of surveillance (in cyberspace) in the spheres of production, circulation, and consumption?

This chapter is understood as a critical contribution to surveillance studies insofar as it is based on the foundations of a critical political economy approach

(Marx 1976). It constructs theoretically founded typologies in order to systemize the existing literature of surveillance studies and to analyse examples of surveillance.

In the second section, Foucault's understanding of surveillance and the idea of the Panopticon are introduced. Based on these findings, the section analyses how surveillance (on the Internet) is defined in the existing literature, what the different notions of (online) surveillance have in common and what distinguishes them from one another. The third section discusses the advantages and disadvantages of such definitions and how different notions treat economic aspects of surveillance. It clarifies if there is a gap in the existing literature in order to study surveillance in the modern economy. In addition, the specific economic mode of (Internet) surveillance is studied. Based on the foundations of a political economy approach, the distinction between production, circulation, and consumption within the economy is introduced in order to establish a typology of surveillance in the economy. This section also provides a systematic analysis of economic surveillance on the basis of current developments in the Internet. The fourth and final section concludes with a summary and makes some political recommendations in order to overcome (online) surveillance in the modern economy.[1]

Foundations of (Internet) surveillance studies

Since Foucault published his book *Surveiller et Punir* in French in 1975 and in English in 1977, the amount of literature on surveillance has increased enormously and represents a diffuse and complex field of research. Lyon (1994, 6–7) states that since "Michel Foucault's celebrated, and contentious, historical studies of surveillance and discipline had appeared ... mainstream social theorists began to take surveillance seriously in its own right". Murakami Wood (2003, 235) emphasizes that "for Surveillance Studies, Foucault is a foundational thinker and his work on the development of the modern subject, in particular Surveillir et Punir (translated as Discipline and Punish), remains a touchstone for this nascent transdisciplinary field". According to Google Scholar, Foucault's book *Discipline and Punish* is cited almost 15,000 times. According to the *Encyclopedia of Philosophy* (Pryor 2006, 898) and to the *Routledge Encyclopedia of Philosophy* (Gutting 1998, 708–713), Foucault is one of the most important historians and philosophers of the twentieth century with wide influence in different disciplines.

Foucault (1995; 2002; 2003; 2007) analyses surveillance in the context of the emergence of disciplinary societies. He traces an evolution from feudal societies of torture, to reformed societies of punishment, and on to modern disciplinary societies. In the age of torture, arbitrary penalties and public spectacles of the scaffold took place in order to exterminate bodies. Afterwards, in the age of punishment, defendants were punished and exterminated. In the age of disciplines, direct violence was replaced with softer forms of power in order to discipline, control, and normalize people in respect of drilling docile bodies and "political puppets" (Foucault 1995, 136).

For Foucault (1995, 195–210), Bentham's Panopticon is a symbol of modern disciplinary society. "On the whole, therefore, one can speak of the formation of a disciplinary society in this movement that stretches from the enclosed disciplines, a sort of social 'quarantine', to an indefinitely generalizable mechanism of 'panopticism'" (Foucault 1995, 216). The Panopticon is an ideal architectural figure of modern disciplinary power. It consists of an annular building divided into different cells and a huge tower with windows in the middle. Prisoners, workers, pupils, as well as patients stay in the cells and a supervisor occupies the middle tower. The architecture allows the supervisor to observe all individuals in the cells without being seen. Not every inmate is observed at every moment, but no one knows if she or he is being monitored. Observation is possible at any time. As a result, everyone acts as if kept under surveillance all the time – individuals discipline themselves out of fear of surveillance. The Panopticon creates a consciousness of permanent visibility as a form of power, where bars, chains, and heavy locks are no longer necessary for domination. Foucault (1995, 228) finally asks: "Is it surprising that prisons resemble factories, schools, barracks, hospitals, which all resemble prisons?"

In summary, Foucault analyses surveillance in the context of the emergence of modern disciplinary societies. He understands disciplines as forms of operational power relations and technologies of domination in order to discipline, control, and normalize people. For Foucault, the Panopticon is an ideal symbol of modern surveillance societies. Foucault's understanding of surveillance and the Panopticon allows one to distinguish panoptic (affirmation of Foucault's notion) and non-panoptic (rejection of Foucault's notion) approaches to defining (Internet) surveillance that may be used to construct a typology of existing surveillance literature and to discuss commonalties and differences among definitions of surveillance.

Non-panoptic definitions of (online) surveillance make one or more of the following assumptions:

- Foucault's notion of the Panopticon is useless for studying surveillance nowadays.
- (Internet) surveillance should be defined in a neutral way.
- This view uses a broad definition of surveillance.
- There are constraining and enabling effects of collecting data.
- Surveillance is primarily understood as a plural and technical process.

In comparison, panoptic definitions of (online) surveillance make one or more of the following assumptions:

- Foucault's notion of the Panopticon is (to a certain extent) useful for studying surveillance nowadays.
- (Internet) surveillance should be defined in a negative way.
- This view uses a narrow definition of surveillance.
- Surveillance should be connected to coercion, repression, discipline, power, and domination.

- Power is primarily centralized and society tends to be repressive and controlled.

Panoptic and non-panoptic approaches to defining surveillance in general and Internet surveillance in particular will be outlined below. The following subsections are therefore structured according to this distinction. The task of this section is to give a representative but still eclectic overview of different (Internet) surveillance definitions (for a more detailed discussion see Allmer 2012a, 24–38, 74–89).

Surveillance technologies are developed by analogy with productive forces in modern societies. New information technologies have generated a "rapid *quantitative* expansion of surveillance, which simultaneously raises questions of a *qualitative* shift" (Lyon 1994, 56). New surveillance is a dialectical sublation of traditional surveillance in the form of elimination, retention, and emergence of new qualities on a higher level. For example, the necessity of face-to-face surveillance is eliminated, but power relations and forms of domination are retained and work on a more intensive and extensive level. Surveillance in the context of new information and communication technologies is a dialectic of continuity and discontinuity.

In order to describe surveillance in the context of the emergence of new information and communication technologies, further scholars accentuated terms such as "social control in the computer age" (Rule 1973), "information technology and dataveillance" (Clarke 1988), "in the age of the smart machine" (Zuboff 1988), "the superpanopticon" (Poster 1990), "hypercontrol in telematic societies" (Bogard 1996), "social Taylorism of surveillance" (Robins and Webster 1999), "the maximum surveillance society" (Norris and Armstrong 1999), "the intensification of surveillance"(Ball and Webster 2003), "digitizing surveillance" (Graham and Murakami Wood 2003), "profiling machines" (Elmer 2004), "surveillance in the interactive area" (Andrejevic 2007b), and "Internet and surveillance" (Fuchs *et al.* 2012b). The Internet is the most important phenomenon of new information and communication technologies, which includes all the different forms of information, communication, and cooperation in one medium (Fuchs 2008, 139). These approaches show that many forms of contemporary surveillance are computer based and Internet based and, as a reaction, a multiplicity of new analytical approaches has emerged.

Non-panoptic theories of (Internet) surveillance

Non-panoptic theories of surveillance

Giddens (1981, 169) defines surveillance as "symbolic material that can be stored by an agency or collectivity" and as "the supervision of the activities of subordinates". He sees surveillance primarily as a phenomenon of the nation-state: "Surveillance as the mobilizing of administrative power – through the storage and control of information – is the primary means of the concentration of authoritative resources involved in the formation of the nation-state" (Giddens 1985, 181). While Foucault's negative and powerful understanding of surveillance is criticized, a neutral notion of surveillance is discussed.

Rule (1973) stresses in his empirical case study the idea of a total surveillance society. Although he describes the political and economic context, he uses a non-judgemental term and a broad definition of surveillance. Rule (2007, 13–17; 2012) still accentuates a broad term of surveillance with advantages and disadvantages in his continuing work on surveillance, published recently in his book *Privacy in Peril*, and in his book chapter " 'Needs' for Surveillance and the Movement to Protect Privacy".

The importance of new information and communication technologies for undercover work and the differentiation between traditional and new surveillance are mentioned by Gary Marx (1988, 221; 2002, 10–12). Surveillance is for Gary Marx (2002, 12) primarily a technical process and is defined as "the use of technical means to extract or create personal data". Gary Marx sees parents monitoring their baby on CCTV (closed-circuit television) as an example of surveillance.

In *Visions of Social Control*, Cohen (1987, 1–12) focuses on crime, punishment, and classification. He stresses that it is not fruitful if social control is used as negative term and if powerful abstractions of ideological and repressive state apparatus are analysed as Marxists did. In modern society power and domination are not centralized, but rather everyone can achieve a powerful position.

For Beniger (1986), control and surveillance are general concepts of "purposive influence toward a predetermined goal" (Beniger 1986, 7), where the "information storage, processing, and communication" (Beniger 1986, 62) are stressed.

For Clarke (1988), surveillance and dataveillance are neither negative nor positive, as it depends on the situation. "I explicitly reject the notion that surveillance is, of itself, evil or undesirable; its nature must be understood, and society must decide the circumstances in which it should be used" (Clarke 1988, 498–499). Although many dangers and disadvantages of surveillance in general and dataveillance in particular are mentioned, benefits like physical security of people and financial opportunities in both the public (social welfare and tax) and private (insurance and finance) sector are listed as well.

Lyon (1994, viii–x) grasps surveillance "as a shorthand term to cover the many, and expanding, range of contexts within which personal data is collected by employment, commercial and administrative agencies, as well as in policing and security" (Lyon 1994, ix). He suggests a neutral understanding of surveillance with positive and negative effects of constraining and enabling. Surveillance is undemocratic, coercive, impersonal or even inhuman on the one hand, but it is also "innocuous or a channel of positive blessing" (Lyon 1994, ix) on the other hand. Lyon (2001, 3) emphasizes watching over a child and taking care of it as positive aspects of surveillance.

In *Forget Foucault*, Baudrillard (2007, 34) dismisses Foucault's concept of the Panopticon:

The same goes for *Discipline and Punish*, with its theory of discipline, of the "panoptic" and of "transparence." A magistral but obsolete theory. Such a theory of control by means of a gaze that objectifies, even when it is pulverized into micro-devices, is passé. With the simulation device we are no doubt as far from the strategy of transparence as the latter is from the immediate, symbolic operation of punishment which Foucault himself describes. Once again a spiral is missing here, the spiral in front of which Foucault, oddly enough, comes to a halt right at the threshold of a current revolution of the system which he has never wanted to cross.

Based on Baudrillard, Bogard (1996, 2006, 2012) focuses on the simulation of hypersurveillant control in telematic societies. Surveillance is considered as both a mode of oppressed capture and a mode of line flights of "escape, deterritorialization, indetermination and resistance" (Bogard 2006, 101).

In *The Maximum Surveillance Society*, Norris and Armstrong (1999, 3–12) consider surveillance as an ambivalent process with protective and enabling elements and totalitarian and powerful effects. Although the power of surveillance is mentioned, they do not want to automatically apply the idea of a powerful Panopticon or a totalitarian Big Brother state to the rise of CCTV (see also Norris and Armstrong 1998, 7; 2012).

According to Haggerty and Ericson (2000), surveillance is a decentralized, non-hierarchical phenomenon without a certain powerful group or institution. Haggerty and Ericson (2000, 607) are neither interested in analysing Foucault's concept of surveillance because it "fails to directly engage contemporary developments in surveillance technology", nor in incorporating new approaches based on Foucault because they are "providing little that is theoretically novel".

Non-panoptic theories of Internet surveillance

As we have seen above, Lyon understands surveillance as a neutral concept which assumes that there are enabling and constraining effects. As a logical result, he also understands the "world wide web of surveillance" (Lyon 1998) as a neutral concept that identifies positive consequences including protection and security as well as negative consequences such as control. The computerization of surveillance makes bureaucratic administration easier (Lyon 2003a, 164) and surveillance in cyberspace permits "greater efficiency and speed, and may well result in increased benefits for citizens and consumers, who experience them as enhancing their comfort, convenience, and safety" (Lyon 2003b, 69). Nevertheless, Lyon singles out the nation-state and the capitalist workplace as the main sites of surveillance on the Internet (Lyon 1998, 95; 2003b, 69; 2003a, 163) and argues that surveillance technologies such as the Internet reinforce asymmetrical power relations on an extensive and intensive level (Lyon 1998, 92). "So surveillance spreads, becoming constantly more routine, more intensive (profiles) and extensive (populations), driven by economic, bureaucratic and now technological forces" (Lyon 1998, 99). The Internet has become a multi-billion-dollar industry, because it is primarily corporations that are interested in collecting, analysing, and assessing a huge amount of personal consumer data in order to target personalized advertising (Lyon 2003a, 162).

Similar to Lyon's notion of Internet surveillance assuming that there are enabling and constraining effects, Miller and Weckert (2000, 255) articulate the advantages and disadvantages of being monitored.

For Albrechtslund (2008; 2012, 187), positive aspects of being under surveillance are worth mentioning. He argues that online surveillance also empowers the users, constructs subjectivity, and is playful. Internet surveillance as a social and participatory act involves mutuality and sharing.

People's active role in the context of surveillance in general and online surveillance in particular is emphasized by Koskela (2004; 2006). For instance, reality shows are based on viewer participation, mobile phones with cameras create an active subject, and home webcams generate new subjectivities. Koskela (2006, 175) wants to analyse "the other side of surveillance", which has resistant and liberating elements. "Webcams can also be argued to contribute to the 'democratization' of surveillance."

In conclusion, non-panoptic notions of (Internet) surveillance either use a neutral concept assuming there are enabling effects (e.g. protection and security) as well as constraining effects (e.g. control) or a positive concept that identifies comical, playful, amusing, and even enjoyable characteristics of surveillance, where everyone has the opportunity to surveil. Surveillance is used as a broad category and understood primarily as a plural, neutral, and technical process. In addition, these approaches tend to reject the proposition that surveillance mechanisms are dominated by political and economic actors and see monitoring not necessarily as annoying or disturbing. In non-panoptic notions (of the Internet), surveillance is understood as a useful and effective management tool and as fair methods and procedures of monitoring individuals online. Nevertheless, there are theorists who analyse surveillance based on Foucault in the context of the Panopticon and stress powerful and disciplinary elements of contemporary surveillance societies.

Panoptic theories of (Internet) surveillance

Panoptic theories of surveillance

Deleuze (1992, 23–46) underlines a mutation of capitalism in "Postscript on the Societies of Control". Based on the ideas of Foucault, he describes the change from the disciplinary societies to the societies of control. He speaks of a change in the mode of institutions, production, culture, and technique that creates a new level of control in social subsystems.

Also interesting in this context is the dystopian novel *Nineteen Eighty-Four* by George Orwell (2004), first published in 1949. Orwell (2004) describes a ruling system called Oceania, which consists of Big Brother, the party, and the proles, and stands for pervasive government surveillance, totalitarian regime, and public mind control.

Every citizen, or at least every citizen important enough to be worth watching, could be kept for twenty-four hours a day under the eyes of the police and in the sound of official propaganda, with all other channels of communication closed. The possibility of enforcing not only complete obedience to the will of the State, but complete uniformity of opinion on all subjects, now existed for the first time.

(Orwell 2004, 255)

Zuboff (1988) studied the emergence of information technologies in the workplace in her book *In the Age of the Smart Machine*. She defines authority as "the spiritual dimension of power" (Zuboff 1988, 219) and technique as "the material dimension of power" (Zuboff 1988, 311). Based on Foucault's disciplinary societies, she stresses the panoptic power of information technology in corporate institutions and presents empirical case studies.

In Foucault's tradition, Poster (1990, 86) understands surveillance as "a major form of power in the mode of information". He emphasizes that technological change has spawned new forms of surveillance and an electronic Superpanopticon in the postmodern and postindustrial mode of information.

For Gandy (1993, 15; see also 2012), panoptic surveillance is a

complex technology that involves the collection, processing, and sharing of information about individuals and groups that is generated through their daily lives as citizens, employees, and consumers and is used to coordinate and control their access to the goods and services that define life in the modern capitalist economy.

Robins and Webster (1993, 1999) refer to Foucault's ideas of the Panopticon and describe surveillance in the context of control, repression, discipline, and power: "To echo Foucault's words, it is not possible for social planning and administration to be exercised without surveillance, it is impossible for surveillance not to reinforce administrative cohesion, efficiency, and power" (Robins and Webster 1999, 90).

Fiske (1999, 125–127, 217–219) focuses on surveillance as the possibility of collecting certain knowledge about other people. In Foucault's tradition, surveillance is stressed as an oppressive and totalitarian method of power. "I believe that surveillance is rapidly becoming the most efficient form of power, the most totalitarian and the hardest to resist" (1999, 218).

Mathiesen (1997) revisits Foucault's Panopticon in "The Viewer Society". He argues that in modern society not only the few see the many as Foucault has articulated, but also the many see the few. Mathiesen (1997, 219) introduces in contrast to the Panopticon the term Synopticon – a combination of the Greek word "syn" = together, at the same time, and "opticon" = visual. Most importantly, in the Synopticon, news reporters, media personalities, and commentators

actively filter and shape information; as has been widely documented in media research, they produce news… they place topics on the agenda and avoid placing topics on the agenda.... Those who are allowed to enter [the media from the outside] are systematically men – not women – from the higher social strata, with power in political life, private industry and public bureaucracy.... The information professionals have become highly visible and valuable sources of information for the media; informational activity has become an occupation. The information professionals are trained to filter information, and to present images which are favourable to the institution or organization in question.

(Mathiesen 1997, 226–227)

Therefore, not only the Panopticon but also the Synopticon makes individuals silent, and directs, controls, and disciplines our consciousness (Mathiesen 1997, 230). As a result, the author concludes: "Taken as a whole, things are much *worse* than Michel Foucault imagined" (Mathiesen 1997, 231).

Sewell and Wilkinson (1992, 271; see also Sewell 2012) scrutinize surveillance in the labour process and draw parallels between Foucault's ideas of power, knowledge, and surveillance and the phenomenon of post-Fordism. According to these authors, Just-in-Time (JIT) and Total Quality Control (TQC) regimes are improved surveillance techniques that aim at the optimization of disciplinary power and the control of the labour process.

Panoptic theories of Internet surveillance

Elmer (1997) understands the Internet predominantly as a powerful space of economic surveillance. "The Internet is first mapped, through indexical search engines, and then diagnosed, via 'spiders' and 'cookies', to actively monitor, survey, solicit and subsequently profile users' online behavior" (Elmer 1997, 182).

Similarly, Winseck (2003) argues that media conglomerates dominate the commercialized cyberspace in modern society and mentions the importance of studying online surveillance in the context of ownership patterns. He considers, just like Foucault, surveillance to be negative and centralized and as being connected to coercion, power, and domination (Winseck 2003, 195). Similar to Foucault, Winseck (2003, 176) stresses that surveillance is primarily undertaken by powerful institutions such as corporations and is installed in order to discipline, control, and to normalize people in respect of drilling conformed individuals.

Likewise, in *The Internet Galaxy*, Castells (2001, 168–187) describes the Internet not only as a space full of opportunities, but also as a technology of control, which has primarily emerged from the interests of economic and political actors such as corporations and state institutions. Castells (2001, 171–173) considers, just like Foucault, surveillance to be negative and centralized, and as being connected to control and power. Hence, although Castells does not refer to the Panopticon directly, his contribution to online surveillance fits into panoptic notions of Internet surveillance.

Turow (2005, 2006) talks about marketing and consumer surveillance in the digital age of media. He stresses that online media are interested in collecting data about their audience in order to sell these data to advertisers. Similar to Foucault, Turow stresses that surveillance is predominately undertaken by powerful institutions such as corporations.

Andrejevic (2002; 2007a; 2007b; 2012) wants to offer an alternative approach to online surveillance in the era of new media. He studies the economic surveillance of interactive media such as interactive TV (Andrejevic 2002) and Google's business model of free wireless Internet access (Andrejevic 2007a), and analyses interactive surveillance in the digital enclosure: "the model of enclosure traces the relationship between a material, spatial process – the construction of networked, interactive environments – and the private expropriation of information" (Andrejevic 2007a, 297). The author argues that Foucault's approach to the Panopticon is suitable in order to study surveillance and hierarchical power asymmetries in the online economy, and talks about a "digital form of disciplinary panopticism" (Andrejevic 2007a, 237).

Also in the context of economic surveillance, Campbell and Carlson (2002) revisit Foucault's idea of the Panopticon as well as Gandy's notion of the panoptic sort. They apply these notions to online surveillance and the commodification of privacy on the Internet.

> The Panopticon was seen as a way of organizing social institutions to ensure a more orderly society by producing disciplined and "rational" (read predictable) citizens. With Internet ad servers, the goal is to provide marketers with the personal information necessary to determine if an individual constitutes an economically viable consumer. The enhanced consumer profiling offered by these third-party ad servers increases the effectiveness and efficiency of advertisers' efforts, reducing the uncertainty faced by producers introducing their goods and services into the marketplace.
>
> (Campbell and Carlson 2002, 587)

Summing up, panoptic notions of (Internet) surveillance argue that power, control, and surveillance have increased. Furthermore, the rise of the Internet has brought a space of electronic surveillance, where the powerful will appropriate the Internet as a technology of control for their own instrumental advantage. These approaches consider (online) surveillance to be negative and as being connected to coercion, repression, discipline, power, and domination. For these authors, power is primarily centralized and society tends to be repressive and controlled. This view emphasizes panoptical elements and uses a narrow definition of surveillance.

Towards a critical theory of (Internet) surveillance

The overall aim of the previous section was to clarify how (online) surveillance is defined in the existing literature and what the different notions of (online) surveillance have in common and what distinguishes them from one another. In doing so, Foucault's understanding of surveillance and the idea of the Panopticon were introduced. Based on these findings, a systematic discussion of the state of the art of surveillance (on the Internet) by establishing a typology of the existing literature and a discussion of commonalties and differences were introduced. Table 4.1 summarizes the results.

In conclusion, non-panoptic concepts use a neutral and general notion of surveillance (in cyberspace), where everyone has the opportunity to surveil; they are represented by scholars such Giddens, Rule, Miller and Weckert, and Albrechtslund. In contrast, panoptic notions consider surveillance to be negative and as being connected to coercion, repression, discipline, power, and domination; they are represented by scholars such as Deleuze, Gandy, Castells, and Andrejevic.

Although private actors monitor and watch over other individuals in everyday life experiences (e.g. parents taking care of their children, providing personal information on Weblogs, and using social networking sites on the Internet), these acts are processes to which people agree and which involve no violence, coercion, or repression. In comparison, economic and political actors use (online) surveillance and exercise violence in order to control a certain behaviour of people and in most cases people do not know that they are being surveilled. Corporations control the economic behaviour of people and coerce individuals in order to produce or buy specific commodities for accumulating profit and for guaranteeing the production of surplus value. Corporations and state institutions

Table 4.1 Foundations of (Internet) surveillance theory

Non-panoptic theories of (Internet) surveillance	Panoptic theories of (Internet) surveillance
Many scholars use a neutral and general notion and stress non-panoptic elements of (Internet) surveillance. This approach applies a broad definition of surveillance and stresses constraining and enabling effects of collecting data. Surveillance is primarily understood as a plural, neutral, and technical process.	This approach considers (Internet) surveillance to be always negative and being connected to coercion, repression, discipline, power, and domination. For these authors, power is primarily centralized and society tends to be repressive and controlled. This view emphasizes panoptical elements and uses a narrow definition of (online) surveillance.
Giddens (1981; 1985), Rule (1973; 2007; 2012), Gary Marx (1988; 2002), Cohen (1987), Beniger (1986), Clarke (1988), Lyon (1994; 2001; 1998; 2003b), Baudrillard (2007), Bogard (1996; 2006; 2012), Norris and Armstrong (1999; 1998), Haggerty and Ericson (2000), Miller and Weckert (2000), Albrechtslund (2008; 2012), Koskela (2004; 2006)	Deleuze (1992), Orwell (2004), Zuboff (1988), Poster (1990), Gandy (1993; 2012), Robins and Webster (1993; 1999), Fiske (1999), Mathiesen (1997), Sewell and Wilkinson (1992), Elmer (1997), Winseck (2003), Castells (2001), Turow (2005; 2006), Andrejevic (2002; 2007a; 2007b; 2012), Campbell and Carlson (2002)

are the most powerful actors in society and are able to undertake mass surveillance extensively and intensively (e.g. the collection and gathering of information on Internet user profiles in order to implement targeted advertising), because available resources decide surveillance dimensions. In the modern production process, electronic surveillance is primarily used to document and control workers' behaviour and communication for guaranteeing the production of surplus value. The commodification of privacy is important to target advertising for accumulating profit. State institutions have intensified and extended state surveillance of citizens in order to combat the threat of terrorism (Gandy 2003, 26–41; Lyon 2003c). There is also a relationship between economic and political surveillance, as PRISM demonstrates (*The Washington Post* 2013). PRISM is a clandestine mass electronic surveillance program operated by the National Security Agency (NSA) of the United States mining data from different Internet companies including Microsoft, Yahoo, Google, Apple, and Facebook. It shows that state surveillance and corporate surveillance interact. One may assume that corporations and state institutions are the main actors in modern surveillance societies and that surveillance is a crucial element for modern societies.

Non-panoptical notions use a broad definition of surveillance (on the Net) and tend to mix up very heterogeneous phenomena on one level of analysis. If, for example, the same term is used to describe harmless experiences like watching a baby on the one hand and powerful economic and political surveillance on the other hand, it becomes difficult to criticize contemporary surveillance phenomena such as CCTV, Internet surveillance, the EU data retention directive, biometrical iris scanners, facial recognition software, Computer Assisted Passenger Prescreening System (CAPPS), and the collection of DNA samples (Fuchs 2008, 273–275). Furthermore, non-panoptic notions understand (Internet) surveillance in a non-hierarchical and decentralized way, where everyone has the opportunity to surveil. This argument overlooks the fact that corporations and state institutions are the most powerful actors in society and are able to undertake mass surveillance, something that private actors are not able to do. Neutral surveillance concepts tend to overlook the power asymmetries of contemporary society and therefore tend to convey the image that private actors are equally powerful as corporations and state institutions. Hence, a general and neutral understanding is not fruitful for studying surveillance as it does not take asymmetrical power relations and repressive aspects of society into consideration. Approaches stressing that everyone today has the opportunity to surveil, that surveillance techniques democratize surveillance societies to a certain degree, and that surveillance has comical, playful, amusing, and even enjoyable characteristics are typical for postmodern scholars and disguise the fact of power and domination in contemporary surveillance societies.

Surveillance studies scholars like Lyon (1994, 119–158; 1998, 95) grasp that economic (online) surveillance such as monitoring consumers or the workplace are central aspects of surveillance societies. Most of the panoptic notions recognize the importance of economic aspects of surveillance in general and Internet surveillance in particular. Panoptic notions of surveillance analyse economic aspects of surveillance in different spheres, namely surveillance in the spheres of production, circulation, and consumption (for a detailed discussion see Allmer 2012a, 45, 94).

Although panoptic notions recognize the importance of the economy, they tend to focus on only one or two spheres as important aspects of contemporary surveillance societies. Furthermore, panoptic notions claim that there are particular forms of economic surveillance without a theoretical criterion for a certain typology. In contrast, a typology of (Internet) surveillance in the modern economy, which is based on Marx's theory of the political economy, allows us to systemize economic surveillance on the Internet and to distinguish online surveillance into the spheres of production, circulation, and consumption. A theoretically founded typology of economic surveillance (online) is important in order to undertake a theoretical analysis of surveillance in the modern economy. A critical contribution to surveillance studies strives for the development of theoretical and empirical research methods in order to focus on surveillance in the context of domination, asymmetrical power relations, resource control, social struggles, and exploitation. It critically analyses surveillance as an important aspect in guaranteeing the production of surplus value and in accumulating profit (Fuchs 2008, 268–270; 2010b, 19–21; Sandoval 2012). Based on the foundations of a critical political economy approach, the distinction of production, circulation, and consumption within the economy is introduced in order to establish a typology of (online) surveillance in the economy and to study surveillance (on the Internet) in the spheres of production, circulation, and consumption.

The Marxian spheres of the economy

In the "Introduction to a Contribution to the Critique of Political Economy", Marx (1986, 26–37) distinguishes between (1) production, (2) circulation (distribution and exchange), and (3) consumption as dialectically mediated spheres of the capitalistic economy. (1) The sphere of production appears as the point of departure. In the capitalist mode of production, entrepreneurs purchase means of production and labour power in order to produce commodities and surplus value. (2) Circulation is the "mediation between production and consumption" (Marx 1986, 27). In the process of circulation, consumers purchase commodities for daily life and proprietors sell the produced commodities to realize profit. (3) In the sphere of consumption as the final point of the process, "the product drops out of this social movement, becomes the direct object and servant of an individual need, which its use satisfies" (Marx 1986, 26). While in the production the person receives an objective aspect, in the consumption the object receives a subjective aspect. The "consumption, as the concluding act, ... reacts on the point of departure thus once again initiating the whole process" (Marx 1986, 27).

Although production, circulation, and consumption are separated spheres, they correlate in an interconnected relationship (see Figure 4.1).

In the sphere of production means of production are consumed, and in the sphere of consumption labour power is (re)produced. "Production is consumption;

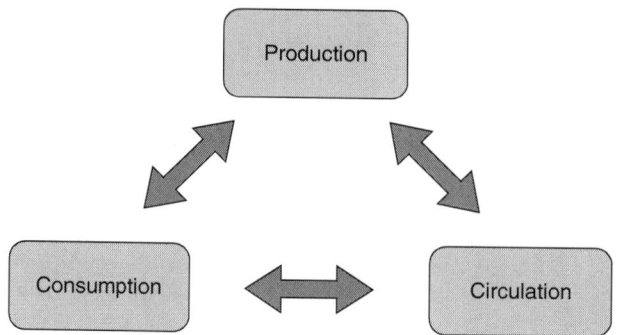

Figure 4.1 Production, circulation, and consumption as dialectically mediated spheres of the economy.

consumption is production. Consumptive production. Productive consumption" (Marx 1986, 30). Production is not possible without demand and consumption does not take place without material. "No consumption without production; no production without consumption" (Marx 1986, 30). Moreover, the process of production is determined by circulation of labour power as well as means of production, whereas circulation itself is a product of production. Production, circulation, and consumption are not "identical, but that they are all elements of a totality, differences within a unity.... There is an interaction between the different moments" (Marx 1986, 36–37). Nevertheless, production, circulation, and consumption are not equal spheres in the economy; production is rather

> the dominant moment, both with regard to itself in the contradictory determination of production and with regard to the other moments. The process always starts afresh with production ... A definite [mode of] production thus determines a definite [mode of] consumption, distribution, exchange and *definite relations of these different moments to one another*. Production *in its one-sided form*, however, is in its turn also determined by the other moments.
>
> (Marx 1986, 36)

Based on the distinction of production, circulation, and consumption, a typology of (online) surveillance in the economy may be constructed. Such a typology will be outlined in the next subsection.

(Internet) surveillance in the Marxian spheres of the economy

Economic surveillance and illustrative examples in the spheres of production, circulation, and consumption will be outlined.

(Internet) surveillance in the sphere of production

Marx analyses the process of producing capital in *Capital, Volume One*. The process starts with commodities and money, continues with labour-produced surplus value and methods for producing absolute and relative surplus value, and concludes with the accumulation of capital. For Marx, production is a unity of the labour process (1) and the process of producing surplus value (2). (1) The labour process is a human activity where, with the help of the instruments of labour, an alteration of material is effected. Marx understands the labour process as a relationship of human activity with its physical and intellectual capabilities on the one hand and the means of production with its instruments and subjects of labour on the other hand, whereas labour is defined as a "process between man and nature, a process by which man, through his own actions, mediates, regulates and controls the metabolism between himself and nature" (Marx 1976, 283). The land is the "universal material for human labour" (Marx 1976, 284). An instrument of labour

> is a thing, or a complex of things, which the worker interposes between himself and the object of his labour and which serves as a conductor, directing his activity onto that object. He makes use of the mechanical, physical and chemical properties of some substances in order to set them to work on other substances as instruments of his power, and in accordance with his purposes.
>
> (Marx 1976, 285)

(2) In the capitalist mode of production, entrepreneurs consume purchased labour power as variable capital (v) and purchased means of production as constant capital (c) in order to produce commodities. Constant capital such as raw materials, operating supplies, buildings, equipment, etc. does not change its value in the process of production, because the value of constant capital is transferred to the commodity, whereas labour power as variable capital changes its value during the process of production and produces surplus value (Marx 1976, 317). The overall aim of capitalists is to produce as much surplus value as possible in order to accumulate profit. There are two different possibilities for doing so: the production of absolute surplus value by extension of the working day and the production of relative surplus value by intensification of the working day and increasing productivity.

> I call that surplus-value which is produced by the lengthening of the working day, absolute surplus-value. In contrast to this, I call that surplus-value which arises from the curtailment of the necessary labour-time, and from the corresponding alteration in the respective lengths of the two components of the working day, relative surplus-value.
>
> (Marx 1976, 432)

Marx develops the concept of producing relative surplus value as instrument to intensify the working day and introduces cooperation as one possibility for doing so. For Marx, cooperation is an essential part of the capitalist process of production being defined as a process of many workers collaborating with each other in one process or many related processes of production in order to work systematically side by side and together (Marx 1976, 442). He highlights the importance and necessity of control, supervision, and surveillance in order to guarantee cooperation, the production of relative surplus value, and therefore achieve accumulation of capital:

> The work of directing, superintending and adjusting becomes one of the functions of capital, from the moment that the labour under capital's control becomes co-operative.... Just as at first the capitalist is relieved from actual labour as soon as his capital has reached that minimum amount with which capitalist production, properly speaking, first begins, so now he hands over the work of direct and constant supervision of the individual workers and groups of workers to a special kind of wage-labourer. An industrial army of workers under the command of a capitalist requires like a real army, officers (managers) and N.C.O.s (foremen, overseers), who command during the labour process in the name of capital. The work of supervision becomes their established and exclusive function.
>
> (Marx 1976, 449–450)

The "Electronic Monitoring and Surveillance Survey" (American Management Association and the ePolicy Institute 2008) offers interesting examples of surveillance in the sphere of production. According to the American Management Association and the ePolicy Institute (2008) which undertake an annual quantitative survey about electronic monitoring and surveillance with approximately 300 US companies, "more than one fourth of employers have fired workers for misusing e-mail and nearly one third have fired employees for misusing the Internet". More than 40 per cent of the studied companies monitor e-mail traffic of their workers, and 66 per cent of the corporations monitor Internet connections. In addition, most companies use software to block non-work-related websites such as sexual or pornographic sites, game sites, social networking sites, entertainment sites, shopping sites, and sport sites. The American Management Association and the ePolicy Institute (2008) also emphasize that companies track "content, keystrokes, and time spent at the keyboard ... store and review computer files ... monitor the blogosphere to see what is being written about the company, and ... monitor social networking sites". Furthermore, about 30 per cent of the companies had fired employees for non-work-related e-mail and Internet usage, including "inappropriate or offensive language" and "viewing, downloading, or uploading inappropriate/offensive content" (American Management Association and the ePolicy Institute 2008). This example shows that companies use surveillance and exercise violence in order to control certain behaviours of workers. Corporations control the economic behaviour of people and coerce individuals in order to produce specific commodities for accumulating profit and for guaranteeing the production of surplus value. In the modern production process, electronic surveillance is primarily used to document and control workers' behaviour and communications in guaranteeing the production of surplus value.

(Internet) surveillance in the sphere of circulation

In order to understand the sphere of circulation of the capitalistic economy and surveillance in it, it is helpful to analyse the circuit of capital. As outlined in Chapter 1, the circuit of capital contains three stages, namely the stage of money capital (sphere of circulation), the stage of productive capital (sphere of production), and the stage of commodity capital (sphere of circulation). By knowing the sphere of circulation in the circuit of capital, one is able to identify surveillance in the sphere of purchasing labour power (L) in the stage of money capital (1), purchasing means of production (mp; objects and instruments of labour) in the stage of money capital (2), and produced commodities (C') in the stage of commodity capital (3).

1 (INTERNET) SURVEILLANCE OF PURCHASING LABOUR POWER

Surveillance of purchasing labour power in the stage of money capital means applicant surveillance. Applicant surveillance is useful for getting the most suitable labour power, which is able to produce the most surplus value and with means of production creates a new commodity of the greatest possible value in order to sell the commodity and to accumulate as much profit as possible. Lyon (2001, 41) stresses in this context that "before an employee is even hired, she or he is likely to be checked, using special databases (including data mining techniques) or genetic screening, to discover the likelihood of this or that person turning out to be a responsible and hard-working employee". Gandy (1993, 62) argues that the corporate file "begins with the application" and that "applications are required to classify the applicant in terms of eligibility or in relation to the assignment of the applicant to one or more classes of service".

Surveillance of purchasing labour power in the stage of money capital means online applicant surveillance. Searle (2006, 343) states in this context that

> checking procedures are increasingly utilised to authenticate candidates' data. In several countries financial services authorities have sanctioned formal vetting, often outsourcing it to external contractors. The growth in the collection and sale of information databases can be seen by the proliferation of information verification firms, such as Kroll and Carratu International.

The New Yorker risk consulting company Kroll is an operating unit of Altegrity Inc. and undertakes off- and online pre-employment screening on a large scale. Kroll offers background screening services of new job applicants for companies and government agencies in order to check information, including address histories, education and employment histories, media coverage, credit reports, civil and bankruptcy records, criminal records, driving histories, liens and judgment histories, and professional licences and certifications (Kroll 2012). If Kroll realizes a company's application procedure, the job candidates have to fill out a detailed questionnaire on the Internet as part of their application, which is sent invisibly to Kroll (Searle 2006, 343). "Kroll has pioneered a secure Internet-based system that collects information from job candidates and provides clients with project updates and final reports. Kroll's Applicant Submission System allows job candidates to fill out a detailed questionnaire online and submit it securely to Kroll" (Kroll 2012). In order to investigate job candidates, Kroll "searches primary sources (including electronic resources), visits courthouses throughout the country to retrieve and review public documents, and conducts telephone interviews with a job candidate's professional and personal references" (Kroll 2012). Kroll is a threat to the job candidates' privacy, because the applicants assume that their personal information is only shared with the company to which they are applying, but the candidates do not know that their information is sent to Kroll. Kroll and its entrepreneurial clients use surveillance and exercise violence in order to control certain behaviours of people. Kroll also offers surveillance services of existing employees involving monitoring e-mail traffic and Internet use (Internet surveillance in the sphere of production). This indicates that economic surveillance also occurs in combinations of different spheres and forms of surveillance in the spheres of production, circulation, and consumption are interconnected.

2 (INTERNET) SURVEILLANCE OF PURCHASING MEANS OF PRODUCTION

Surveillance of purchasing means of production in the stage of money capital includes screening of suppliers. Kroll (2012) provides a so-called off- and online commercial intelligence program in order to check existing and potential suppliers. According to Kroll (2012), the service "goes beyond the published data" and gives the company "a real sense of who you are doing business with". Kroll (2012) screens primary source data and analysis of suppliers, performance benchmarking in the sector of suppliers, and collects information based on industry knowledge and contacts. As claimed by Kroll (2012), the

> advantage lies in being able to give you the right information, at the right time, to help you make the best possible decision.... By accessing reliable and effective commercial intelligence from Kroll, you will gain the confidence to make sound business decisions that will enhance your corporate reputation and bottom line performance.

3 (INTERNET) SURVEILLANCE OF PRODUCED COMMODITIES

Surveillance of produced commodities in the stage of commodity capital contains (material and immaterial) property surveillance as well as surveillance of vendors.

Interesting in this context is the corporate investigation company Carratu, which is headquartered in London. Carratu operates around the world with national and multinational corporations, insurance companies, law firms, and financial institutions, which are primarily found in the Fortune 500 and the Financial Times Top 100 rankings (Carratu 2012). Carratu offers so-called Intellectual Property Protection Services (IPPS) off- and online on behalf of brands, trademarks, and patent owners. It includes services such as anti-counterfeiting investigations, trademark infringement and passing-off investigations, market watch, patent investigations, and parallel trade investigations. In order to avoid product counterfeiting, Carratu (2012) offers

> brand owners and their legal representatives a unique range of anti-counterfeiting programmes, tracking infringements from point of sale to source, identifying those responsible and building up a comprehensive supply chain diagnosis. We obtain the evidence needed to bring an enforcement action and support clients through the entire process.

Furthermore, the corporate investigation company undertakes trademark infringement and passing-off investigations: "Whether it is your company name or one of your registered or un-registered trademarks, we investigate those individuals behind the infringement and provide you with sufficient evidence to take the appropriate action" (Carratu 2012). The company also offers a market watch service. This service

> constantly monitors all likely distribution centres with each area covered by a watcher, or watchers, who submit monthly intelligence reports on the outlets and venues checked. If an infringement is found, a test purchase is completed and, when requested, we liaise with the local authorities to ensure that wherever possible, enforcement action is taken.
>
> (Carratu 2012)

In addition, Carratu (2012) carries out parallel trade investigations and assists "trademark owners in determining who is behind the supply of parallel goods and to secure the necessary evidence to take enforcement action and so safeguard regional markets and profits".

Kroll (2012) provides a so-called off- and online vendor integrity program in order to check whether existing and potential vendors "have criminal records, financial troubles, or business relationships that could create costly conflicts or be deeply embarrassing" or "could have a negative impact on your company's revenues and reputation". Therefore, Kroll (2012) screens criminal records, bankruptcy records, illegal activity allegations, civil cases, liens, as well as media coverage of vendors. In doing so, vendors have to "complete a detailed online questionnaire that's electronically submitted to Kroll ... Kroll's staff screens the information provided by vendors and collect additional intelligence" (Kroll 2012) and publishes an online report.

In conclusion, the circuit of capital contains three stages, namely the stage of money capital, the stage of productive capital, and the stage of commodity capital. Based on these findings, surveillance in the sphere of circulation consists of applicant surveillance, screening of suppliers, property surveillance, and surveillance of vendors. The next point of discussion is the sphere of consumption.

(Internet) surveillance in the sphere of consumption

Marx (1986) notes that "production produces consumption: (1) by creating the material for consumption; (2) by determining the mode of consumption; (3) by creating in the consumer a need for the products which it first posits as objects" and concludes that production "produces the object of consumption, the mode of consumption and the urge to consume". Nevertheless, in order to know which mode of production generates which mode of consumption of different consumers, knowledge of consumption matters is required. Although the emergence of mass consumption in modern societies promises individuality, free choice, sovereignty, and freedom of consumers, it synchronously requires knowledge of consuming activities in order to stimulate and steer consumption (Lyon 1994, 137). Advertising as a product of modern society is an important instrument for realizing profit, because it induces people to consume more products or services through branding. The more data are available, the more precise and effective are the targeted advertisements. Consumer surveillance may be seen as a product of the capitalistic economy (Lyon 1994, 138; Gill 2003, 25–27; Ogura 2006, 293–295; Brown 2006, 18–20; Hewson 1994). In order to target advertising, market research such as analysing behaviour, preferences, and interests of consumers is important. The basic question for market research is who buys where, when, what, and why. The overall aim is to access certain behaviours, preferences, usages, interests, and choices of customers in order to identify, classify, and assess (Gandy 1993, 80–87) certain groups and supply them with targeted advertisements. As Adorno and Horkheimer (2002, 98) put it: "Sharp distinctions like those between A and B films, or between short stories published in magazines in different price segments, do not so much reflect real differences as assist in the classification, organization, and identification of consumers". So, "for the consumer there is nothing left to classify, since the classification has already be preempted by the schematism of production". Corporations are interested in collecting and generating as much data as possible (qualitative level) from as many people as possible (quantitative level).

For surveillance in the sphere of consumption, the example of Google and DoubleClick may be outlined. According to the top sites of the Web by Alexa Internet (2013), Google has the most visits on the Internet. Google uses a wide range of methods in order to collect data on its users, namely click tracking (to log clicks of users), log files (to store server requests), JavaScript and web bugs (to check user visits), as well as cookies (to record individual actions) (Stalder and Mayer 2009, 102). DoubleClick is one of the main projects of Google (Google 2008). It is a global leader in ad serving and has developed sophisticated methods in order to collect, analyse, and assess huge amounts of users' data on the Internet (Campbell and Carlson 2002, 596–597). Google (2007, 2008) acquired DoubleClick in 2008 for US$3.1 billion. DoubleClick is headquartered in New York City. It was founded in 1996 and works for leading digital publishers, marketers, and agencies around the world including About, Durex, Ford, Friendster, Optimedia, Scripps, and MTV (DoubleClick 2012). Ad serving companies such as DoubleClick use methods such as placing advertisements on websites and analysing their efficiency. DoubleClick develops and provides Internet ad serving services being primarily sold to advertisers and publishers. DoubleClick collects personal data on many websites, sells this data, and supports targeted advertising. DoubleClick's main product is known as DART (Dynamic Advertising, Reporting, and Targeting). DART is an ad serving programme working with a complex algorithm and is primarily developed for publishers and advertisers in order to "ensure you get the right message, to the right person, at the right time, on the right device" (DoubleClick 2012). DoubleClick collects personal data including individual behaviours, preferences, and interests on many websites with the help of systematic and automated computer processes. DoubleClick sells these data to advertising agencies in order to guarantee the production of surplus value and to accumulate profit.

Conclusion: capitalist surveillance vs. counter-surveillance

The overall aim of this chapter was to clarify how we theorize and systemize surveillance in the modern economy. This chapter constructed theoretically founded typologies in order to systemize the existing literature of surveillance studies and to analyse examples of surveillance.

Foundations of surveillance studies were discussed in the second section. In the third section, a critical contribution to surveillance studies was drawn in order to distinguish surveillance into the spheres of production, circulation, and consumption. Based on these findings, we were able to systemize economic surveillance on the basis of current developments on the Internet such as the Electronic Monitoring and Surveillance Survey, Kroll, Carratu, and DoubleClick into the spheres of production, circulation, and consumption.

As shown in this contribution, economic actors such as corporations undertake surveillance and exercise violence in order to control a certain behaviour of people and in most cases people do not know that they are being surveilled. Corporations control the economic behaviour of people and coerce individuals in order to produce or buy specific commodities for guaranteeing the production of surplus value and for accumulating profit. Therefore, one may assume that surveillance is a negative phenomenon of modern societies, which should be questioned and struggled against. Based on Gandy (1993, 230–231), Castells (2001, 182–184), Parenti (2003, 207–212), Ogura (2006, 291–293), Lyon (1994, 159–225; 2007b, 159–178; 2007a, 368–377), and Fuchs (2009a, 115–117), some political recommendations may be drawn in order to overcome economic (online) surveillance:

- The first recommendation is that support is needed for critical surveillance movements in order to develop counter-hegemonic power and advance critical awareness of surveillance.
- "Such public awareness of surveillance issues could further be raised through professional groups and organizations, especially those directly concerned with computing, information management, and so on" (Lyon 1994, 223).
- Furthermore, Lyon (2001, 127) states the importance of political activism by critical citizens: "Films, consumer groups, Internet campaigns and international watchdogs are just some of the ways that ongoing surveillance practices are brought to the surface of our consciousness, and thus overtly into the realm of ethical evaluation and political response."
- According to Fuchs (2009a, 116),

  > critical citizens, critical citizens' initiatives, consumer groups, social movement groups, critical scholars, unions, data protection specialists/groups, consumer protection specialists/groups, critical politicians, critical political parties observe closely the relationship of surveillance and corporations and document instances where corporations and politicians take measures that threaten privacy or increase the surveillance of citizens.

- In addition, it is recommended to support cyberactivism and "counter-surveillance" (Lyon 1994, 159) in order to surveil corporate surveillants or rather to watch the watchers.
- Parenti (2003, 212) suggests civil disobedience, rebellion, and protest:

  > It will compel regulators to tell corporations, police, schools, hospitals, and other institutions that there are limits. As a society, we want to say: Here you may not go. Here you may not record. Here you may not track and identify people. Here you may not trade and analyze information and build dossiers.

- A further recommendation is to create non-profit, non-commercial social networking platforms on the Internet such as Kaioo and diaspora* (Fuchs 2009a, 116; Sevignani 2012). Diaspora* is a non-profit and user-owned social networking site managed by the Diaspora Foundation. The platform has been available since 2010 and has currently more than one million accounts. The Diaspora Foundation is not interested in targeting advertising as it does not need to produce surplus value and to accumulate profit:

  > To try to advance critical awareness and to surveil corporate and political surveillers are important political moves for guaranteeing civil rights, but they will ultimately fail if they do not recognize that electronic surveillance is not a technological issue that can be solved by technological means or by different individual behaviours, but only by bringing about changes of society.

  (Fuchs 2009a, 116)

Therefore, surveillance has to be put into the larger context of societal problems in public discourse. "We should look at the whole macro picture" (Ogura 2006, 292).

- Finally, surveillance is caused by economic and political issues and is inherent in modern society. It is neither just a technical issue nor an individual problem, but a societal problem. Surveillance is a crucial phenomenon, but there are many other features in contemporary society such as information, neoliberalism, globalization, and capital.

The economic and political logic shaping the strategies of profit-oriented social media platforms produces an antagonism between communicative opportunities and privacy and surveillance threats. This points out the antagonistic structure of communication technologies in capitalism. The overall aim of the subsequent part is to study the users' knowledge, attitudes, and practices towards this antagonistic character and the potentials and risks of social media. Part II may be considered as a case study of the critical theory and dialectics of media, technology, and society and as an ontological approach, because it focuses on the analysis of digital media and the concrete use of social media.

Note

1 An earlier version of this chapter was published in *Towards a Critical Theory of Surveillance in Informational Capitalism*, Peter Lang, 2012. See: www.peterlang.com/ ?263220.

Part II
Case study

5 Traditional and critical research of privacy and surveillance on social media

Introduction

Horkheimer (2002, 188–243) distinguishes between traditional and critical theory. Traditional theory is considered as a form of academic thinking based on instrumental reason, where the reason becomes an instrument for the advancement of external and alienated interest. Instrumental reason is oriented on utility and productivity. In contrast, critical theory may be described as a form of academic, normative, and partial reflection based on critical reason. Critical reason operates with Marxian categories such as class, exploitation, and oppression. Critical theory struggles for the transformation of society and the realization of human potentialities. Based on these ideas, I distinguish between traditional and critical research of privacy and surveillance on social media. The subsequent sections are structured according to this distinction.

In the second section, existing empirical research of privacy on web 2.0 is analysed. A discussion of some of the most cited studies should give a representative overview of typical empirical research approaches that assess privacy on social networking sites. I will show that there is a predominance of traditional and uncritical research in the context of privacy on web 2.0. This research does not reflect structural power asymmetries in capitalism. Some critical theoretical studies about surveillance on digital and new media are thus examined in the third section. The studies and any important findings are briefly summarized in order to provide an overview of the existing research. The fourth and final section summarizes and concludes the results, and argues for the need for a critical empirical study of privacy and surveillance on social media.

Traditional research of privacy on social media

Studies of privacy on web 2.0 focus primarily on privacy-related issues on corporate social networking sites. These studies pay attention to one or more of the following issues concerning SNS users:

- Individual knowledge and information towards or about privacy.
- Individual privacy-related attitudes or concerns.
- Individual behaviour and practices towards or about privacy (settings).

Acquisti and Gross (2006, 37) conducted an online survey of students, staff, and faculty members (N=294; 147 male and 147 female participants) at a US academic institution in order to study their privacy concerns as well as their use and knowledge of and attitudes towards Facebook (FB). The questionnaire contained around 40 questions including an initial set of screening questions, a set of calibration questions, a consent section, and questions relating to Facebook (Acquisti and Gross 2006, 39). In the questionnaire, the participants were asked to rank agreement, concern, worries, or importance on a 7-point Likert scale (where 1 is "not important at all" and 7 is "very important"); the questions ranged from general, to increasingly specific, and personal (Acquisti and Gross 2006, 43).

According to Acquisti and Gross (2006, 47), "members claim that the FB is very useful to them for learning about and finding classmates (4.93 mean on a 7-point Likert scale) and for making it more convenient for people to get in touch with them (4.92), but deny any usefulness for other activities". Among the stated reasons for using Facebook, having fun and revealing useful information were ranked top (Acquisti and Gross 2006, 53). The study stresses that the users' knowledge about privacy issues on Facebook is very low:

> Thirty percent claim not to know whether FB grants any way to manage who can search for and find their profile, or think that they are given no such control. 18% do not know whether FB grants any way to manage who can actually read their profile, or think that they are given no such control.... 22% of our sample do not know what the FB privacy settings are or do not remember if they have ever changed them. Around 25% do not know what the location settings are.
>
> (Acquisti and Gross 2006, 51–52)

In addition,

> almost 77% of respondents claimed not to have read FB's privacy policy (the real number is probably higher); and that many of them mistakenly believe that FB does not collect information about them from other sources regardless of their use of the site (67%), that FB does not combine information about them collected from other sources (70%), or that FB does not share personal information with third parties (56%).
>
> (Acquisti and Gross 2006, 53)

The survey further shows that although privacy concerns may drive older and senior university members away from Facebook, primarily undergraduate students join the network regardless of their privacy concerns (Acquisti and Gross 2006, 47). To a certain extent, privacy attitudes determine who joins Facebook but, once joined, there are only minor differences in information disclosure across different social groups (Acquisti and Gross 2006, 50).

Fogel and Nehmad (2009) carried out a quantitative survey with students at a University in New York City (N=205; equal percentages of men and women;

average age: 22 years). The study analyses risk taking, trust, and privacy concerns among students in the context of social networking sites (Facebook and MySpace). Participants were asked at the university campus to complete an anonymous questionnaire.

In the survey, more than three-quarters of the students had registered at a social networking site and nearly three-quarters of the participants were allowed to view their profile without restrictions (Fogel and Nehmad 2009, 156–157).

> In conclusion, those who have profiles on social networking websites have greater risk taking attitudes than those who do not have profiles on social networking websites. Also, risk taking attitudes are greater among men than women. Facebook has a perception of being a trustworthy social networking website. General privacy concerns and identity information disclosure concerns are of greater concern to woman than men. Lastly, there are greater percentages of disclosure of phone numbers and home addresses among men than women.
>
> (Fogel and Nehmad 2009, 160)

boyd and Hargittai (2010) conducted a quantitative paper-pencil survey with 1115 participating students in 2009 at the University of Illinois, Chicago, and followed up with the same group using a quantitative paper survey sent by postal mail in 2010 (495 valid completed survey responses). The study examines the attitudes and practices of 18- and 19-year-old students about privacy settings on Facebook.

boyd and Hargittai (2010) asked participants to indicate to which degree they agreed with the following statement: "I feel confident changing the privacy settings of my Facebook account" ("strongly disagree" to "strongly agree"). In addition, the respondents were asked how often they change their Facebook privacy settings ("never", "have done it once", "have done it two to three times", and "have done it four or more times").

Eighty-seven per cent of the respondents were members of Facebook in 2009 and 90 per cent had joined the network in 2010. boyd and Hargittai (2010) found that:

> while not universal, modifications to privacy settings have increased during a year in which Facebook's approach to privacy was hotly contested. We also find that both frequency and type of Facebook use as well as Internet skill are correlated with making modifications to privacy settings. In contrast, we observe few gender differences in how young adults approach their Facebook privacy settings, which is notable given that gender differences exist in so many other domains online.

Furthermore, the data showed that

> far from being nonchalant and unconcerned about privacy matters, the majority of young adult users of Facebook are engaged with managing their

privacy settings on the site at least to some extent. The frequency with which they adjust their settings and their confidence in doing so may vary, but most report modifying their settings.

Christofides and colleagues (2009) undertook a quantitative online survey with 343 participating undergraduate students (261 women, 81 men; age: 17 to 24) at a university in Ontario, Canada. The survey endeavoured to analyse information disclosure and information control on Facebook and to explain the personality factors that effect levels of disclosure and control. In detail, the authors were interested in receiving answers to what information students disclose, how they control access to that information, and personality factors (need for popularity, levels of trust, and likelihood of disclosing personal information) related to online information control and disclosure (Christofides *et al.* 2009, 342).

The questionnaire contained demographic questions, questions about information disclosure, the likelihood of using available privacy settings on Facebook, and types of posted pictures.

Students disclose more personal information on Facebook than they disclose in general (Christofides *et al.* 2009, 342). In addition,

> participants were very likely to have posted information such as their birthday and e-mail address, and almost all had joined an online network. They were also very likely to post pictures such as a profile picture, pictures with friends, and even pictures at parties and drinking with friends.
>
> (Christofides *et al.* 2009, 341)

The authors also found out that:

> information disclosure and information control were not significantly negatively correlated, and multiple regression analyses revealed that while disclosure was significantly predicted by the need for popularity, levels of trust and self-esteem predicted information control. Therefore, disclosure and control on Facebook are not as closely related as expected but rather are different processes that are affected by different aspects of personality.
>
> (Christofides *et al.* 2009, 341)

Debatin *et al.* (2009) conducted an online quantitative (N = 119) and qualitative (N = 8; open-ended in-depth face-to-face interviews) empirical research exercise with undergraduate students at a US academic institution. The study strives to analyse the relationship between Facebook privacy issues, privacy settings, recognized benefits and risks on Facebook, as well as restrictions of privacy.

The online questionnaire contained 36 multiple-choice questions classified into thematic groups such as Facebook habits, types of personal information available on the users' profile, users' practices with regard to privacy, role of friends in Facebook use, potential risks of Facebook, negative incidents, differences between perceived negative incidents to oneself and to others, and demographic variables.

From the online survey respondent pool, eight students (six female, two male) were asked for open-ended in-depth face-to-face interviews. The eight interviewees were selected according to their survey answers and their availability. After recording and transcribing the interviews, the data were analysed based on a combination of typological reduction analysis, qualitative content analysis, and hermeneutical/rhetorical interpretation. In order to identify and interpret relevant statements, the authors used the following categories: invasion of privacy, breach of trust, gossip and rumours, violation of boundaries, and habitual or ritualized use of Facebook (Debatin *et al.* 2009, 92).

One result of the study was as follows:

> While the majority of Facebook users report having an understanding of privacy settings and make use of their privacy settings, it is also apparent, however, that they may have a skewed sense of what that exactly entails. Additionally, as hypothesized, perceived benefits of online social networking outweighed risks of disclosing personal information. Risks to privacy were ascribed more to others than to the self. If Facebook users reported an invasion of personal privacy, users are more likely to change privacy settings than if they reported hearing of an invasion of privacy happening to others.
>
> (Debatin *et al.* 2009, 100)

The authors further stress that:

> the interviews exemplified how deeply Facebook is integrated into daily routines and rituals, and how much it has produced its own routines and rites. The habitual use of Facebook and its integration into daily life indicates that it has become an indispensable tool of social capital and connectedness with large numbers of people. The benefits of Facebook outweigh privacy concerns, even when concrete privacy invasion was experienced.
>
> (Debatin *et al.* 2009, 100)

Although Ellison and colleagues (2007) focused in their survey on the relationship between the use of Facebook and the maintenance of social status, the authors also analysed privacy concerns of individuals. Ellison and colleagues carried out a quantitative online survey with undergraduate students (N = 286) at the Michigan State University (MSU). Their instrument included four broad types of measures, namely measures of demographic variables (gender, age, local/home residence, ethnicity, year in school), measure of Internet use, measure of Facebook use (time spent on Facebook, reasons for use), and measure of individual well-being and social status. Ellison and colleagues' (2007, 1165) findings may be summarized as follows:

We asked Facebook users whether or not they had set the privacy settings on their accounts to control who viewed their profiles. More than two thirds (70%) either did not know (suggesting that they left the default setting of all members of the MSU network) or said that their profile was visible by the entire MSU network. Only 13% limited access only to their friends, while the rest blocked only certain individuals.

Hinduja and Patchin (2008) conducted a quantitative content analysis of Myspace. They collected and analysed types of information found on randomly sampled Myspace profile pages that were publicly accessible (N=1475; age: 16–17 years). In order to record certain kinds of information of Myspace profile pages, the researchers used a data collection form. The data collection form contained variables such as name, birth date, telephone number, postal address, last login date, evidence of alcohol, tobacco, or drug use, number of pictures, and swear words in profile (Hinduja and Patchin 2008, 141–142).

The authors summarized their findings as follows:

> Almost 40% of the profiles included the youth's first name, and approximately 9% included their full name. This information, along with their current city (81%) and school (28%), may also assist those seeking to identify profile owners offline. While it is effortless to contact youth via their Myspace profiles (using private messages or public comments), some youth also included their instant messaging name (4%, usually a screen name for AOL, Yahoo, or MSN Messenger) or an additional email address (1%). In rare cases (*n*=4) youth reported their personal (usually cell) phone number. In addition to the phone numbers reported within the profile by its owner, we noticed a few cases where friends would include their own phone numbers in a public comment they left.... Four profiles out of approximately 1500 represents a small percentage (about one-third of 1%), however, this number extrapolated to all adolescents on MySpace suggests that up to 75,000 youth may be including this very private information.
>
> (Hinduja and Patchin 2008, 136)

Hinduja and Patchin (2008, 136) concluded:

> this review of MySpace profiles also revealed that many adolescents seek to demonstrate familiarity with adult-oriented behaviors. For example, many youth indicated they had recently consumed alcohol (18%), while others noted that they had smoked cigarettes (8%) or used marijuana (2%).

Lewis and colleagues (2008) undertook an analysis of college students' privacy settings on Facebook and endeavoured to find out factors being predictive of a student having a private or public profile. In order to reach full access to the student's profiles, the scholars created an undergraduate account and participated in the university network on Facebook (Lewis *et al.* 2008, 84). The authors realized a quantitative content analysis of Facebook profiles of 1564 undergraduate students at a private university in the northeastern United States. The dataset was extracted directly from Facebook and included variables such as sex, friends, home town, race/ethnicity, socioeconomic status, and online activity.

As a result of the study, Lewis and colleagues (2008, 94–95) stress that privacy behaviour is a consequence of both social influences and personal interests and sum up:

> A student is significantly more likely to have a private profile if (1) the student's friends, and especially roommates, have private profiles; (2) the student is more active on Facebook; (3) the student is female; and (4) the student generally prefers music that is relatively popular (high mean) and only music that is relatively popular (low SD).

In the Greater London area, Livingstone (2008) conducted qualitative interviews with 16 teenagers (eight females, eight males; age: 13–16 years), who use social networking sites. Livingstone was interested in showing that online opportunities on the one hand and risks such as privacy threats on the other hand are interconnected and that both issues characterize social media. In the study, the interview schedule addressed three main topics, namely motivations and literacies forming the teenagers' profile, the semiotic understanding of others' profiles, and the social meanings of the contacts encouraged online and their connection to offline relations (Livingstone 2008, 398). After recording and transcribing the interviews, the data were coded based on participants' responses and the asked questions.

Although Livingstone (2008, 406) found that teenagers see the maintenance of old and the establishment of new friendships as a central opportunity of social networking sites, she discovered that the interviewees were concerned about privacy settings on these sites:

> A fair proportion of those interviewed hesitated to show how to change their privacy settings, often clicking on the wrong options before managing this task, and showing some nervousness about the unintended consequences of changing settings (both the risk of "stranger danger" and parental approbation were referred to here, although they also told stories of viruses, crashed computers, unwanted advertising and unpleasant chain messages).

Livingstone (2008, 406) concluded: "when asked whether they would like to change anything about social networking, the operation of privacy settings and provision of private messaging on the sites are teenagers' top priorities, along with elimination of spam and chain messages – both intrusions of their privacy."

Dwyer and colleagues (2007, 2010) conducted quantitative online surveys with 115 MySpace and 107 Facebook users in the US, and 388 studiVZ (a German-based social networking site) users in the German-speaking world in order to study the influence of trust and privacy concerns on the use of social networking sites for social interaction. The questionnaire contained questions about general use of the site, perceptions of trust, Internet privacy concerns, information sharing, and the development of new relationships (Dwyer *et al.* 2007).

The authors conclude:

> Facebook members reveal more information, but MySpace members are more likely to extend online relationships beyond the bounds of the social networking site. Paradoxically, MySpace has stronger evidence of new relationship development, despite weaker trust results. Even MySpace subjects with high distrust in other members report strong levels of relationship development. The results suggest that for MySpace, trust is not as necessary in the building of new relationships as it is in face to face encounters.
>
> (Dwyer *et al.* 2007)

In addition, the authors found out that there is a significant difference of privacy settings between the US-based (Facebook and MySpace) and the German (studiVZ) social networking sites:

> StudiVZ users are the most familiar with their privacy settings.... StudiVZ users also generally feel confidence in their ability to modify their privacy settings.... Members of StudiVZ express a higher level of familiarity ... and facility ... with their privacy settings, but express less comfort ... with their abilities.
>
> (Dwyer *et al.* 2010, 2975)

TNS Opinion & Social (2011) interviewed 26,574 people aged 15 and over in the 27 member states of the EU in 2010. The overall aim was to find out citizens' behaviours and attitudes concerning identity management, data protection, and privacy in the European Union. The interviews were conducted face-to-face with the help of a structured questionnaire in people's homes and in the appropriate national languages. The questionnaire contained 39 questions. These ranged from general ones, to increasingly specific, and personal questions.

In the context of social networking sites, TNS Opinion & Social (2011, 1–2) conclude that "over half of Internet users are informed about the data collection conditions and the further uses of their data when joining a social networking site or registering for a service online (54%).... Just over a quarter of social network users (26%) ... feel in *complete* control (TNS Opinion & Social 2011, 2)

The analysis of existing research literature shows that empirical studies of privacy on web 2.0 focus mainly on privacy-related issues on commercial social networking sites. These studies pay attention to issues of users on social networking sites, namely individual knowledge and information about privacy, individual privacy-related attitudes, and individual behaviour towards privacy.

Next we move on to critical theoretical approaches of surveillance on social media.

Critical research of surveillance on social media

There is a predominance of uncritical research in the context of privacy on web 2.0. This research does not reflect structural power asymmetries in capitalism. Some theoretical considerations of what is missing will now be provided (1–4).

1   Some authors have advanced critique of this kind of studying privacy (Beer 2008; Fuchs 2009a, 11–12; 2010b; 2010d; 2011c) and have contributed filling the identified gap with critical arguments.

For Beer (2008), a more political analysis focusing on the workings of capitalism is missing:

> By focusing solely upon the user … we are overlooking the software and concrete infrastructures, the capitalist organisations, the marketing and advertising rhetoric, the construction of these phenomena in various rhetorical agendas, the role of designers, metadata and algorithms, the role, access and conduct of third parties using SNS, amongst many other things…. Capitalism is there, present, particularly in the history, but it is at risk of looming as a black box in understandings of SNS…. So, when we ask about who are using SNS and for what purpose, we should not just think about those with profiles, we should also be thinking about capitalist interests, of third parties using the data, of the organising power of algorithms … of the welfare issues of privacy made public, of the motives and agendas of those that construct these technologies in the common rhetoric of the day, and, finally, of the way that information is taken out of the system to inform about the users, or, in short, how SNS can be understood as archives of the everyday that represent vast and rich source of transactional data about a vast population of users.
>
> (Beer 2008, 523–526)

Fuchs (2009a; see also Fuchs 2010b; 2010d; 2011c) criticizes the existing approaches to studying privacy on web 2.0 as uncritical and individualistic, and says that they tend to overlook the greater societal context:

> The authors only see individual and interpersonal reasons and attitudes as causes of certain behaviour. They are strictly focusing on individual usage and do not consider that tools and usage are conditioned by the larger societal context, such as corporate profit maximization in the economic systems and state regulation in the political system…. It focuses on the analysis of individual usage behaviour without seeing and analysing how this use is conditioned by the societal context of information technologies, such as

surveillance, the global war against terror, corporate interests, neoliberalism, and capitalist development,... One needs to change society for finding solutions to problems. There are no technological fixes to societal problems. Societal problems, such as state surveillance after 9/11, corporate interests, or the commodification of personal data in the form of spam and advertising, that frame Internet use are political problems, not individual ones.... It does not focus on how technology and technology use are framed by political issues and issues that concern the development of society, such as capitalist crises, profit interests, global war, the globalization of capitalism, or the rise of a surveillance society.... The crucial point here is that no matter if users set their profiles to visible or invisible, commercial ISNS [Integrated Social Networking Sites] will always pass on the data to the state as long as there are interests in establishing a "surveillance society", and to other companies and advertisers, as long as they have a profit interest. Therefore the only solution to privacy threats is to overcome new imperialism, surveillance society, and capitalism. If research just focuses on issues such as individual privacy settings and how they can be adjusted, or individual empowerment, then one neglects these issues and therefore conducts uncritical research.

(Fuchs 2009a, 13–22)

2   In addition, some authors have conducted critical empirical case studies of economic surveillance and targeted advertising (Sandoval 2012; Fernback and Papacharissi 2007; Fuchs 2012b) and have thereby helped in advancing a critique of the political economy of online/web 2.0 surveillance.

Sandoval (2012) conducted a content analysis of the terms of use and privacy statements of the 52 most popular web 2.0 platforms such as wikis, weblogs, social networking sites, and file-sharing sites. She wanted to find out how "surveillance contribute to capital accumulation on web 2.0" and how "the owners of commercial web 2.0 sites collect and disseminate user information" (Sandoval 2012, 147). The coding scheme used four main categories, namely general characteristics, advertising, data collection, and data dissemination (Sandoval 2012, 154). From the 52 analysed web 2.0 platforms, 51 were privately owned and commercially organized (Sandoval 2012, 154). In addition, the vast majority of web 2.0 platforms displayed advertisements (Sandoval 2012, 155).

The terms of use and privacy statements of commercial web 2.0 platforms allow the widespread use of user data in a way that supports the profit interests of platform owners. The business model of most commercial web 2.0 platforms is based on personalized advertising. Capital is accumulated by selling space for advertisements as well as by selling user data to third-party advertising companies.

(Sandoval 2012, 166)

Fernback and Papacharissi (2007) conducted a discourse analysis of online privacy statements of four websites with web 2.0 applications, namely MSN, Google, Real.com, and Kazaa. The survey was undertaken in order to find out how these sites are able to deal with personal information about their users (Fernback and Papacharissi 2007, 722). The authors conclude:

> The MSN use of language articulates a concern for Microsoft's legal standing rather than for consumer protection. The Google privacy statement offers consumers little protection. The Kazaa statement is dismissive of consumer concerns, and the Real statement is a contradictory promotional apparatus.
>
> (Fernback and Papacharissi 2007, 722)

In addition, Fernback and Papacharissi (2007, 730) state that:

> each privacy statement initially assures consumers of a commitment to privacy and subsequently dismantles any true protection of consumer data. These portals are businesses and must be free to operate as such; they must be able to profit responsibly, without undue restriction. However, these privacy statements pose virtually no restriction on businesses to profit excessively from the collection and use of consumer information.... The rhetoric of these privacy statements reveals business practices that favor profit initiatives over consumer protection.

Based on terms of use and privacy policies, Fuchs (2012b) analysed an empirical sample of the most-used web 2.0 platforms in the USA regarding ownership and advertising rights. His findings show that the majority of popular web 2.0 platforms in the USA including Facebook, YouTube, MySpace, Blogspot, and Flickr are corporate based. With the help of legal instruments such as privacy policies and terms of use, these platforms have the right to store, analyse, and sell personal data of their users to third parties for targeted advertising in order to accumulate profit (Fuchs 2012b, 43). Fuchs (2012b, 53) further stresses that an asymmetrical economic power relation characterizes web 2.0, because companies own the data of their users, while the users do not have any ownership rights in these companies, although they produce economic value for these companies and may be considered as an unpaid and infinitely exploited labour force. The structure of web 2.0 primarily maximizes power of the dominating economic class that owns such platforms and benefits the few at the expense of the many (Fuchs 2012b, 53). Fuchs (2012b, 53) argues that it is important to study web 2.0 based on the approach of the critique of the political economy of media and communication by employing terms such as class, exploitation, and surplus value. The creation of profit on platforms like Google, Facebook, or MySpace is mainly achieved through the exploitation of the work of users of these platforms. They produce user-generated content being commodified and sold to advertising clients, who target the users with ads being individually customized with the help of surveillance procedures (Fuchs 2012b, 54). "New media corporations do not (or hardly) pay the users for the production of content. One accumulation strategy is to give them free access to services and platforms, let them produce content, and to accumulate a large number of produsers that are sold as a commodity to third-party advertisers" (Fuchs 2012b, 54). The productive labour time involves "all of the time that is spent online by the users" that is "produced completely for free" and characterizes an extreme form of infinite exploitation and "an essential part of the capitalist production process" (Fuchs 2012b, 54–55). This means that users generate profit for large corporations during web 2.0 activities. It is the "total commodification of human creativity" (Fuchs 2012b, 56). On web 2.0, "producers are consumers and consumers producers of information. Therefore, producer surveillance and consumer surveillance merge into web 2.0 prosumer surveillance" (Fuchs 2012b, 57).

3   Some other theoretical studies have tried to situate the logic of web 2.0 surveillance in light of:
   • Exploitation and exchange value (Andrejevic 2010; Petersen 2008).
   • Culture of connectivity (Dijck 2013).
   • Exception and dispossession (Jakobsson and Stiernstedt 2010).
   • Digital disconnection (McChesney 2013).
   • Social factory and netslaves (Terranova 2004).
   • New strategies of capital accumulation in post-Fordism (Cohen 2008).
   • Digital commodification (Coté and Pybus 2007, 2011; Kang and McAllister 2011).
   • Rent and primitive accumulation (Böhm *et al.* 2012).
   • Alienation and exploitation (Fisher 2012; Rey 2012).
   • (Immaterial) free labour (Terranova 2004; Petersen 2008; Scholz 2008).
   • Cultural work and digital labour (Murdock 2013, 168).

To name but a few, Andrejevic (2010) wants to help develop a theory of exploitation on commercial social networking sites. "This chapter argues that more work need to be done to clarify the relationship between willing participation and commercial exploitation. What is needed is an explanation of how a theory of exploitation might apply to the conditions under which user-generated content creates value" (Andrejevic 2010, 83). For Andrejevic (2010, 94), "exploitation entails some form of coercion" and "obtains when there is loss of control over one's creative, productive activity". The users' activities on social networking sites are treated as free resources. Web 2.0 platforms have the right to store, analyse, and sell personal data of their users to third parties for targeted advertising and "the use of this information will be shaped by existing power relations and structures of ownership" (Andrejevic 2010, 85). Terms of use and privacy policies of commercial social networking sites aim at asserting rights to store, analyse, and sell personal data of their users (Andrejevic 2010, 87). Web 2.0 activities such as creating profiles and sharing ideas, announcing personal messages, uploading or watching videos, and writing personal entries on commercial social networking sites have the capacity to produce value (Andrejevic 2010, 89). These activities are "both unpaid (outside of established labor markets) and freely given, endowed with a sense of autonomy" (Andrejevic 2010, 90). Andrejevic further stresses that commercial social networking platforms strive to appear as open, interactive, and participatory networks, where users are able to control their own activities. In fact, these promises "enlist the participatory public in the process of marketing to itself" (Andrejevic 2010, 95), influence users' behaviour with the help of targeted marketing more effectively (Andrejevic 2010, 96), and overlook asymmetrical power relations and structures of ownership. Greater participation of web 2.0 users leads to greater and more exclusive forms of proprietary knowledge (Andrejevic 2010, 95). The users' "free participation is redoubled as a form of productive labor captured by capital. In a self-generating cycle, the offer to overcome estrangement or alienation produces a second-order form of separation: that of users form the data they generate" (Andrejevic 2010, 94). Andrejevic (2010, 96) describes commercial social networking sites as part of the "social factory":

> In the social factory, the boundaries between spheres of labor and leisure, domesticity, and consumption upon which the distinction between consumer choice and workplace coercion relies, become blurred. To the extent that our communicative, educational, and social lives are folded into the social factory and become the resources that we draw upon and sell to employers, access to resources for online networking becomes a crucial component of generating value.
>
> (Andrejevic 2010, 97)

Andrejevic (2010, 99) therefore argues for a not-for-profit online infrastructure, a non-commercial web 2.0, and a real networked interactivity. Andrejevic's notion of a theory of exploitation on commercial social networking sites may be summarized as follows:

> This chapter's premise is that the new forms of communication, transaction, consumption, and interaction made possible by digital technologies need to be situated within their larger economic context, namely, the creation of a privately owned and operated commercial media structure. When we explore what people do on Facebook or MySpace and the forms of community such sites enable, we must also keep in mind what gets done with the products of this activity, who controls its use and re-use, who profits from its transformation into commercial commodities and marketing campaigns, as well as who is targeted by these campaigns and to what end. Contrary to conventional wisdom, social networking sites don't publicize community, they privatize it. Commercial social networking sites are ostensibly collaborative productions, except when it comes to structuring terms-of-use agreements, and, of course, allocating the profits they generate.
>
> (Andrejevic 2010, 97)

Terranova (2004, 73–74) speaks in the context of the digital economy about "netslaves", "free labour", and (following Antonio Negri) the "social factory":

> Simultaneously voluntarily given and unwaged, enjoyed and exploited, free labour on the Net includes the activity of building web sites, modifying software packages, reading and participating in mailing lists and building virtual spaces. For from being an 'unreal', empty space, the Internet is animated by cultural and technical labour through and through, a continuous production of value which is completely immanent in the flows of the network society at large.... In the overdeveloped countries, the end of the factory has spelled out the marginalisation of the old working class, but it has also produced generations of workers who have been repeatedly addressed as active consumers of meaningful commodities. Free labour is the moment where this knowledgeable consumption of culture is translated into excess productive activities that are pleasurably embraced and at the same time often shamelessly exploited.... The new Web was made of the big players, but also of new ways to make the audience work.
>
> (Terranova 2004, 74, 78, 95)

Cohen (2008) stresses the need for research on the political economy of web 2.0 and to analyse social networking sites (with special focus on Facebook) in the larger context of commodification and new strategies of capital accumulation under post-Fordist conditions:

> In an effort to draw attention to these dynamics, this paper makes two inter-related arguments about the ongoing, extensive commodification in which Facebook is engaged. Extensive commodification refers to the way in which market forces shape and re-shape life, entering spaces previously untouched, or mildly touched, by capitalist social relations.... Facebook facilitates this process through the valorisation of surveillance. Not only is surveillance the method by which Facebook aggregates user information for third-party use and specifically targets demographics for marketing purposes, but surveillance is the main strategy by which the company retains members and keeps them returning to the site. This leads to the second argument of this paper: it is the unpaid labour of producer-consumers that facilitates this surveillance. Like other Web 2.0 businesses, Facebook is engaged in the commodification of what can be understood as free labour, or what has been called immaterial labour. What distinguishes this particular social network is the way in which surveillance is fundamental to this process. Although Facebook and other Web 2.0 ventures have implemented strategies that break with those of "old" media, these sites can be situated within more general capitalist processes that follow familiar patterns of asymmetrical power relations between workers and owners, commodification, and the harnessing of audience power.
>
> (Cohen 2008, 7–8)

For Cohen (2008, 9–10), the conflation of production and consumption and the effort of free labour on web 2.0 must be situated in the context of flexible production under neoliberal and neo-Fordist conditions. Free labour furthermore may be considered as the tendency of capital shifting labour costs onto consumers and to bring knowledge, social relationships, and creativity under the logic of capital accumulation in the digital age. "Web 2.0 as a business strategy can be understood as capital reacting to and attempting to exploit the way in which people seek non-commodified relationships online" (Cohen 2008, 17). Privately owned social networking sites extend work out of the direct production process of factories and offices into society at large in the form of social labour power in order to accumulate capital (Cohen 2008, 17–18).

In the context of social networks, Coté and Pybus (2007; see also 2011) state that corporations circulate digital commodities, which are sold to third parties:

> However, its political-economic foundation demonstrates how such user-generated content – immaterial labour 2.0 – is the very dynamic driving new revenue streams. Thus, it is the tastes, preferences, and social narratives found in user entries which comprises the quotidian motherlode of these new revenue streams. It is this user-generated content that spyware and adware monitor to microtarget those same online subjectivities. This is what has excited media conglomerates like News Corp who realize the value of mining these new networked subjectivities to extend existing and produce new markets – indeed, to construct a new paradigm of capitalist market relations.... Part of what enables the management of the immanent networked relations is the juridical forms of the site's "Privacy Policy" where it is clearly stated that all information recorded on the website can be shared with third parties.
>
> (Coté and Pybus 2007)

Petersen (2008) analyses social networking sites in the context of exploitation, free labour, and enclosure. For Petersen (2008), the huge amount of user-generated content, personal information, and network structures makes it easy for private corporations to deal with this information.

> It is when the technological infrastructure and design of these sites is combined with capitalism that the architecture begins to oscillate between exploitation and participation.... In this way the architecture of participation turns into an architecture of exploitation and enclosure, transforming users into commodities that can be sold on the market.... What is seriously needed is a theory of labor that is able to map both exploitation and free labor, along with considering the value using these sites creates for their users.
>
> (Petersen 2008)

Scholz (2008) argues:

> A fine example of the Web 2.0 Ideology is immaterial free labor, a fairly unpopular and very complex subject. The Web makes people easier to use. By "surfing" it, people serve their virtual hosts and they are not unhappy about it. Online, service platforms, rather than products are offered and users are encouraged to participate, communities become the brand. The Web makes it possible to "out-source" many tasks to the users who can create in "self-service" mode.... They enjoy using these platforms: from entertainment, to staying in touch with friends and family, to chatting, remixing, collaborating, sharing, and gossiping, to getting a job through the mighty power of weak links. It's a tradeoff. Presence does not produce objects but life as such that is put to work and monetary value is created through the affective labor of users who are either not aware of this fact or do not mind it (yet).

Murdock (2013, 168) states in this context that

> the voluntary labor of audiences and users online also offers corporations a new source of value. Increasingly, consumers are encouraged to also become producers, "prosumers" contributing ideas, energy, and expertise that can be used to develop new cultural commodities for sale or market them more effectively. This push to commandeer the activity of audiences without payment raises urgent questions of exploitation.

4   There is an ongoing debate in academia about studying social and new media critically. Dallas Smythe's (2006) concept of "audience work" has recently gained importance in discussions about value creation and labour on the Internet. Research at different levels has been carried out touching on the digital labour concept and (un)paid Internet labour that is also related to the context of surveillance.

Burston and colleagues (2010) edited a special issue based on a conference called "Digital Labour: Workers, Authors, Citizens", held at the University of Western Ontario in 2009 (see http://ir.lib.uwo.ca/digitallabour). The conference was organized by the Digital Labour Group, a collection of scholars from within the Faculty of Information and Media Studies at the University of Western Ontario. The special issue provides a strong showing of autonomist Marxism and Marxist political economy analyses of digital labour. In 2011, Peters and Bulut (2011) edited a book called *Cognitive Capitalism, Education and Digital Labor*, studying "cognitive capitalism" and focusing on the question of digital labour primarily from an Autonomist Marxist perspective. As an outcome of the European Cooperation in Science and Technology (COST) Action "Living in Surveillance Societies", Fuchs *et al.* (2012b) published the book *Internet and Surveillance: The Challenges of Web 2.0 and Social Media*. Fuchs and colleagues (2012a, 6) mention in the introduction of the book that "the study of online surveillance and web 2.0 surveillance is situated in the context of the continuities and changes of the Internet, conflicts and contradictions, power structures and society". Scholz organized a conference, "The Internet as Playground and Factory: A Conference on Digital Labour", at New York City in 2009 (see http://digitallabor.org). The outcomes of the conference have been published recently (Scholz 2013). Scholz (2013) states on the cover that the book "claims that the divide between leisure time and work has vanished so that every aspect of life drives the digital economy. The book reveals the anatomy of *playbor* (play/labor), the lure of exploitation and the potential for empowerment." In 2013, Lovink and Rasch (2013) edited the *Unlike Us Reader*, offering a "critical examination of social media". The reader asks questions such as "We know very well that monopolies control social media, but what are the alternatives?" The Unlike Us research network was launched in July 2011 (see networkcultures.org/unlikeus). Unlike Us "is a research network of artists, designers, scholars, activists, and programmers, with the aim to combine a critique of the dominant social media platforms with work on 'alternatives in social media'" (Institute of Network Cultures 2013). The book *Critique, Social Media & The Information Society* (Fuchs and Sandoval 2013) is the outcome of the conference "Critique, Democracy, and Philosophy in 21st Century Information Society: Towards Critical Theories of Social Media: The Fourth ICTs and Society-Conference" (see www.icts-and-society.net/events/uppsala2012) organized by Fuchs and Sandoval in Uppsala in 2012.

> This volume addresses the question of how to critically make sense of a world in crisis, discussing issues such as what kind of society and what kind of Internet are desirable; how capitalism, power structures, class, labour and social media are connected; what the main problems, risks, opportunities and challenges are for the current and future development of Internet and society; what current developments of the Internet and society tell us about potential futures; what an alternative Internet can look like; and how a participatory, commons-based Internet and a co-operative, participatory, sustainable information society can be achieved.
>
> (Fuchs and Sandoval 2013)

As a reaction to a debate between Fuchs (2010e; 2012a) and Arvidsson and Colleoni (2012), Proffitt *et al.* (2014) edited a special issue in the journal *The Information Society*, addressing the following questions, among others:

- "Do the theory and concepts that are part of a labor theory of value limit our understanding of user-generated content? Should we choose a different point of departure for our theoretical endeavors?"
- "Is the notion of 'labor time' relevant to the production of user-generated content?"
- "How can Marxist and historical-critical perspectives engage with the new organization of information economies and information societies?"

(The Information Society 2013)

McGuigan and Manzerolle edited a book called *The Audience Commodity in a Digital Era*, published in 2013. The collection provides new and reprinted material re-examining and critiquing Dallas Smythe's "audience commodity" thesis in the context of the commodification of new media. Critical scholars of new trends in the ICT sector and the emerging field of virtual work and digital labour are also assembled in the COST Action "Dynamics of Virtual Work" (see: http://dynamicsofvirtualwork.com). The action is chaired by Huws and vice-chaired by Fuchs, and runs from 2012 to 2016. The project "aims to explore the shifting boundaries between paid and unpaid work and between 'work' and 'play' and to develop an understanding of how new forms of virtual work emerge and how new value is created in the process" (COST 2012). A first outcome of this project is a special issue called "Philosophers of the World Unite! Theorizing Digital Labour and Virtual Work: Definitions, Forms and Transformations" which was published in the journal *tripleC: Communication, Capitalism and Critique*" (Sandoval *et al.* 2014). The questions being addressed in the special issue range from:

- "Is the traditional distinction between the material base and superstructure in the realm of social media and digital labour still valid or does it become blurred or undermined?" over
- "What is the role of agricultural, industrial, service and knowledge work in the world of digital labour and how are they related?" to
- "How can blurring boundaries between toil and play, labour and leisure time, the factory and society, production and consumption, public and private, the sphere of production and reproduction, economic value and social wealth in the realm of digital media be conceptualized?"

(tripleC 2013)

This indicates the actuality of a renewed interest in theories of value creation and its relation to digital labour, and that many scholars are interested in studying digital and social media critically.

Conclusion: a critical empirical study of privacy and surveillance on social media

The previous sections provided an overview of the existing empirical and theoretical research of privacy and surveillance on social media. Table 5.1 summarizes the results.

The analysis of existing research literature shows that empirical studies of privacy on web 2.0 focus mainly on privacy-related issues on commercial social networking sites (e.g. Acquisti and Gross, boyd and Hargittai, and TNS Opinion and Social). These studies focus on issues of users on social networking sites, namely individual knowledge and information about privacy, individual privacy-related attitudes, and individual behaviour towards privacy. Some authors have advanced critiques of this kind of studying privacy and have contributed filling

Table 5.1 Traditional and critical research of privacy and surveillance on social media

Traditional research of privacy on social media	Critical research of surveillance on social media
Studies of privacy on web 2.0 focus primarily on privacy-related issues on corporate social networking sites. These studies pay attention to one or more of the following issues concerning SNS users: • Individual knowledge and information towards/about privacy. • Individual privacy-related attitudes/concerns. • Individual behaviour and practices towards/about privacy (settings).	1 Some authors have advanced critiques of this kind of studying privacy and have contributed by filling the identified gap with critical arguments. 2 Some authors have also conducted critical empirical case studies of economic surveillance and targeted advertising, and have thereby helped advance a critique of the political economy of online/web 2.0 surveillance. 3 Some other theoretical studies have tried to situate the logic of web 2.0 surveillance in light of the social factory and free labour, alienation and exploitation, exception and dispossession, etc. 4 There is an ongoing debate in academia about studying social and new media critically. Dallas Smythe's concept of "audience work" has recently gained importance in discussions about value creation and labour on the Internet. Research at different levels has been carried out touching on the digital labour concept and (un)paid Internet labour that is also related to the context of surveillance.
Acquisti and Gross (2006), Fogel and Nehmad (2009), boyd and Hargittai (2010), Christofides *et al.* (2009), Debatin *et al.* (2009), Ellison *et al.* (2007), Hinduja and Patchin (2008), Lewis *et al.* (2008), Livingstone (2008), Dwyer *et al.* (2007; 2010), TNS Opinion & Social (2011)	Beer (2008), Fuchs (2009a; 2010b; 2010d; 2011c; 2012b), Sandoval (2012), Fernback and Papacharissi (2007), Andrejevic (2010), Petersen (2008), Dijck (2013), Jakobsson and Stiernstedt (2010), McChesney (2013), Terranova (2004), Cohen (2008), Coteì and Pybus (2011), Kang (2011), Böhm *et al.* (2012), Fisher (2012), Rey (2012), Terranova (2004), Scholz (2008), Murdock (2013), Burston *et al.* (2010), Peters and Bulut (2011), Fuchs *et al.* (2012b), Scholz (2013), Lovink and Rasch (2013), Fuchs and Sandoval (2013), Proffitt *et al.* (2014), Manzerolle and McGuigan (2014), COST (2012), Sandoval *et al.* (2014)

the identified gap with critical arguments (Beer and Fuchs). In addition, some authors have conducted critical empirical case studies of economic surveillance and targeted advertising, and have thereby helped advance a critique of the political economy of online/web 2.0 surveillance (Sandoval, Fernback and Papacharissi, and Fuchs). Some other theoretical studies have tried to situate the logic of web 2.0 surveillance in light of the social factory and free labour, alienation and exploitation, exception and dispossession, etc. (for example: Terranova,

Fisher, and Jakobsson and Stiernstedt). There is an ongoing debate in academia about studying social and new media critically. Dallas Smythe's concept of "audience work" has recently gained importance in discussions about value creation and labour on the Internet. Research at different levels has been carried out touching on the digital labour concept and (un)paid Internet labour that is also related to the context of surveillance (e.g. Burston, Dyer-Witheford, and Hearn, Fuchs and Sandoval, and COST).

Most empirical studies of privacy on social networking sites pay attention to individual user aspects. The issue of surveillance is more a macro-topic requiring that usage behaviour is framed by societal context variables such as state surveillance, economic surveillance, and modernity. The analysis of surveillance and SNS is therefore is in need of a research approach taking into account political contexts (Beer 2008). Surveillance has thus far, with single exceptions, been rather ignored as a topic in SNS studies (Fuchs *et al.* 2012b; Andrejevic 2010). The absence of critical empirical studies of social media characterizes the academic landscape. The existing empirical studies show that there is much more focus on the privacy topic than on surveillance. Advertising mechanisms and the connection between surveillance and privacy attitudes on the one hand and SNS advertising settings on the other hand have thus far hardly been studied. This is a task for the survey that is still missing in the state of the art. Given the fact that the majority of the most popular web 2.0 platforms are privately owned and commercially organized and that the business model of most web 2.0 platforms is based on personalized advertising, I find it more appropriate to study web 2.0 in the context of economic surveillance and targeted advertising. What is missing within the current research on privacy is a critique of the political economy and a critical theory of privacy and surveillance taking into account the larger societal context of class, ideology, commodity, and exploitation. Apart from a few exceptions (e.g. Fernback and Papacharissi 2007; Fuchs 2012b; Sandoval 2012), there are no studies combining critical theoretical and empirical research in the context of digital and social media. This is the task for the following study.

The fact that one can find web 2.0 platforms including Facebook (rank 2), YouTube (rank 3), Twitter (rank 14), and LinkedIn (rank 13) among the most frequently accessed websites worldwide indicates the enormous popularity of these sites (Alexa Internet 2013). In Austria, websites that allow social networking, such as Facebook (rank 2), LinkedIn (rank 29), and XING (rank 48), or are among the most popular websites (Alexa Internet 2013). With single exceptions (e.g. Fuchs 2012b; Sandoval 2012; Fernback and Papacharissi 2007), there are no studies that combine critical theoretical and empirical research of privacy and surveillance in the context of web 2.0. The overall aim of this survey is to study electronic surveillance on social networking sites that are used by Austrian students.

Social networking site users are primarily young and educated people. Thus, for example, 45 per cent of the users of MySpace are aged 18 to 34, 42 per cent of the users of Facebook are aged 18 to 34, and 53 per cent of Facebook users have attended college or graduate school (all data: Quantcast 2013). We may thus assume that young people are early adopters of new technologies. It is therefore important to study their usage behaviour because they may anticipate future trends. Owing to their education standards, students tend to be very sensitive towards new issues that confront society. Given that students are early adopters and sensitive citizens, it is important to study their usage of SNS in the context of the issue of surveillance. The next chapter offers a critical empirical study of privacy and surveillance on social media.

6   Empirical results

(Dis)advantages of social media

Introduction

This is the general research question being addressed in this study:

Which major advantages and disadvantages of social networking platforms do Austrian students see?

The specific research questions are:

- What is the role of surveillance for users in the context of social networking sites?
- What are the disadvantages and advantages that are seen by users in relation by decreased privacy?
- Concerning the disadvantages, do they see more individual disadvantages or disadvantages for society?
- Are privacy reduction and surveillance seen as legitimate if in return there is free access to platforms and to certain Internet services?

In order to test if maintaining existing relationships over spatio-temporal distances and creating new social relationships is considered as the main advantage of social networking platforms (SNS), I asked students what in their opinion were the greatest advantages of social networking sites such as Facebook and MySpace (open question):

Was sind für dich die größten Vorteile von Social Networking Plattformen wie Facebook, MySpace, LinkedIn, etc? [What are the greatest advantages of social networking platforms such as Facebook, MySpace, LinkedIn, etc. for you?]

For analysing whether the surveillance threat is considered as the major disadvantage of SNS, I asked what the greatest concerns of social networking sites such as Facebook and MySpace are (open question):

Was sind deine größten Besorgnisse über Social Networking Plattformen wie Facebook, MySpace, LinkedIn, etc? [What are your greatest concerns about social networking platforms such as Facebook, MySpace, LinkedIn, etc?]

We conducted an online survey (Batinic *et al.* 2002; Johns *et al.* 2004; Couper 2000; Schmidt 1997; Sills and Song 2002; Zhang 2000; Hewson *et al.* 1996) which focused on Austrian students. We identified how important students consider the topic of surveillance in relation to SNS by analysing their answers to our questions with the help of PASW Statistics 18 (formerly SPSS Statistics) for the quantitative data (Field 2009) and SPSS Text Analytics for Surveys 4 for the open questions. Our questions focused on the most frequently used SNS in Austria, namely Facebook (Alexa Internet 2011). The reason why we confine our sample to one country is a practical one.

We constructed a questionnaire that consisted of single and multiple choice, open-ended, interval-scaled, matrix, and contingency questions. The survey was conducted in German, but the questionnaire was translated for the analysis into English. Depending on the contingency level, students had to answer at least three questions, but no more than 78 questions. Filling out the whole questionnaire lasted about 20 minutes. The participants were asked if they would agree to allow their data to be used for purposes of research, as well as that the results of the survey – in compliance with the protection of anonymity – may be published. The questionnaire was thematically grouped into different subsections. Some questions required special instructions to facilitate proper answering. For questions about personal settings on Facebook, we asked the participants if they could log into their Facebook profile (if any) for checking their settings. In order to help the respondents to find the right settings quickly, we further implemented Facebook screen shots including short instructions into the survey.

We conducted the survey as part of the project "Social Networking Sites in the Surveillance Society" (see: http://sns3.uti.at):

- Funded by: Austrian Science Fund (FWF)
- Project number: P 22445-G17
- Project coordination: Professor Christian Fuchs
- Duration: September 2010 to February 2013
- Amount of funding: 267,284 Euro
- Executing organization: Unified Theory of Information Research Group.

We aimed to achieve two main objectives in the survey. On the one hand, we tried to figure out which major advantages and disadvantages of social networking platforms Austrians students recognize and whether privacy is rather considered as extrinsic value and based on the control theory (part one). On the other hand, we made an effort to find out if knowledge and attitudes towards surveillance and privacy of Austrian students and their information behaviour on social networking platforms are connected (part two). Although the survey was undertaken as one combined questionnaire, my colleague, Verena Kreilinger, focused on the analysis of part two and I elaborated part one.

We asked open-ended questions about what students perceive as the major advantages and disadvantages of social networking sites. By asking students about benefits and concerns of SNS, we used open-ended instead of closed-ended questions, because "the researcher's structuring of responses may overlook some important responses" and a "checklist of issues might omit certain issues that respondents would have said were important" (Babbie 2010, 256–257). This allowed us to conduct a quantifying qualitative analysis of the answers given. For reasons of impartiality, we placed the open-ended questions about advantages and disadvantages of social networking sites at the very beginning of the survey. Privacy is rather considered as extrinsic value and as based on the control theory measured with the help of indices that were calculated using the answers given to single and multiple choice questions that tested such considerations. In the final part of the questionnaire, we collected data on sociodemographic factors (gender, age, number of studied semesters, level of study, and field of study), socio-economic status (monthly income, highest education achievement of parents, and main occupation of parents), and the respondents' use of social networking sites. All in all, we tried to make the questionnaire interesting and exciting, but kept the items short and clear, and we made an effort to avoid double-barrelled questions, negative items, and biased terms (Babbie 2010, 255–262).

The questionnaire was implemented as an electronic survey with the help of the online survey tool SurveyMonkey (Gordon 2002; Babbie 2010, 286). The research was carried out from 20 June to 23 November 2011. The survey was available to the students for five months. The poll could be reached by clicking the following SSL-cryptographic link: www.surveymonkey.com/s/social_networking_sites (the survey is no longer available). The questionnaire operated in all commonly used web browsers including Internet Explorer, Mozilla Firefox, Google Chrome, Safari, and Opera. No further special technical requirements such as Java were necessary to open the online poll. In order to convey the progress of the task, a dynamic progress bar was integrated into the survey and was shown at the top of each site. By clicking the next button after having answered all questions on one particular site, the next site appeared. No more than eight questions were shown at once. In order to avoid double responses from one person, the poll could only filled out once from each computer. It was possible to interrupt the survey and to continue at a later time.

A typical critique on web surveys is that a sampling error could arise insofar as those without Internet or Web access are underrepresented in the survey sample. The Internet is not appropriate for empirical research due to the fact that the group of non-adopters may remain significantly too large for the new technology (Babbie 2010, 284). "The primary drawback of using the Web to collect survey data is the presence of sample bias. The population of individuals with access to the Web is small as compared to those with mail addresses and telephones" (Tuten *et al.* 2002, 17).

In our survey, the respondents were students at Austrian universities. It is the norm for Austrian students to attend university immediately after having finished high school. Most students are therefore young people aged under 30 (Austrian Federal Ministry for Science and Research 2012). According to the Federal Institute Statistics Austria (2011), 95.2 per cent of people aged 16 to 24 and 91.8 per cent of people aged 25 to 34 had accessed the Internet within the last three months before the point in time when they were interviewed. Due to the fact that students are early adopters of new technologies and the Internet has become an integral part for research and teaching at universities (for example, many Austrian universities including the University of Salzburg and the University of Vienna have implemented e-learning platforms in recent years), we may assume that the Internet usage rate of students at Austrian universities is even higher than the Federal Institute Statistics Austria (2011) claims for young people in general. I therefore believe that conducting an online survey with a group where such a technology is frequently used, popular, and widespread is an appropriate way for empirical research. A dynamic and interactive online survey offers enormous opportunities for self-administered surveys using a wide variety of multimedia material (sound, images, video, etc.), delivers the inclusion of different design features (e.g. customization of wording, real-time editing), may increase respondent motivation, may reduce the effect of social desirability of sensitive data (such as privacy topics), and provides large-scale data collection (which used to be to a large extent restricted to powerful political and economic actors including governments and large corporations), and helps thereby to democratize the survey-taking process (Couper 2000, 476–477; Schmidt 2006, 274–275; Brenner 2002, 93; Babbie 2010, 283–285; Johnston and Walton 1995).

Our potential respondents were male and female students all attending Austrian universities. According to the Austrian Federal Ministry for Science and Research (2012), there are in total 272,169 students (53.4 per cent women, 46.6 per cent men) at 21 public Austrian universities.[1] We included national and international people who have been matriculated in one of Austria's universities. We focused on part-time and full-time as well as short-term and long-term undergraduate, graduate, and doctoral students of all age groups and in all fields of studies.

A total of 5213 respondents participated in the survey; 1655 datasets were deleted from the dataset, because the respondents had not completed the survey, had not agreed to allow their data to be used for purposes of research, as well as that the results of the survey may be published, had not used social networking sites (the study focuses on the use of social networking sites), or had not studied at one of Austria's universities (the study focuses on students in Austria). The remaining N=3558 datasets were analysed (comprising 1.31 per cent of the Austrian student population). The task of this chapter is to answer the question of what the greatest advantages and disadvantages of social networking sites are. In doing so, the following main points may be listed:

- General characteristics of the respondents.
- Advantages of social networking sites.
- Disadvantages of social networking sites.

The sections in this chapter are structured according to this distinction.[2]

General characteristics of the respondents

We collected data on sociodemographic factors (gender, age, number of studied semesters, level of study, and field of study), socioeconomic status (monthly income, highest education achievement of parents, and main occupation of parents), and the respondents' use of social networking sites. These general characteristics of our survey participants are presented below.

Socio-demographic factors of the respondents

There were 63.8 per cent female and 36.2 per cent male respondents. This reflects very well the overall gender distribution of students in Austria, although women were slightly overrepresented in the survey. According to the Austrian Federal Ministry for Science and Research (2012), there were 53.4 per cent female and 46.6 per cent male students at Austrian universities in the winter term 2011/2012.

The mean age of our respondents is 24.3 years and the mean number of studied semesters is 6.6 (including summer term 2011). More than two-thirds of the respondents (70.8%) are undergraduate students, about one-fifth are graduate students (21.2%), and 8 per cent are doctoral students. Note that Bachelor and diploma students (so-called Magister studies, a discontinuing type of study at Austrian universities) are counted as undergraduate students, Master students as graduate students, and Ph.D. students as doctoral students.

Figure 6.1 shows the share of different fields of study in the sample and at Austrian universities.

More than half of the respondents (56.9%) were studying social sciences and humanities, and nearly one-third (31.3%) were students of natural and engineering sciences. According to the Austrian Federal Ministry for Science and Research (2012), there were 55 per cent students of social sciences and humanities, 40.8 per cent students of natural and engineering sciences, 15.1 per cent students of law, 4.8 per cent students of medical science, and 2.8 per cent students of arts at Austrian universities in the winter term 2011/2012. By comparing the share in our study with the share at Austrian universities, one may see that our dataset reflects very well the distribution of fields of study in Austria. Please note that there are 113.9 per cent at the sample and 118.5 per cent at Austrian universities in total, because multiple responses were possible for people enrolled in more than one field of study. Social sciences and humanities include social sciences, economics, humanities and cultural studies, and theology. Natural and engineering sciences consist of natural sciences, technical sciences, engineering, agricultural sciences and forestry, veterinary medicine, and sport science.[3]

Socioeconomic status of the respondents

Table 6.1 shows the monthly income of our respondents.

A total of 3558 students were asked what their average monthly income was (including receiving subsidies from parents, the state, or grants, etc.). Table 6.1

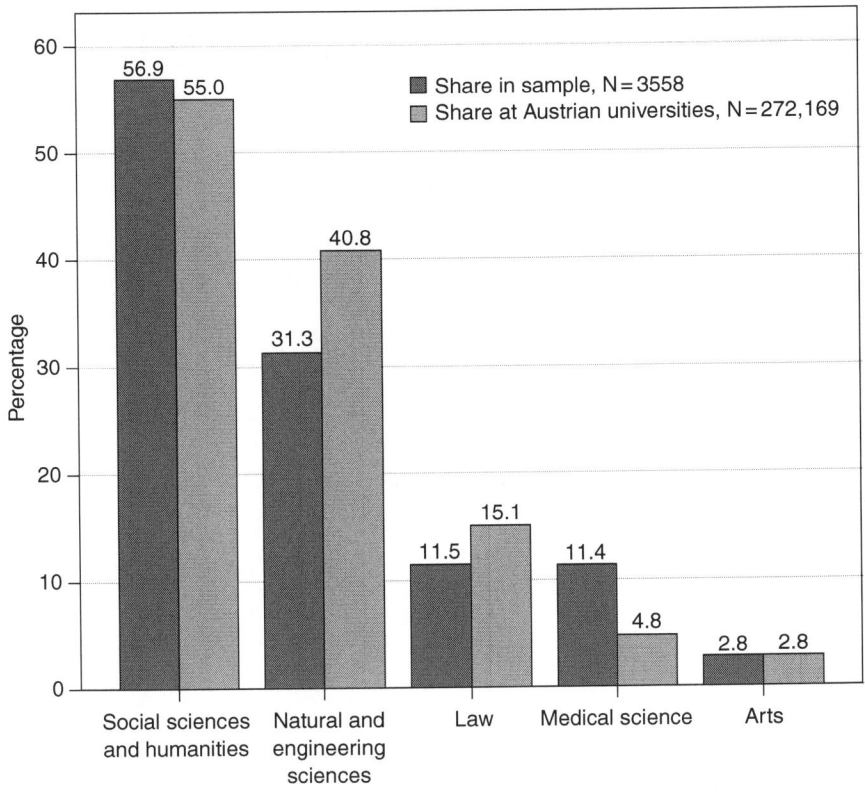

Figure 6.1 Share in sample and at Austrian universities of fields of study.

demonstrates that the income of more than two-thirds of the students (68.8%) was less than or of 800 Euro per month. Due to the fact that the minimum level of monthly income deemed adequate in Austria is 994 Euro (Statistical Office of the European Union 2012), one may argue that more than two-thirds of our respondents lived below the poverty line. This indicates the low economic status of the participants and Austrian students in general.

Figure 6.2 presents the educational achievement of the respondents' parents.

On the one hand, the majority of the respondents' parents (mother: 55.8%, father: 52.3%) have only achieved compulsory school or college. On the other hand, almost one-third of the respondents' parents (mother: 27.5%, father: 31.7%) have completed an academic education. Please note that in order to present the data in a manageable form (Babbie 2010, 433), some answer options of the questionnaire appear as a combined category in the bar chart.

We collected data on the usage rate of social media: 3558 students were asked which social networking sites they use. The vast majority of the respondents

Table 6.1 Monthly income of respondents

Monthly income (in Euro), N = 3558

		Frequency	%	Valid %	Cumulative %
Valid	0–400	783	22.0	22.0	22.0
	401–600	940	26.4	26.5	48.5
	601–800	720	20.2	20.3	68.8
	801–1000	384	10.8	10.8	79.6
	1001–1200	244	6.9	6.9	86.4
	1201–1400	154	4.3	4.3	90.8
	1401–1600	105	3.0	3.0	93.7
	1601–1800	61	1.7	1.7	95.4
	1801–2000	51	1.4	1.4	96.9
	2000–	111	3.1	3.1	100.0
	Total	3553	99.9	100.0	
Missing	System	5	0.1		
Total		3558	100.0		

(96.8%) use Facebook. This reflects very well the popularity of this site in Austria. Facebook is the second most popular website in Austria (Alexa Internet 2011). Only 6.4 per cent of the respondents use Google+. Google+ was open to everyone without the need for an invitation in September 2011. Our research was carried out from June to November 2011. It may therefore be assumed that the usage rate of Google+ by Austrian students is much higher now than it was during our survey period. Also worth mentioning is the fact that 7 per cent of the survey participants indicated that they use other social networking sites; mentioned examples are diaspora* (0.3%), Orkut, Szene 1 (an Austrian social networking site), and Lokalisten (a German social networking site). Please note that there are more than 100 per cent in total, because multiple responses were possible; 553 non-social networking site users were deleted from the dataset, because the study focuses on the usage of social networking sites. Google+ was not separately listed in the answer options, but 6.4 per cent of the respondents mentioned it in the answer option "other". The results of the advantages of social networking sites are presented in the next section.

Advantages of social networking sites

Perceived advantages of social networking sites

In order to test if maintaining existing relationships over spatio-temporal distances and creating new social relationships are considered to be the main advantages of SNS, I asked the students what in their opinion were the greatest advantages of social networking sites such as Facebook and MySpace (open question). I received N = 3531 qualitative answer texts to the question that addressed advantages. I identified 17 categories for the advantages and analysed the answers to the questions by content analysis (Krippendorff 2004; Berg 2001). On the one hand, the categories were adopted from theoretical and empirical

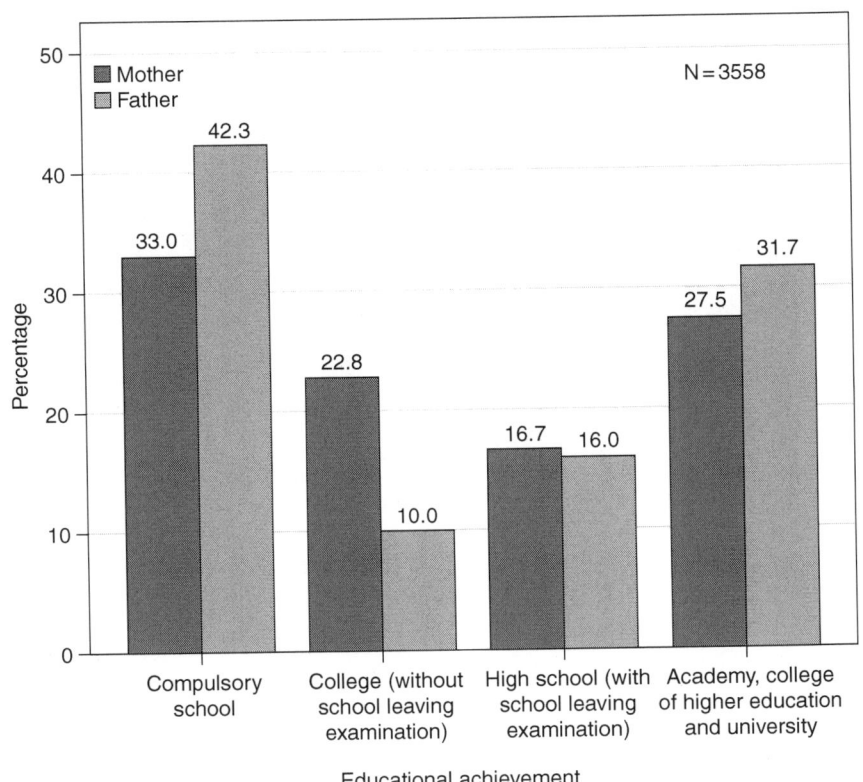

Figure 6.2 Highest educational achievement of respondents' parents.

studies about social networking sites (Fuchs 2010b; Acquisti and Gross 2006), and were revised and expanded regarding the provided answers by summarizing, paraphrasing, abstracting, and generalizing groups of answer texts to categories on the other hand; that is, a combination of inductive and deductive methods (Berg 2001, 248–249; Babbie 2010, 339). The respondents tended to list more than one major advantage. Many answers are therefore mapped with more than one category (Berg 2001, 247–248). Figure 6.3 presents the major advantages of social networking sites that our respondents mentioned.

Figure 6.3 shows that maintaining existing relationships and communication over distances are considered as the greatest advantages of social networking sites. More than 40 per cent of our respondents stress the maintenance of existing contacts, friendships, and family relations as major opportunities of SNS. One-third (33.8%) say that social relationships over spatial distances are very important. Almost a quarter (23.4%) see social networking platforms as a medium of information and news, and 22.5 per cent mention finding and renewing old contacts as a major benefit. Some 7.5 per cent of the participants state that an important aspect of

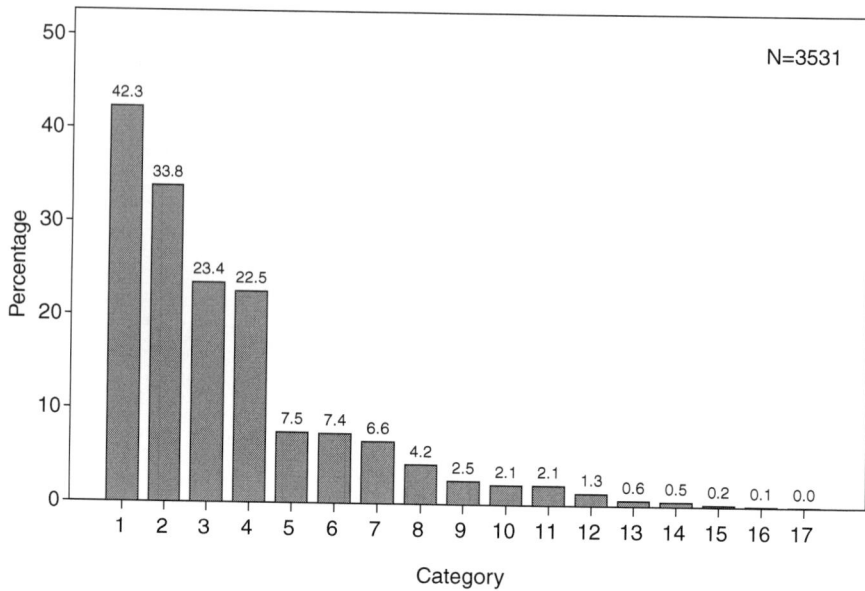

Figure 6.3 Greatest perceived advantages of social networking platforms.

Table 6.2 Identified categories of greatest perceived advantages of social networking platforms

No.	Category
1	Maintaining existing contacts, friendships, family relations, etc.
2	Communication and contacts over spatial distances (national and international)
3	Medium of information and news
4	Finding and renewing old contacts
5	Free communication that saves money
6	Sharing and accessing photos, music, videos
7	Establishing new contacts with unknown people or with people whom one hardly knows and can easily contact online
8	Communication and contacts in general (no further specification)
9	Communication in political groups and interest groups
10	Mobility, access from anywhere
11	Entertainment, fun, pastime, amusement
12	Overview and reminder of birthdays
13	Self-presentation to others (for non-business reasons)
14	I see no advantages
15	Business communication, finding jobs, self-presentation to potential employers
16	Browsing other profiles, 'spying' on others
17	Flirting, sex, love

Table 6.3 Examples of advantages listed by respondents

Respondent ID	Answer (German)	Answer (English)	Categories
1560377386	Kontakt mit Freunden.	Contact with friends.	1
1568235826	Aufrechterhaltung der Kontakte, neue Freunde finden, Echtzeit-Kommunikation, Globale Verbindung aller Menschen, Schnelle Nachrichtenverbreitung.	Maintaining contacts, finding new friends, real-time communication, global connection of all people, fast spreading of news.	1, 2, 3, 7, 8
1560016493	internationale Kontakte.	International contacts.	2
1580232644	Man kann auch mit Freunden aus dem Ausland leicht in Kontakt bleiben. Man kann Freunde von früher wieder finden.	You are able to stay in contact with friends from abroad easily. You are able to find old friends again.	1, 2, 4
1568268592	Neuigkeiten erfahren.	Getting news.	3
1479119303	Man wird ständig über neuigkeiten informiert. Ich nutze es oft um mich mit klassenkameraden über schulisches auszutauschen. Man kann mit freunden und verwandten, die weit entfernt wohnen, den kontakt aufrecht erhalten.	You are permanently informed about news. I often use it to communicate with classmates about school matters. You are able to maintain contact with friends and relatives who live far away.	1, 2, 3
1567786081	Leute von früher finden.	To find people from former times.	4
1572592810	Es ist leichter geworden Kontakt mit Freunden aus aller Welt aufrecht zu erhalten. Kontakte zu knüpfen ist für im normalen Leben schüchterne Leute keine so große Hürde mehr. Man kann Freunde von früher, mit denen man sich aus den Augen verloren hat, wieder ausfindig machen. Kurz gesagt, man kann sein Freunde- bzw. Bekanntennetzwerk schnell vergrößern.	It has become easier to maintain contact with friends from all around the world. It is no longer a major obstacle for normally shy people to establish contact. You are able to catch up with friends from former times with whom you have lost contact. In short, you are able to expand your network of friends quickly.	1, 2, 4, 7
1551285273	Kontakt mit Freunden ohne Kosten.	Contact with friends at no cost.	1, 5
1567739679	gratis Kommunikation mit Freunden, Bekannten, Verwandten, auch wenn diese in anderen Ländern sind.	Communication for free with friends, relatives, even if they are from other countries.	1, 2, 5, 7
	Neue Leute (auch aus dem Ausland) kennenlernen.	Meeting new people (also from abroad).	

continued

Table 6.3 Examples of advantages listed by respondents

Respondent ID	Answer (German)	Answer (English)	Categories
1557035103	Teilen von Fotos, Informationsaustausch.	Sharing photos, exchange of information.	3, 6
1550759823	Austausch mit Menschen, die man nicht mehr so oft sieht. Gleichzeitig das Ansehen von Bildern, Videos usw.	Exchange with people, who you just see rarely. Viewing pictures, videos, etc. simultaneously	4, 6
1566170073	Neue Leute kennenzulernen, soziale Kontakte!	Meeting new people, social contacts!	7, 8
1559706248	lernt neue Freunde kennen, findet eventuell alte Freundschaften wieder, kann seine Gedanken mit anderen teilen, eignet sich gut um Veranstaltungen zu planen, organisieren.	Meeting new friends, possibly finding old friendships again, you are able to share your thoughts with others, suitable for planning and organizing events.	4, 7, 8, 9
1564705747	Kommunikation.	Communication.	8
1559810724	Einfache Kontaktaufnahme und Newsaustausch.	Ease of making contact and exchanging news.	3, 8
1567625028	Einfaches Aufrechterhalten des Kontakts mit FreundInnen, die auf einem anderen Kontinent leben.	Maintaining contact with friends easily who are living on another continent.	1, 2, 9
1580667756	Demonstrationen können leichter organisiert werden. Ich kann viele Menschen erreichen ... meine Statusmeldungen sind meistens Botschaften und Zitate, um Leuten eine positive Sicht auf die Welt zu geben (Beispiel: „man sieht nur mit dem Herzen gut"). Ich hoffe damit ein Lächeln auf manche Gesichter meiner Freunde zu zaubern. Auch für manche politische Zwecke ist es hilfreich: Unibrennt.	Organizing demonstrations easily. I am able to reach a lot of people . . . my status messages are at the most time good news and quotes in order to give people a positive view of the world (example: "you only see good with your heart"). I hope with it that there will be smiles on some of my friends' faces. It is also helpful for political purposes: Unibrennt.[1]	3, 9
15655455	Leichte Erreichbarkeit.	Simple accessibility.	10
1566262210	Schnelle Information, ständige Erreichbarkeit.	Quick information, permanent accessibility	3, 10
1559714377	Unterhaltung, Kontake knüpfen, Ablenkung	Entertainment, establishing contacts, diversions.	7, 11
1549540851	Nehme etwas Teil am Leben von Freunden & Familie in anderen Städten, Ländern, Kontinenten. Kann mit Freunden zuhause chatten, wenn ich mal weg bin. Organisatorisches lässt sich auch ganz praktisch erledigen. Unterhaltung. Klatsch.	To take part in the lives of friends and family, who live in other cities, countries, continents. To be able to chat with friends at home if I am away. To carry out organizational matters easily. Entertainment. Gossip.	1, 2, 8, 11

ID			
1559724915	Um Kontakt mit Freunden/Bekannten zu halten.	To maintain contact with friends.	1, 3, 12
1558332265	Veranstaltungen, Geburtstage im Überblick. Aufrechterhalten von Kontakten, Vernetzung, Erinnerungen an Geburtstage, leichte Planungsmöglichkeiten für gemeinschaftliche Aktivitäten.	Events, overview of birthdays. Maintaining contacts, networking, reminder of birthdays, an easy possibility of planning collective activities.	1, 8, 9, 12
1556033638	Kommunikation: viele Freunde/Bekannte sind einfach und unkompliziert über eine Plattform zu erreichen. Selbstdarstellung.	Communication: to reach many friends in a simple and straightforward way by means of a platform. Self-presentation.	1, 13
1565685686	In Verbindung treten und in Verbindung bleiben mit anderen Social Platform Usern, Selbstdarstellung, Nutzung zur späteren Kundenakquise für Grafikdesign, kultureller Austausch, usw.	Contacting and staying in touch with other social platform users, Self-presentation, usage for prospective customer acquisition for graphic design, cultural exchange, etc.	1, 7, 9, 13, 15
1560098106	Keine.	None.	14
1572561434	Sehe ich keine.	I do not see any.	14
1573341562	Arbeitskontakte.	Business contacts.	15
1565038921	Facebook hat reinen persönlichen Zweck; finden von alten Bekannten, in Kontakt bleiben mit Freunden, Bekannten aus dem Ausland. LinkedIn und MySpace haben rein professionellen Nutzen, zum finden und suchen von Jobs und professionelle Kontakte.	Facebook is only for personal purposes; meeting old friends, staying in contact with friends from abroad. LinkedIn and MySpace do have professional benefits, namely to find and search jobs and professional contacts.	1, 2, 4, 15
1558232492	Spionage.	Espionage.	16
1559729071	In Kontakt zu bleiben. Man kann Menschen ausfindig machen und etwas über sie erfahren wenn sie das im Profil nicht gesperrt haben (kurz: stalken).	To keep in touch. You are able to locate people and to be kept informed about them, if they haven't blocked that on their profile (in short: stalking).	1, 16
1565035091	Leichtigkeit mit Freunden Sachen zu teilen. Events Infos. Subscriptions von Produkten, VIPs, usw. Mädels aufreißen.	Simplicity of sharing stuff with friends. Information about events. Subscriptions of products, VIPs, etc. Pulling girls.	3, 17

Note
1 Unibrennt was an Austrian student protest in 2009 against the commodification of higher education and the undemocratic decision-making structures at universities, where many universities' lecture halls and rooms were occupied. The protest spread to other countries such as Germany and Switzerland. Unibrennt used social media for organizing and communicating the protest (Unibrennt 2013).

a social networking site is that it enables free communication, thereby saving money. In addition, 7.4 per cent mention sharing photos and other media with friends and accessing such media as a major opportunity, and 6.6 per cent of the students say establishing new contacts is very important. Some 4.2 per cent list communication and contacts in general with no further specification as the greatest advantage. It is also interesting that only 0.04 per cent of our respondents mention flirting, sex, and love as important aspects of social media, which could be caused by social desirability.

Table 6.3 presents some characteristic examples of answers that were given to the question of what the major advantages of social networking platforms are (one or two examples for each category).

The minimum amount of a received answer text consisted of one word; the maximum amount was 184 words. Please note that the survey was conducted in German, but the questionnaire was translated for the analysis into English.

Advantages of social networking sites in comparison: bivariate analysis

Figures 6.4 to 6.6 display the results of the greatest perceived advantages of social networking platforms (N=3531) in comparison with gender, level of study, and field of study.

A total of 41.5 per cent of the female and 44 per cent of the male respondents stress the maintenance of existing contacts, friendships, and family relations as a major opportunity of social networking sites. Moreover, 38.7 per cent of women and 24.3 per cent of men indicate that social relationships over spatial distances are the greatest advantage, and 23.3 per cent of the female and 23.5 per cent of the male students consider social networking platforms as a medium of information and news. Some 25.1 per cent of women and 17.5 per cent of men mention finding and renewing old contacts as major benefit.

Some 41.1 per cent of the undergraduate, 43.3 per cent of the graduate, and 50.9 per cent of the doctoral students stress the maintenance of existing contacts, friendships, and family relations as major opportunities of social networking sites, and 35.3 per cent of undergraduates, 33.7 per cent of graduates, and 20.8 per cent of postgraduates indicate that social relationships over spatial distances are the greatest advantage. In addition, 23.5 per cent of the undergraduate, 24.1 per cent of the graduate, and 20.3 per cent of the Ph.D. students consider social networking platforms as a medium of information and news.

In all, 40.1 per cent of the students of social sciences and humanities, 37.2 per cent of the students of natural and engineering sciences, 44.1 per cent of the students of law, 41.0 per cent of the students of medical science, and 38.2 per cent of the students of arts stress the maintenance of existing contacts, friendships, and family relations as major opportunities of social networking sites. Besides, 34.6 per cent of the students of social sciences and humanities, 26 per cent of the students of natural and engineering sciences, 32.8 per cent of the students of law, 34.3 per cent of the students of medical science, and 31.6 per cent of the students of arts indicate that social relationships over spatial distances are the greatest

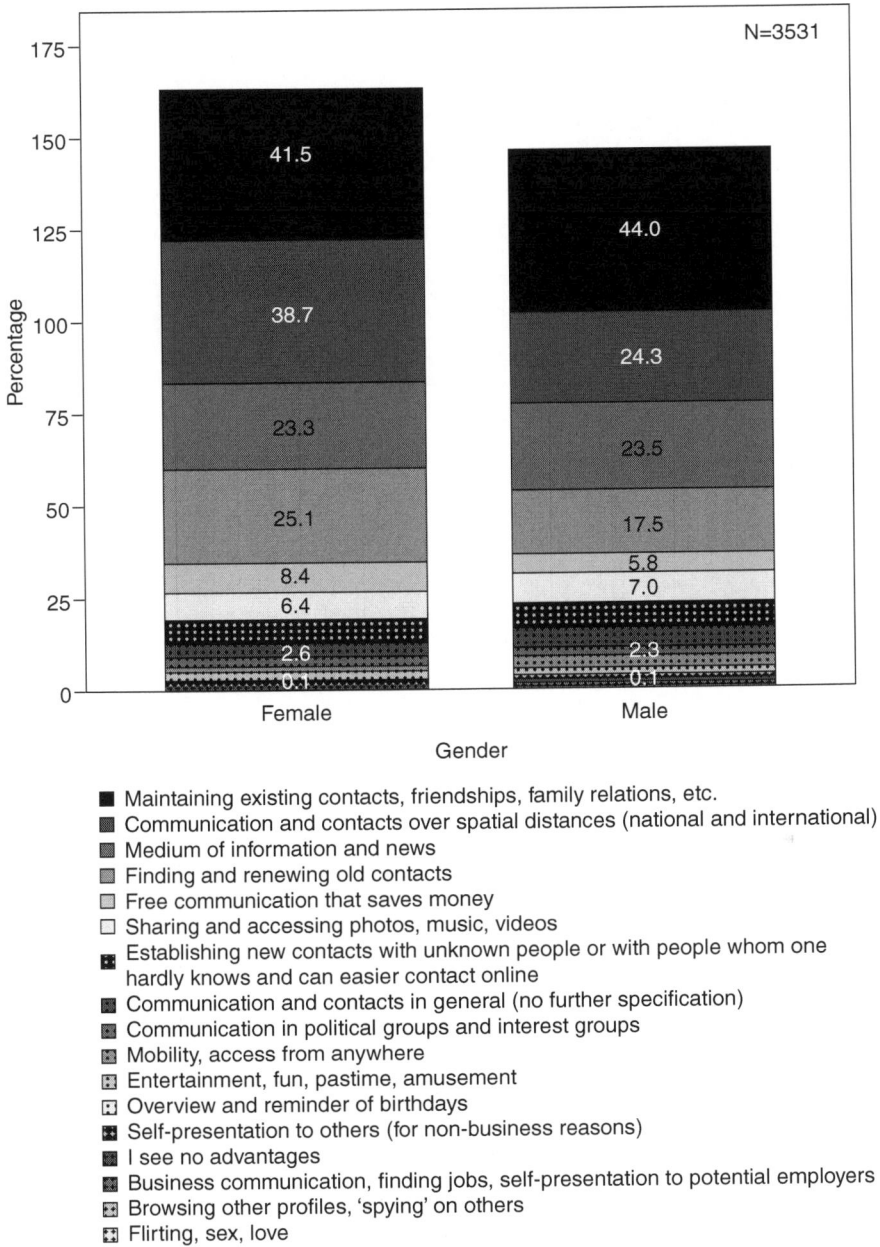

Figure 6.4 Greatest perceived advantages of social networking platforms and gender.

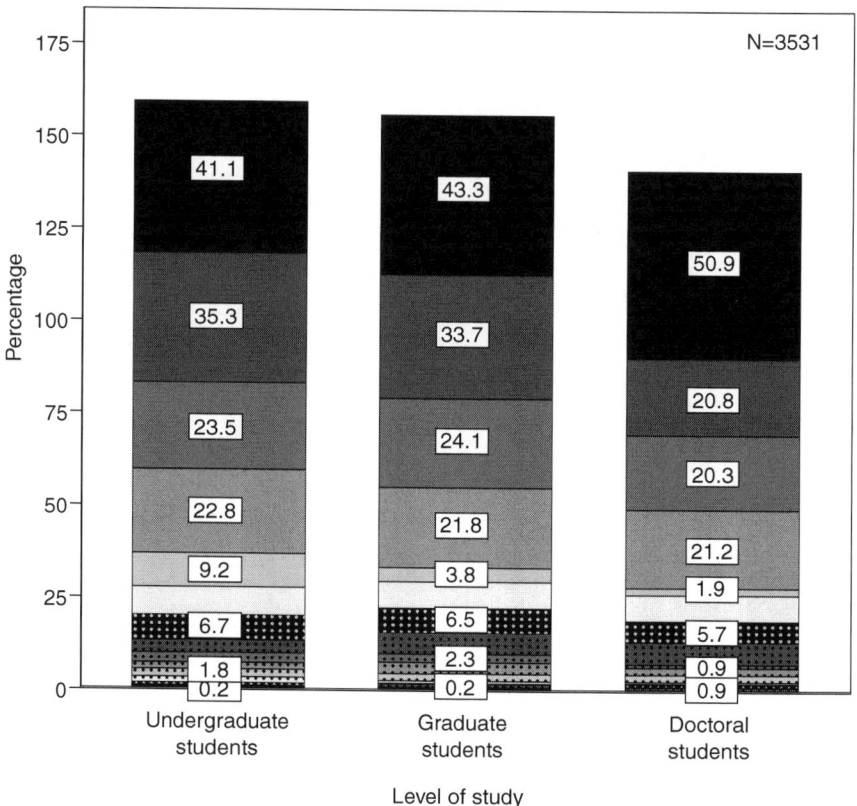

Figure 6.5 Greatest perceived advantages of social networking platforms and level of study.

The chart legend:

- Maintaining existing contacts, friendships, family relations, etc.
- Communication and contacts over spatial distances (national and international)
- Medium of information and news
- Finding and renewing old contacts
- Free communication that saves money
- Sharing and accessing photos, music, videos
- Establishing new contacts with unknown people or with people whom one hardly knows and can easier contact online
- Communication and contacts in general (no further specification)
- Communication in political groups and interest groups
- Mobility, access from anywhere
- Entertainment, fun, pastime, amusement
- Overview and reminder of birthdays
- Self-presentationto others (for non-business reasons)
- I see no advantages
- Business communication, finding jobs, self-presentation to potential employers
- Browsing other profiles, 'spying' on others
- Flirting, sex, love

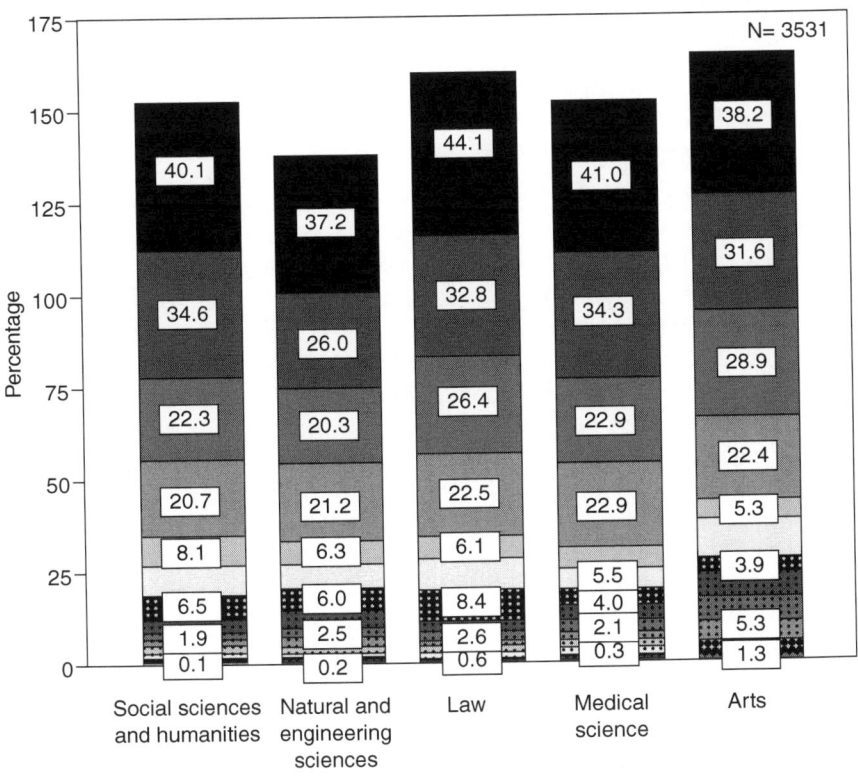

Field of study

- ■ Maintaining existing contacts, friendships, family relations, etc.
- ■ Communication and contacts over spatial distances (national and international)
- ▨ Medium of information and news
- ▨ Finding and renewing old contacts
- □ Free communication that saves money
- □ Sharing and accessing photos, music, videos
- ▦ Establishing new contacts with unknown people or with people whom one hardly knows and can easier contact online
- ▨ Communication and contacts in general (no further specification)
- ▨ Communication in political groups and interest groups
- ▨ Mobility, access from anywhere
- ▨ Entertainment, fun, pastime, amusement
- ▨ Overview and reminder of birthdays
- ▨ Self-presentation to others (for non-business reasons)
- ▨ I see no advantages
- ▨ Business communication, finding jobs, self-presentation to potential employers
- ▨ Browsing other profiles, 'spying' on others
- ▨ Flirting, sex, love

Figure 6.6 Greatest perceived advantages of social networking platforms and field of study.

advantage. The results of the disadvantages of social networking sites are presented in the next section.

Disadvantages of social networking sites

Perceived disadvantages of social networking sites

In analysing whether the surveillance threat is considered as the major disadvantage of SNS, I asked what the greatest concerns of social networking sites such as Facebook and MySpace are (open question). I received N=3534 qualitative answer texts to the question that addressed disadvantages. I identified 14 categories for the concerns and analysed the answers to the questions by content analysis (Krippendorff 2004; Berg 2001). The categories were adopted from theoretical and empirical studies about social networking sites (Fuchs 2010b; Livingstone 2008) on the one hand, and were revised and expanded regarding the answers by summarizing, paraphrasing, abstracting, and generalizing groups of answer texts to categories on the other hand; that is, a combination of inductive and deductive methods (Berg 2001, 248–249; Babbie 2010, 339). Our respondents tended to list more than one major disadvantage. Many answers are therefore mapped with more than one category (Berg 2001, 247–248). Figure 6.7 shows the major concerns of social networking sites that our respondents mentioned.

Figure 6.7 shows that surveillance is considered to be the greatest concern of social networking sites. Almost 60 per cent of our respondents stress that economic, political, or cultural surveillance as a result of data abuse, data

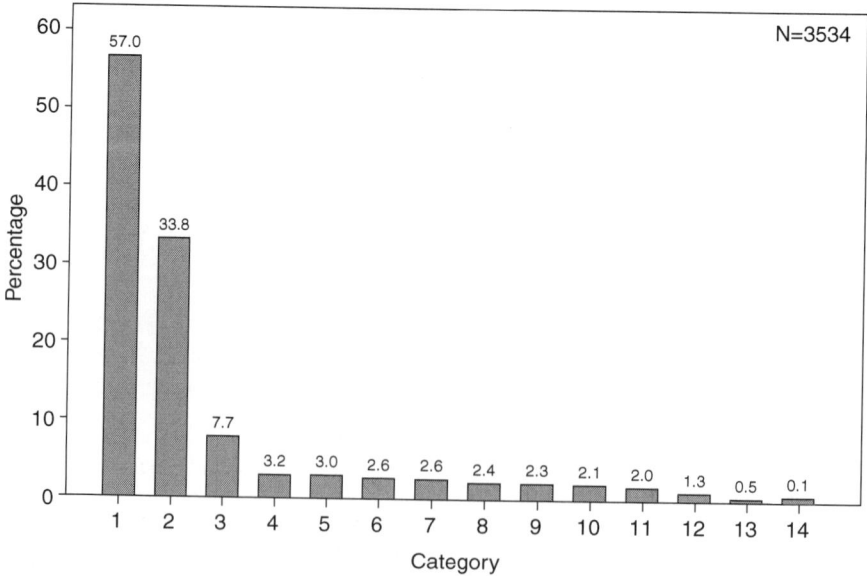

Figure 6.7 Greatest perceived concerns of social networking platforms.

Table 6.4 Identified categories of greatest perceived concerns of social networking platforms

No.	Category
1	Data abuse, data forwarding or lack of data protection that lead to surveillance by companies, state, or individuals
2	Private affairs become public and result in a lack of privacy and privacy control
3	Personal profile data (images, etc.) are accessed by employers or potential employers and result in job-related disadvantages (such as losing a job or not getting hired)
4	Internet addiction
5	Data and identity theft
6	Receiving advertising or spam
7	I see no disadvantages
8	Stalking, harassment, becoming a victim of crime
9	Commercial selling of personal data
10	Lack or loss of personal contacts, superficial communication and contacts, impoverishment of social relations
11	Virus, hacking and defacing of profiles, data integrity
12	It is a waste of time
13	Unrealistic, exaggerated self-presentation, competition for best self-presentation
14	Disadvantages at university because professors can access profiles

forwarding, or a lack of data protection is the main threat of SNS. One-third (33.8%) say that it is problematic that personal affairs that should better be kept private and should not be known to others tend to become public, and 7.7 per cent state that it is also a danger that current and potential employers can access profiles, which could result in job-related disadvantages. In addition, 3.2 per cent mention Internet addiction, and 3 per cent stress data and identity theft as the greatest risks of social media. Some 2.6 per cent express concerns about advertising or spam. Also interesting is that 2.6 per cent of the students do not see disadvantages in the use of commercial social networking platforms.

Although the general surveillance threat (category one) is considered to be the major disadvantage, it may be argued that economic surveillance (category three, six, and nine) also plays an important role as perceived concern and risk of SNS, because it is the third most mentioned major concern (12.6%). It is likely that many answers subsumed under category one are also directly or indirectly linked to targeted advertising and commercial selling of personal data, but brief responses such as "surveillance" or "data forwarding" do not expose whether it is meant in a political, economic, or cultural sense. For reasons of impartiality, we put the open-ended questions about advantages and disadvantages of social networking sites at the very beginning of the survey. Although the above figure already indicates the importance of economic surveillance, students obviously tend to be more concerned about targeted advertising if they are confronted with closed-ended questions (Allmer *et al.* 2014).

Table 6.5 presents some characteristic examples of answers that were given to the question of what the major disadvantages of social networking platforms are (one or two examples for each category).

Table 6.5 Examples of concerns listed by respondents

Respondent ID	Answer (German)	Answer (English)	Categories
1567657160	Missbrauch der Daten.	Data abuse.	1
1569094635	Speicherung bzw. Aufzeichnungen aller Handlungen auf Facebook, das nicht Bestehen der Möglichkeit seine Handlungen komplett zu löschen, Datenmissbrauch (Veröffentlichung) durch Facebook.	Storage resp. recording of all actions on Facebook, absence of the possibility to delete stored actions completely, Facebook's data abuse (publication).	1
1564258061	Ende der Privatsphäre.	End of privacy.	2
1567625679	Die Öffentlichkeit, vor allem die Zugänglichkeit von persönlichen Daten und Informationen.	The public, especially accessibility of personal data and information.	2
1519050546	Dass Arbeitgeber private Informationen erhalten könnten.	That employers are able to receive private information.	3
1567729690	dass Bilder, Kommentare, usw. von Leuten gesehen werden, welche diese nicht sehen sollten. z.B. Arbeitgeber → Schwierigkeiten bei der Jobsuche.	That pictures, comments, etc. are seen by people who should not see them e.g. employer. → difficulties in finding a job.	2, 3
1559723549	Süchtig zu werden.	To become addicted.	4
1566733372	Abhängigkeit, das Gefühl, jeden Tag online sein zu müssen, Aspekte wie Datenschutz und Privatsphäre.	Addiction, feeling to have to be online every day, aspects such as data protection and privacy.	1, 2, 4
1557650353	Datendiebstahl, Identitätsdiebstahl.	Data theft, identity theft.	5
1559750909	Privatsphäre; Identitätsdiebstahl, Risiko der Belästigung und Begegnung mit Online-Verbrechern; veröffentlichten Inhalte können in der ganzen Welt gesehen werden.	Privacy; identity theft, risk of harassment and encounter with online criminals; published content may be viewed all over the world.	2, 5, 8
1559706802	Unrechtliche Nutzung der Daten, Weitergabe, Personalisierte Werbung, Gesichtserkennungsalgorithmus, Entfremdung des Wortes „Freund", Gruppenzwang und mittlerweile sozialer Druck bei sowas mitzumachen.	Unlawful use of data, forwarding, personalized advertising, algorithm of face recognition, alienation of the term "friend"; meanwhile group pressure and social pressure to join in.	1, 6, 10

ID	German	English	
1559719051	Das persönliche Informationen, die ich oft auch unbewusst über mich selbst Preis gebe, gegen mich verwendet werden. Außerdem nervt mich personalisierte Werbung.	That personal information, which I often expose unconsciously, is used against me. Besides, I am annoyed by personalized advertising.	2, 6
1557047480	Keine.	None.	7
1550525803	Eigentlich keine.	Actually none.	7
1564999544	Cyber stalking.	Cyber stalking.	8
1559760035	* Leute die ich nicht kenne sehen mein Profil (z.B.: Kriminelle, Arbeitgeber) * FB verändert sich andauernd → mann muss die Privatsphäreeinstellungen immer anpassen.	* Unknown people are able to view my profile (e.g. criminals, employers) * Facebook is always changing → one has always to adjust the privacy settings.	2, 3, 8
1566130533	Gläserner Mensch, kommerzielle Nutzung von UserImendaten.	Transparent individual, commercial usage of user data.	2, 9
1525388777	...die (zukünftig gewiss) stärker werdende Verwendung aller gesammelten Daten, Nutzerangaben zur Marktforschung dh. Profitmaximierung ... ein weiterer Schritt in Richtung „globaler Überwachungsstaat", über welchen tatsächlich bald nicht mehr die Völker/die Politiker herrschen werden, sondern Konzerne und Lobbies ... untrasparent, benutzerunfreundliche Privatsphäre-Einstellungen.	...(prospective) increasing use of all collected data, user details for market research; that is, profit maximization ... a further step towards "global police state", which the people/politicians will no longer rule, but corporations and lobbies ... opaque, non-user-friendly privacy settings.	1, 2, 9
1561084176	Sehr oberflächliche konversationen, zu leichtsinniges teilen von information.	Very superficial conversations, too careless sharing of information.	2, 10
1565288593	Datenschutz, Vereinsamung, falsche Vorstellungen von der Realität, normale Gespräche mit dem Gegenüber – man weiß ja eh schon alles, denn es wird ja von manchen „alles" gepostet.	Data protection, loneliness, misconception of reality, normal conversations with a guy – you already know all stuff, because some people post "everything".	1, 10

continued

Table 6.5 Examples of concerns listed by respondents

Respondent ID	Answer (German)	Answer (English)	Categories
1561247966	Hacker.	Hackers.	11
1567638641	Das es Hecker gibt, die in meinem Namen, meine Seite „verunstalten".	That there are hackers who "deface" my site in the name of me.	11
1559785387	Zeitverschwendung.	Waste of time.	12
1567639535	Privatsphäre, Zeitverschwendung (Leute schreiben zu viel rein, was mich nicht interessiert; Spieleanfragen nerven).	Privacy, waste of time (people write too much into it that does not interest me; inquiries about games annoy).	2, 12
1560127276	dass diese Plattformen zur reinen Selbstinszenierung verwendet werden.	That these platforms are used for pure self-presentation.	13
1550551373	Datenschutz, „Stasi auf freiwilliger basis", wenn das System kippt sind die Leute leicht einzuteilen nach politischen Interessen, usw., falsche Selbstdarstellung der Nutzer → oft will man sich profilieren.	Data protection, "stasi on a voluntary basis", if the system overturns, it is easy to classify people according political interests, etc., false description of oneself → often one wants to show off oneself.	1, 13
1565224564	* Die Privatsphäre ist sehr angegriffen, da Freunde oft Fotos hochladen, in denen man verlinkt wird (und sichtbar ist) .... * Die Pflege sozialer Netzwerke „im real life" könnte vernachlässigt werden. * V.a. junge Leute sind sich der Auswirkungen ständiger (eig. privater) Status-Erneuerungen nicht bewusst, bzw. des Umstandes, dass diese auch Professoren und zukünftige Vorgesetzte usw. lesen könnten.	* Privacy is violated, because friends often upload photos, where you are linked (and visible) .... * Cultivation of social networks "in real life" could be neglected. * Especially young people are not aware of the consequences of permanent (actually private) status changing, resp. the fact that this could also read professors and prospective superiors, etc.	2, 10, 14

The minimum amount of a received answer text consisted of one word; the maximum amount was 229 words. Please note that the survey was conducted in German, but the questionnaire was translated for the analysis into English.

Disadvantages of social networking sites in comparison: bivariate analysis

Figures 6.8 to 6.10 show the results of the greatest perceived concerns of social networking platforms (N=3534) in comparison with gender, level of study, and field of study.

Some 55.1 per cent of the female and 60.2 per cent of the male respondents stress that data abuse, data forwarding, or a lack of data protection is the greatest concern of social networking platforms. Moreover, 36.1 per cent of women and 30 per cent of men indicate that it is problematic that personal affairs tend to become public, and 8.8 per cent of the female and 5.9 per cent of the male students state that it is also a danger that current and potential employers can access profiles; 3.3 per cent of women and 3.1 per cent of men mention Internet addiction as the main risk of social media.

Some 55.5 per cent of the undergraduate, 62.3 per cent of the graduate, and 57.5 per cent of the doctoral students stress that data abuse, data forwarding, or a lack of data protection is the greatest concern of social networking platforms, and 33.9 per cent of undergraduates, 32.8 per cent of graduates, and 35.5 per cent of postgraduates indicate that it is problematic that personal affairs tend to become public. In addition, 8.4 per cent of the undergraduate, 6.8 per cent of the graduate, and 3.8 per cent of the Ph.D. students state that it is also a danger that current and potential employers can access profiles.

Some 55.2 per cent of the students of social sciences and humanities, 49.4 per cent of the students of natural and engineering sciences, 66.8 per cent of the students of law, 49.8 per cent of the students of medical science, and 46.2 per cent of the students of arts stress that data abuse, data forwarding, or a lack of data protection is the greatest concern of social networking platforms. Besides, 33.7 per cent of the students of social sciences and humanities, 30.5 per cent of the students of natural and engineering sciences, 27.4 per cent of the students of law, 29.7 per cent of the students of medical science, and 40 per cent of the students of arts indicate that it is problematic that personal affairs tend to become public. By comparing the greatest concerns with the field of study, one can see that a high amount of the students of law (two-thirds) stress data abuse, data forwarding, or a lack of data protection as the greatest drawbacks. One reason that one can imagine is that jurists tend to learn more about rights, are more frequently confronted with unwarranted intrusions and violations, and are also interested in legal protection. For example, the group "Europe-v-facebook" was founded by a group of Austrian students of law in order to fight against Facebook's policy in terms of personal data abuse and forwarding (Europe-v-Facebook 2013). The Irish Data Protection Commissioner started an investigation after receiving 22 complaints by the group in August 2011. It could be an outcome that Austrian

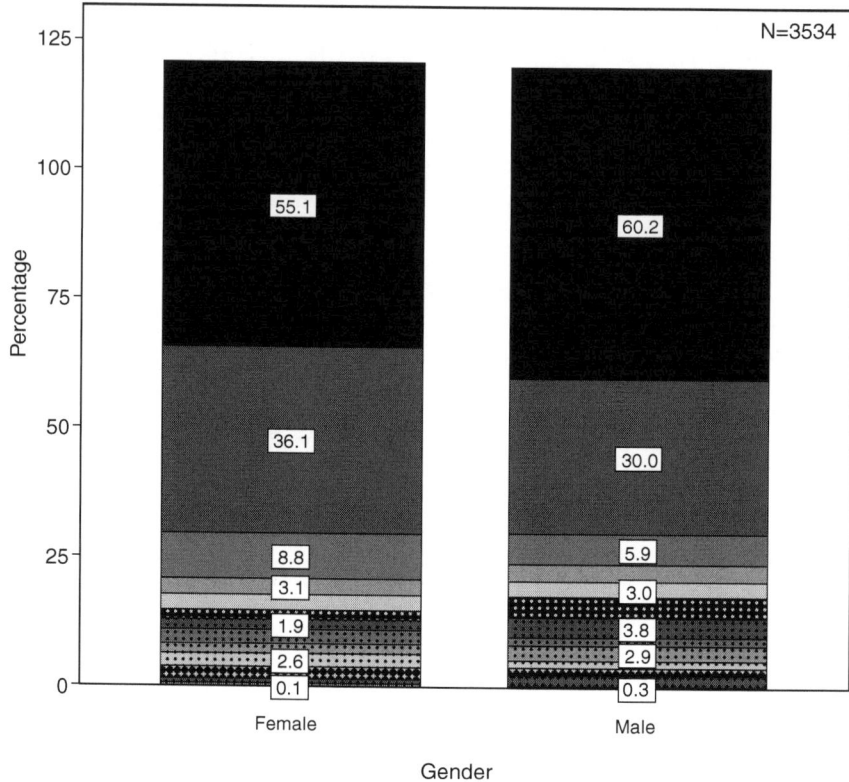

N=3534

Female   Male

Gender

■ Data abuse, data forwarding or lack of data protection that lead to surveillance
▨ Private affairs become public and result in a lack of privacy and privacy control
   Personal profile data (images, etc.) are accessed by employers or potential
■ employers and result in job-related disadvantages (such as losing a job or not
   getting hired)
▨ Internet addiction
☐ Data and identity theft
▣ Receiving advertising or spam
▨ I see no disadvantages
▨ Stalking, harassment, becoming a victim of crime
▥ Commercial selling of personal data
▨ Lack or loss of personal contacts, superficial communication and contacts,
   impoverishment of social relations
▣ Virus, hacking and defacing of profiles, data integrity
▨ It is a waste of time
▨ Unrealistic, exaggerated self-presentation, competition for best self-presentation
▦ Disadvantages at university because professors can access profiles

Figure 6.8 Greatest perceived concerns of social networking platforms and gender.

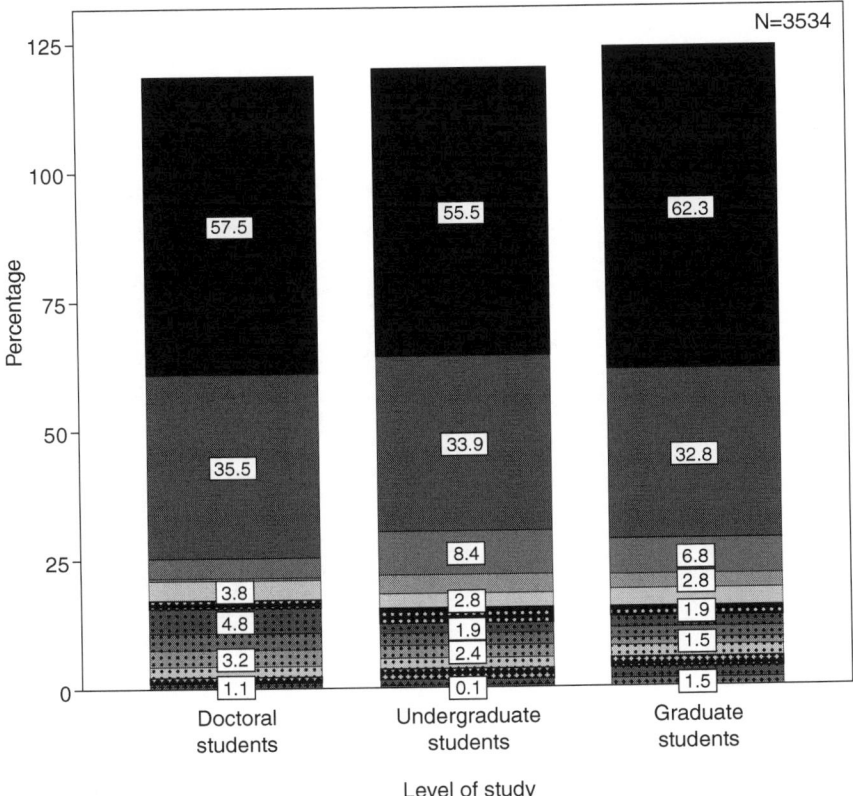

- ■ Data abuse, data forwarding or lack of data protection that lead to surveillance
- ■ Private affairs become public and result in a lack of privacy and privacy control
- ■ Personal profile data (images, etc.) are accessed by employers or potential employers and result in job-related disadvantages (such as losing a job or not getting hired)
- ■ Internet addiction
- □ Data and identity theft
- ■ Receiving advertising or spam
- ■ I see no disadvantages
- ■ Stalking, harassment, becoming a victim of crime
- ■ Commercial selling of personal data
- ■ Lack or loss of personal contacts, superficial communication and contacts, impoverishment of social social relation
- ■ Virus, hacking and defacing of profiles, data integrity
- ■ It is a waste of time
- ■ Unrealistic, exaggerated self-presentation, competition for best self-presentation
- ■ Disadvantages at university because professors can access profiles

Figure 6.9 Greatest perceived concerns of social networking platforms and level of study.

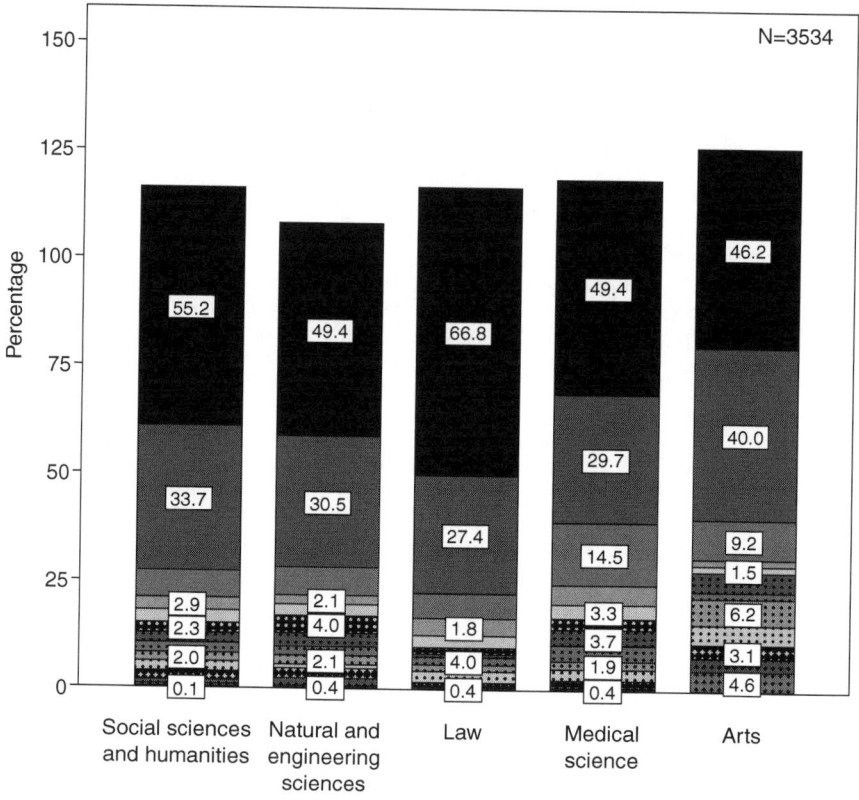

■ Data abuse, data forwarding or lack of data protection that lead to surveillance
■ Private affairs become public and result in a lack of privacy and privacy control
  Personal profile data (images, etc.) are accessed by employers or potential
■ employers and result in job-related disadvantages (such as losing a job or not
  getting hired)
■ Internet addiction
□ Data and identity theft
■ Receiving advertising or spam
■ I see no disadvantages
■ Stalking, harassment, becoming a victim of crime
■ Commercial selling of personal data
■ Lack or loss of personal contacts, superficial communication and contacts,
  impoverishment of social relations
■ Virus, hacking and defacing of profiles, data integrity
■ It is a waste of time
■ Unrealistic, exaggerated self-presentation, competition for best self-presentation
■ Disadvantages at university because professors can access profiles

Figure 6.10 Greatest perceived concerns of social networking platforms and field of study.

students of jurisprudence are more concerned about data abuse and data forwarding.[4]

Conclusion

The results are based on N = 3558 analysed datasets. For answering the research question, the general characteristics of the respondents, advantages of social networking sites, and disadvantages of social networking sites have been presented. This may be summarized as follows:

- There were 63.8 per cent female and 36.2 per cent male respondents. The mean age of our respondents is 24.3 years and the mean number of studied semesters is 6.6. The vast majority of the respondents (96.8%) use Facebook.
- The study shows that maintaining existing relationships and communication over distances are considered to be the greatest advantage of social networking sites. More than 40 per cent of our respondents stress the maintenance of existing contacts, friendships, and family relations as major opportunities of SNS, and 6.6 per cent of the students say establishing new contacts is very important.
- The results also indicate that surveillance is considered to be the greatest concern of social networking sites. Almost 60 per cent of our respondents stress that economic, political, or cultural surveillance as a result of data abuse, data forwarding, or a lack of data protection is the main threat of SNS.

Based on certain foundational concepts of a critical theory of media, technology, and society and the dialectics of productive forces and relations of production of Chapter 1, Chapter 7 contains a theoretical interpretation of the empirical results. This chapter deals with the dialectics of technological design and assessment and the (dis)advantages of social media. It also treats the dialectical relationship of productive forces and relations of production of social media. Chapter 8 summarizes the results of this work and draws some conclusions. It evaluates the prospects and limitations of the objective and subjective characteristics in the realm of digital and social media in terms of achieving a commons-based information society. Part III may be considered to be a praxiological approach, because it discusses political implications and argues for the need for political interventions.

Notes

1 The universities of applied sciences ("Fachhochschulen", 39,276 students in 2011, Austrian Federal Ministry for Science and Research 2012) and the private universities (6301 students in 2010, Austrian Federal Ministry for Science and Research 2012) were for reasons of practicabillity not included in our survey.

2 For a more detailed outline of the research questions, hypotheses, survey questions (conceptualization and operationalization), research methods, as well as population and sampling, see Allmer 2012b.

3 The UNESCO Institute for Statistics has developed the International Standard Classification of Education (ISCED) and suggests nine groups of fields of education: education, humanities and arts, social sciences, business and law, science, engineering, manufacturing and construction, agriculture, health and welfare, and services (UNESCO Institute for Statistics 2012). Although this classification seems appropriate in order to facilitate comparisons of education statistics across countries, we have applied a more simplified classification with five broad groups in our study in order to present the data in a manageable form (Babbie 2010, 433).

4 For a more detailed outline of the data analysis, presentation, and interpretation, see Allmer 2012b.

Part III
Techno-social revolution

7 Critical theory, dialectics, and the (dis)advantages of social media

Introduction

Based on some foundational concepts of a critical theory of media, technology, and society and the dialectics of productive forces and relations of production of Chapter 1, this chapter contains a theoretical interpretation of the empirical results. The second section deals with the dialectics of technological design and assessment, and the (dis)advantages of social media. The third section treats the dialectical relationship of productive forces and relations of production of social media. The fourth and final section concludes with a summary of the findings.

Foundational concepts of a critical theory of media, technology, and society and the (dis)advantages of social media

I have argued in Chapter 1 that asymmetrical social relationships of power and domination are already embedded in the conception, construction, maintenance, as well as modification of technics and the technological design must be rooted in capitalist interests and social forces. Dominating the architecture of the Internet and social media platforms, the client–server computer network may be seen as empirical evidence for this theoretical consideration.

The client–server architecture is the standard computer network model that is applied in most e-mail services and the World Wide Web. This network topology arranges the roles of computers in a network; that is, a computer is either a server or a client. A server is a computer system that is consistently available and shares its resources, and a client is a computer contacting a server in order to make use of these resources. Following a common language and certain rules (communication protocol), a client sends a request and the server returns a request. The model allows multiple clients to communicate with the server synchronously (Brookshear 2009).

The client–server computer network is a hierarchical and centralized architecture of a powerful server with data and files in the centre and relatively powerless clients at the edge. The client–server architecture structures the contemporary online world basically consisting of web servers operated by powerful political and economic actors such as Google and Facebook, and clients used by individuals including social media users. The physical architecture of the Internet and the corresponding software entail hierarchical and structural forms of controls, which enable centralized processing and storage of user data and log files.

The dominant client–server technology fits well into the business model of corporate social media platforms being based on selling personal data. "And the Net, once it became a hierarchically architected zone with servers in the center and increasingly dis-empowered clients at the edge, becomes the zone of platforms and platform making becomes the order of the day" (Moglen 2010). Marx argues that capitalists are not doing any injustice in the process of production by following simply the law of exchange. "There is here therefore an antinomy, of right against right, both [capitalist and worker] equally bearing the seal of the law of exchange" (Marx 1976, 344). Following Marx, one may argue that corporate social networking sites are doing nothing more than applying and improving an already designed technology and following the client–server structure on the Internet. Social platform owners have refined the hierarchical client–server architecture on their platforms and have lifted it to a new qualitative level.

Facebook put its data centre, which includes a 10,916-square-metre computer server equipment room topped with a 4831-square-metre mechanical equipment penthouse, into operation in Prineville, Oregon in April 2010 (Facebook 2013). A similar data centre for the European market opened in Luleå, Sweden in 2014 (Facebook 2015). Facebook uses the client–server model for its platform. Profile information, photos, videos, personal settings, and log files of Facebook users are collected, stored, and processed on servers in the data centre. Users around the world with their digital devices such as desktops, tablets, and smart phones make use of these resources by clients sending requests and servers in Facebook's data centre returning requests. The servers are able to respond to more than one request at the same time. In this technological architecture, Facebook's servers with data and files are in the powerful centre, whereas users' digital devices as clients are at the powerless edge.

The client–server computer network model is a hierarchical organized technology, which includes the idea of the existence of proprietors of such data centres and incorporates the potential of centralized control. The client–server architecture dominating the Internet is designed and constructed as control and surveillance technology, which is embedded in the capitalist relations of production. This technology may increase the risks that people do not know where their data are stored and what is happening to those data. It may strengthen intransparency and uncontrollability of personal data and files (Moglen 2010). This is reflected in the perceived fears and risks of the survey participants when it comes to the greatest disadvantages of social networking sites. The vast majority of our respondents stress that economic, political, or cultural surveillance as a result of data abuse, data forwarding, or a lack of data protection is the main threat of social media. Following Marx, one may argue that the current physical architecture of the Internet indicates that by technology domination "preserves not only social ... but so to say technological realization" (Marx

1982, 2059, my translation).[1] This example shows that capitalist technology may in its foundational form be also a technology of power and domination. The repressive elements of technology in capitalist societies are not solely in its applications, but technology may inherently be a means of power and domination. Technology is a form of organization and maintenance of social relations and a means of control and domination. Technological control is internal to their very structure (Feenberg 2002, 51), and therefore a transformation and redesign of technology is necessary in order to strengthen the idea of the commons and a real liberation of society.

In contrast, the peer-to-peer system is a computer network where each computer can act as a client or server for other computers sharing access to various digital contents such as audio, video, and data files. Peers are equally privileged participants and are both suppliers and consumers of resources. Every switch is an independent and free-standing entity, which makes digital data available to other network participants without the need for a central server or host. The network of peers is a decentralized and non-hierarchical architecture which is hardly applied on the current Net (Brookshear 2009).

In order to provide a mobile version of the peer-to-peer system, Moglen (2010) argues for personal webservers that everyone can put into his or her pocket. A mobile webserver could be plugged in at any place, synced up to any router, could be connected to the Internet, could keep one's log files, and store all one's personal online data. Everyone would be the owner of his or her server and could control what to share online. According to Moglen (2010), such architecture would be easy to realize.

The best-known realizations of the peer-to-peer technology are file-sharing applications such as Napster, Kazaa, LimeWire, Vuze, and The Pirate Bay. These applications enable the direct exchange of files and data between computers on the Net. Peer-to-peer file sharing allows open access to and free distribution and common ownership of digital knowledge (music, films, software, books, etc.). The knowledge, music, and film industry has often complained about file-sharing organizations' economic threats and copyright infringements. File sharing is a thorn in capital's flesh and it attempts over and over again to criminalize the communities, and it creates precedents and deterring examples of court convictions, high fines, and arrests, as The Pirate Bay trial in Sweden showed. But the recent past has also displayed that blocks and forced shutdowns of peer-to-peer networks also evoke protests and result in the emergence of new, similar services or mirror sites (exact copies of the original site) on the Net (TorrentFreak 2012). This indicates that such technologies are hard to control and capital's and communities' interests collide, resulting in social struggles and conflicts. However, the Internet commodity economy also makes use of the peer-to-peer computer network system, as the following example will demonstrate. μTorrent is a proprietary peer-to-peer file-sharing service owned by the US-based corporation BitTorrent Inc. μTorrent standard version is free of charge and its business model is based on advertising and selling personal data. μTorrent (2013) states in its privacy policy:

We collect ... data to improve ... targeted advertising.... We may merge information about you into group data, which may then be shared on an aggregated basis with our advertisers.... Data in an aggregate form without any personally identifiable information may be provided to other parties for marketing, advertising, or other uses.

This indicates that the peer-to-peer technology is not immune to surveillance and commodification. "Everything becomes a commodity" (Gorz 2010, 23). Such a decentralized model may also be subsumed under capital, but with some structures it is more difficult. Overall this points to the need for class struggle, revolution, and politics beyond technology.

I have also claimed in Chapter 1 that technological effects depend on how technologies are used and technology cannot be isolated from its application. I will show exemplarily in the following that the effects of the Internet and new media depend on how they are used in society.

Social movements such as the Occupy movement and Anonymous, and alternative media including Democracy Now! and Indymedia, have potentials to establish a "counterpublic sphere" (Negt and Kluge 1993) and question capitalist logics. Or, speaking in terms of autonomist Marxism, the multitude is able to undermine capitalist hegemony in order to strengthen the idea of a commons-based society. The following are some characteristics of the multitude (Hardt and Negri 2004, 99–105):

- The multitude is composed of a set of singularities.
- The multitude is a, active social subject that acts on the bases of the common.
- The multitude is a class concept.
- The multitude is also a concept of race, gender, and sexuality differences.
- The multitude is composed of all diverse figures of social production.
- The multitude remains plural and multiple, but not fragmented, anarchical, or incoherent.
- The multitude is an open, dynamic, and expansive network.
- The multitude is a global movement.

The rise of the Internet has brought new opportunities for social movements and alternative media that often suffer from a lack of resources. Social movements are able to publish and spread alternative views and raise critical awareness cost-effectively on a global level. The Internet can support digital grassroots democracy and give the powerless a say. Real technological potentials of cyberspace could be brought to fruition having "not yet" (Bloch 1986) been realized. The appearance of the World Wide Web and social media also contains potentials, and it is important to uncover and reveal those hidden and suppressed potentials for a real liberation of human beings. However, the multitude is confronted with problems of gaining visibility, attracting publicity, and attracting attention on the web, which is characterized by capitalist logics, marketing strategies, information overflows, and a loss in cyberspace. Table 7.1 shows the most accessed websites on the Internet.

Table 7.1 Most accessed websites on the Internet

Top sites on the Web

Rank	Website	Ownership	Economic orientation	Country
1	Google	Google Inc.	Profit	USA
2	Facebook	Facebook Inc.	Profit	USA
3	YouTube	Google Inc.	Profit	USA
4	Yahoo!	Yahoo! Inc.	Profit	USA
5	Baidu	Baidu Inc.	Profit	China
6	Wikipedia	Wikimedia Foundation	Non-Profit	USA
7	Windows Live	Microsoft Corporation	Profit	USA
8	QQ	Tencent Holdings Limited	Profit	China
9	Amazon.com	Amazon.com Inc.	Profit	USA
10	Twitter	Twitter Inc.	Profit	USA
11	Taobao Marketplace	Alibaba Group	Profit	China
12	Blogspot.com	Google Inc.	Profit	USA
13	Google India	Google Inc.	Profit	USA
14	LinkedIn	LinkedIn Corporation	Profit	USA
15	Yahoo! Japan	Yahoo! Japan Corporation[1]	Profit	Japan
16	Sina	Sina Corporation	Profit	China
17	eBay	eBay Inc.	Profit	USA
18	MSN	Microsoft Corporation	Profit	USA
19	Google Japan	Google Inc.	Profit	USA
20	Bing	Microsoft Corporation	Profit	USA
21	Yandex	Yandex Company	Profit	Russia
22	WordPress.com	Automattic Inc.	Profit	USA
23	Google Germany	Google Inc.	Profit	USA
24	Google Hong Kong	Google China Inc.[2]	Profit	China
25	VK	VKontakte	Profit	Russia

Source: Alexa Internet (2013).

Notes
1 Yahoo! Japan Corporation is a joint venture between Yahoo! and SoftBank, and is headquartered in Tokyo, Japan.
2 The website Google Hong Kong (formerly Google China) is operated by Google China Inc., which is a subsidiary of Google Inc.

According to Alexa (2013), profit-oriented corporations own 24 of the 25 most accessed websites on the Internet. Only the Wikimedia Foundation as a non-profit organization operates Wikipedia. In comparison, the website of WikiLeaks is ranked 20,686, and diaspora* (an alternative social networking site) is ranked 69,256 on the list of the most accessed websites worlwide (Alexa Internet 2013). Google, Facebook, YouTube, Baidu, Wikipedia, QQ, Twitter, Blogspot.com, LinkedIn, Sina, WordPress, and VK are web 2.0 services, because they also provide communicative and cooperative tools. This shows that commercial companies, based mainly in the USA, dominate the Internet, and indicates the imperialistic character of the social media market (Jin 2013).

The powers that can be marshaled through platforms are not exclusively centered in the U.S. However, as Lenin argued, the conflicts for hegemony between great powers, in this case, U.S.-based SNSs and local-based SNSs have been evident, and Facebook and Twitter have become dominant powers. In other words, a few U.S.-based platforms dominate the global order, which has resulted in the concentration of capital in a few hands within major TNCs [transnational corporations] and start-ups…. A handful of U.S.-owned platforms have rapidly expanded their dominance in the global market, which has caused the asymmetrical gap between a few Western countries and the majority of non-Western countries.

(Jin 2013, 161)

This tendency is also expressed in the use of social networking sites in the survey, because the vast majority of the respondents use commercial web 2.0 platforms (96.8 per cent use Facebook, 16.8 per cent use studiVZ, and 11.9 per cent use Xing) and only 0.3 per cent use alternative social media such as diaspora*.

In 2007, a group of people started the DataPortability Project (2013). The basic idea of the project is to enable data portability that people can move easily between social networking services and reuse their data. Likewise, the European Commission (2012, 9) suggests in its data protection regulation proposal to implement a right to data portability. This would enable users to "transfer data from one electronic processing system to and into another, without being prevented from doing so by the controller". Due to the fact that users could easily choose between corporate and alternative social media platforms and could export all their contacts and data from Facebook to diaspora* and import them there, it may be possible that such attempts could serve as progressive political agendas. But it may also be possible that many people would just use it to transfer photos and data from one profit-oriented social platform to another, which would result in an even more powerful position of major commercial companies in the social media market. Facebook, Google, and others have already joined the DataPortability workgroup. The effects of the realization of the DataPortability Project and the implementation of the data portability right are open, subject to users, and not predetermined, but are also linked to the question of who is able to attract publicity in the future.

Powerful political and economic actors are very successful in raising visibility and attracting publicity in cyberspace. Due to capitalist structures of the Internet and asymmetrical distributions of material resources between the multitude and the empire on the one hand as well as the logic of one-dimensional thoughts (Marcuse), instrumental rationality (Horkheimer), manipulative culture industry (Adorno and Horkheimer), and global false consciousness of society (Marx) on the other hand, critical social movements and critical (social) media are confronted with marginalization and disappearing attention (on the Internet). Marcuse (1965, 81–117) analysed these tendencies in his essay "Repressive Tolerance", where he speaks about tolerance in modern capitalism. He argues that a liberal term of tolerance is defended in advanced industrial society, although the function of tolerance has changed and serves the interests of oppression. Liberal tolerance inevitably mutates to repressive tolerance in a repressive society, where manipulated human beings have developed desires for things that are forced anyway. Technical and intellectual coordination of individuals, dissemination of bourgeois consciousness, and active and passive rejection of social transformations result from the logic of social relations.

> Other words can be spoken and heard, other ideas can be expressed, but, at the massive scale of the conservative majority (outside such enclaves as the intelligentsia), they are immediately 'evaluated' (i.e. automatically understood) in terms of the public language – a language which determines 'a priori' the direction in which the thought process moves.
>
> (Marcuse 1965, 96)

This means that radical and critical movements and media are deliberately tolerated, because such movements are at the edge anyway due to one-dimensional thoughts in society. In this respect, the ruling class has no problems with extending tolerance. The following tables try to further illustrate these tendencies. Table 7.2 displays the most searched terms on Google Web.

Whitney Houston was the most searched term on Google in 2012, followed by Gangnam Style, Hurricane Sandy, iPad 3, and Diablo 3 (Google 2013). In contrast, global political and ecological problems that are central to modern society are not among them. Table 7.3 displays the most popular pages by Likes on Facebook.

According to PageData (2013), Facebook for Every Phone is the most (193.8 million Likes), Facebook the second most (85.9 million Likes), YouTube the third most (69.1 million Likes), Texas HoldEm Poker the fourth most (68 million Likes), and Rihanna the fifth most popular page on Facebook (65.9 million Likes). In contrast, the Facebook page of Anonymous has 940,946 Likes,

Table 7.2 Most searched terms on Google in 2012 (worldwide)

Top searches on Google

Rank	Search term
1	Whitney Houston
2	Gangnam Style
3	Hurricane Sandy
4	iPad 3
5	Diablo 3
6	Kate Middleton
7	Olympics 2012
8	Amanda Todd
9	Michael Clarke Duncan
10	BBB12

Source: Google (2013).

Table 7.3 Most popular pages by Likes on Facebook

Top pages on Facebook

Rank	Page name	Likes
1	Facebook for Every Phone	193,793,376
2	Facebook	85,871,922
3	YouTube	69,067,024
4	Texas HoldEm Poker	68,048,029
5	Rihanna	65,884,512
6	Eminem	65,557,345
7	The Simpsons	60,192,933
8	Shakira	59,800,254
9	Harry Potter	58,773,112
10	Coca-Cola	58,195,469

Source: PageData (2013).

Occupy Wall St. 413,366 Likes, Democracy Now! 318,467 Likes, Indymedia 21,491 Likes, and Europe-v-Facebook 6,303 Likes. Mark Zuckerberg (16.4 million Likes) has far more Likes than the page of Karl Marx (141,343 Likes). Just as personal profiles are for individuals, so pages are for organizations, well-known people, businesses, brands, products, services, or concepts on Facebook. People can create pages allowing fans to like or subscribe to page posts and updates. Users have the option expressing to like the page by pressing the Like button. A Facebook page can have an unlimited number of likes and subscribers. The survey result that only 2.5 per cent of the students list communication in political and interest groups as an important aspect and beneficial characteristic of social media shows that such platforms are not a priori political and critical places. Although social networking is shaped by individualized communication and corporate interests, it also poses possibilities for group formation and cooperation might being channelled into collective political projects (Fuchs 2009b, 83), as the Occupy movement, the Indignados movement in Spain, or the Arab Spring demonstrated. Table 7.4 shows the most viewed videos on YouTube.

PSY – Gangnam Style is the most viewed video of all time on YouTube with 1.3 billion views, followed by Justin Bieber – Baby ft. Ludacris with 825.8 million views, and Jennifer Lopez – On The Floor ft. Pitbull with 644.1 million views (YouTube 2013). Corporate social media are ideological platforms, because they provide the illusionary impression that everyone now has the opportunity to present oneself to the public and to receive attention, while most people on web 2.0 are marginalized and invisible, and cannot influence political decisions and define cultural values compared to powerful political and economic actors, as the above examples indicate. "One *believes* that one's contribution matters, that it means something to and within a context broader than oneself. Contributing to the information stream thus has a subjective registration effect detached from any actual impact or efficacy" (Dean 2009, 31). The

Table 7.4 Most viewed videos on YouTube

Top videos on YouTube		
Rank	Video name	Views
1	PSY – GANGNAM STYLE	1,253,075,141
2	Justin Bieber – Baby ft. Ludacris	825,820,315
3	Jennifer Lopez – On the Floor ft. Pitbull	644,059,561
4	Eminem – Love the Way You Lie ft. Rihanna	534,735,242
5	Lady Gaga – Bad Romance	506,310,140
6	Michel Teló – Ai Se Eu Te Pego	477,669,033

Source: YouTube (2013).

material resources of participation are asymmetrical and show the limitations of freedom of speech on new media. Structural inequalities and power relations stratify public visibility and participation online (Sandoval and Fuchs 2010, 144). New technologies such as social software are an ideology and an expression of repressive tolerance in capitalist society. This is not caused through technics by itself or by design, but rather results from the application of technology in society. Social media may be applied differently to another society.

In summary, power and domination are embedded in the design of the Internet and social media, and at the same time the effects of the Internet and new media depend on how such technologies are used (see Figure 7.1).

The client–server architecture dominating the Internet is designed and constructed as control and surveillance technology, which is embedded in the capitalist relations of production. But the peer-to-peer system and mobile webservers operated with the help of free software could clean up the servers of Facebook, Google, and so on and may undermine the capitalist logic of centralized data storage, surveillance, and the data commodity. In addition, the Internet and corporate social media serve primarily as ideological and repressive platforms

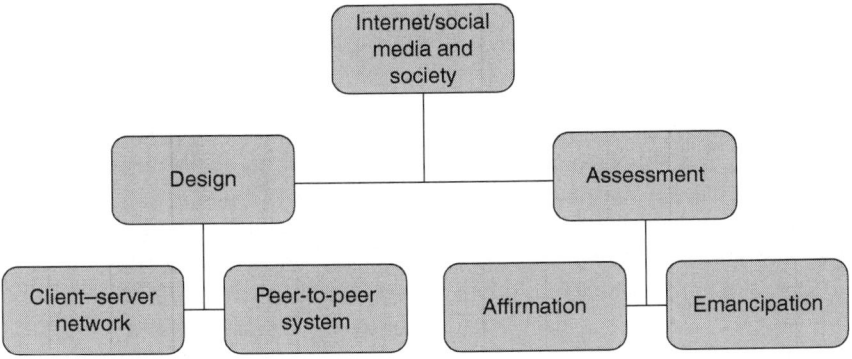

Figure 7.1 Different possibilities of design and assessment of the Internet/social media and society.

(affirmation), but may also be used alternatively (emancipation). These insights are partially reflected in the survey questions about the greatest (dis)advantages of social networking sites.

The dialectics of productive forces and relations of production and the (dis)advantages of social media

Marx describes land and nature primarily as the objects of labour, but one may argue that information and knowledge might also serve as objects of labour in the mode of production. Marx himself traces this possibility in the "Grundrisse". The technological development of the productive forces causes a rising importance of science, information, and general social knowledge in the capitalist process of production. Knowledge becomes a direct force of production. In this context, Marx has raised the notion of the "general intellect".

> Nature builds no machines, no locomotives, railways, electric telegraphs, self-acting mules etc. These are products of human industry; natural material transformed into organs of the human will over nature, or of human participation in nature. They are organs of the human brain, created by the human hand; the power of knowledge, objectified. The development of fixed capital indicates to what degree general social knowledge has become a direct force of production, and to what degree, hence, the conditions of the process of social life itself have come under the control of the general intellect and been transformed in accordance with it. To what degree the powers of social production have been produced, not only in the form of knowledge, but also as immediate organs of social practice, of the real life process.
>
> (Marx 1997b)

There has been an intensification and extension of informational commodities being based on knowledge, ideas, communication, relationships, emotional artefacts, cultural content, etc. in the last decades of capitalist production. That is to say, labour is not only based on information, but information and communication are now direct forms of labour. Different types of work include agricultural, industrial, and informational labour (Fuchs and Sevignani 2013, 257). Autonomist Marxism has coined the notion of "immaterial labour" in this context. "That is, labor that produces an immaterial good, such as a service, a cultural product, knowledge, or communication" (Hardt and Negri 2000, 290).

In the following, I will apply the analysis of the dialectics of productive forces and relations discussed in Chapter 1 to the survey results and social media. The mode of production of social media is based on productive forces including social media users and objects and instruments of labour as well as relations of production of social media owners and users (see Figure 7.2).

The productive forces of social media are a system of social media users and facts and factors of the process of social media production that cause and influence online labour. The relationship between social media users (subject) and

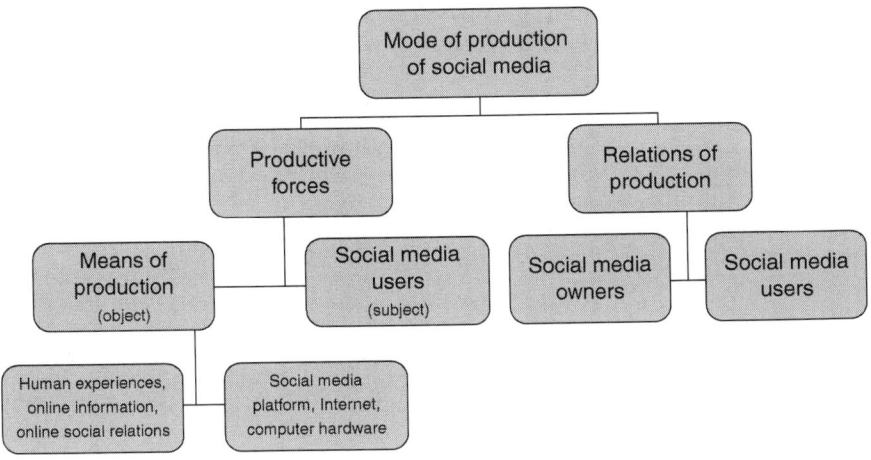

Figure 7.2 Mode of production of social media.

means of production (object) forms the productive forces of social media. On the one hand, subjective productive forces are the unity of physical and intellectual abilities of a social media user. On the other hand, objective productive forces are factors of the process of digital labour; that is, objects of digital labour such as human experiences, online information, and online social relations (Fuchs and Sevignani 2013, 255) and instruments of digital labour including social media platforms, the Internet, and digital devices (desktop, laptop, tablet, mobile phone, etc.). Social media users make use of PCs, the Internet, and social media platforms in order to establish and organize human experiences, online information, and online social relations. These are "the general productive forces of the social brain" (Marx 1997b). The process is extinguished in the product and includes online profiles, new social relationships, and new community buildings.

The process of social media production takes place within certain social structures; that is to say, relations of production of the social media owner and users. The principle of web 2.0 platforms is the massive provision and storage of personal(ly) (identifiable) data being systematically evaluated, marketed, and used for targeted advertising. With the help of legal instruments including privacy policies and terms of use, social networking sites have the right to store, analyse, and sell personal data of their users to third parties for targeted advertising in order to accumulate profit. Social media activities such as creating profiles and sharing ideas on Facebook, announcing personal messages on Twitter, uploading or watching videos on YouTube, and writing personal entries on Blogger enable the collection, analysis, and sale of personal data by commercial web platforms. Web 2.0 applications and social software sites collect and analyse personal behaviour, preferences, and interests with the help of systematic and automated computer processes and sell these data to advertising agencies in order to accumulate profit. Online time is monitored, stored, and packaged to data commodities, and advertising clients purchase these online data packages in order to be able to advertise their products to user groups. An asymmetrical economic power relation characterizes web 2.0, because companies own the platform, the data of their users, and the profit, and decide on terms of use and privacy policies. Users do not share ownership rights, do not control corporate social media platforms, have no right to decide on terms of use and privacy policies, and do not benefit from the profit being created out of user data produced for free. Commercial new media accumulate capital by the dispossession (Harvey 2003) of personal information and data being produced in social and creative processes. This process may be considered to be the accumulation by dispossession on web 2.0 (Jakobsson and Stiernstedt 2010). From the point of view of the productive forces, social media are tools that entail social and communicative characteristics. From the point of view of the relations of production, the structure of corporate social media primarily maximizes the power of the dominating economic class that owns such platforms and benefits the few at the expense of the many. Social media platforms are unsocial capitalist corporations. It thus make sense to speak about (un)social media in capitalist society.

The business model of social media is very advantageous for another reason. While the productive forces of industrial forms of capitalist production such as oil, silicon, technology, and science are costly, the productive forces of social media including the Internet, computer hardware, human experiences, online information, and online social relations make users available at their own costs and with enjoyment and amusement.

Marx's dialectically mediated spheres of the capitalistic economy of production, circulation, and consumption as outlined in the surveillance chapter now work the other way around. Individuals produce personal data on the Internet, which are circulated by companies such as Google and Facebook, and these personal data are consumed by advertising agencies (Allmer 2012a, 112). The distinction between the spheres of production and consumption tends to become blurred. "Production is consumption; consumption is production. Consumptive production. Productive consumption" (Marx 1986, 30). Andrejevic (2011) speaks in this context about social media as a new mode of production, Fuchs (2010c; 2010e) about the "Internet prosumer commodity", and Comor (2010) talks about "digital prosumption and alienation".

The mode of production of social media is based on a dialectical relationship of productive forces and relations of production. The economic structure enables and constrains the development of the productive forces, which form the relations of production. The competition between Facebook, Google, MySpace, Twitter, Blogger, LinkedIn, etc. forces every company to increase users on a quantitative and qualitative level and to integrate ever more services into their platform in order to accumulate profit. The social networking business may be considered as a dynamic and very competitive online field with potential economic ups and downs. For example, the social networking service Google+ was launched in June 2011. The launch of Google+ was a further attempt by Google to rival Facebook and others after previous forays into the social media economy such as Orkut (launched in 2004, now operated entirely by Google Brazil), Google Friend Connect (launched 2008, retired 2012), and Google Buzz (launched 2010, retired in 2011) had failed. Google+ is operated by Google and now has 135 million active monthly users (Google Official Blog 2012). This shows that the relations of production and competition drive the development of the productive forces of corporate social media forward. When people (having a digital device and an Internet access) sign up as users and create profiles on Facebook, accepting the data use policy, and expressing their experiences and enter online relations being controlled by capital, they simultaneously accept the ownership of the platform and reproduce the relation between Facebook and their users. This indicates that the productive forces form the relations of production of social media.

One of the main results of the survey is that students perceive social, informative, and communicative aspects as major opportunities of social networking sites. Commercial social media present themselves as platforms enabling sociability, networking, connectivity, and communication. Facebook (2012) says that its "mission is to give people the power to share and make the world more open and connected". In reference to Marx, the social and communicative qualities may be interpreted as the use value of social media. A use value reveals different qualities of products and exists if usefulness occurs and human needs can be fulfilled. The usefulness emerges out of the material nature of things. Use values are only realized in consumption. According to our respondents' answers, the maintenance of existing contacts, friendships, and family relations, social relationships over spatial distances, information and news, finding and renewing old contacts, sharing photos and other media, and establishing new contacts occur as the usefulness of new media fulfilling human needs. The use value of social media is realized through using such platforms. Just as sitting on it may be the use value of a chair, so the realization of social and communicative characteristics is the use value of social media.

But the specific characteristic of the capitalist mode of production is that a use value of a commodity is only a means to an end in order to produce an exchange value of a commodity. The use values "are also the material bearers [*Träger*] of ... exchange-value" (Marx 1976, 126). The use value is therefore the condition of the exchange value. The exchange value is a social form and is only realized through social exchange. If a thing is not only a use value, but also an exchange value, it evolves into a commodity. The exchange value expresses the commodity value in the form of money.

Because commercial web platforms exchange data for money in terms of selling the data commodity on the market that is expressed in the form of money, one may argue that the monitoring, surveillance, analysis, and sale of private data are the exchange value of social media transforming personal data to commodities. The following examples of answers that were given to the survey question of the major disadvantages of social networking platforms indicate that targeted advertising and the commercial selling of personal data are considered to be concerns (authors' translations from German to English):

- "Unlawful usage of data, forwarding, personalized advertising, algorithm of face recognition, alienation of the term 'friend', meanwhile group pressure and social pressure to join in" (Respondent ID 1559706802).
- "That personal information, which I often expose unconsciously, is used against me. Besides I am annoyed of personalized advertising" (Respondent ID 1559719051).
- "Transparent individual, commercial usage of user data" (Respondent ID 1566130533).
- "(Prospective) increasing usage of all collected data, user details for market research; that is profit maximization ... a further step towards 'global police state', in which not the people/politicians will rule any longer, but corporations and lobbies ... opaque, non-user-friendly privacy settings" (Respondent ID 1525388777).

These examples may be interpreted as answers to the exchange value of privately owned social media platforms. However, almost 60 per cent of our respondents stress that surveillance as a result of data abuse, data forwarding, or a lack of data protection is the main threat of SNS, but only 2.6 per cent of the Austrian students mention receiving advertising or spam and 2.3 per cent list commercial selling of personal data as the greatest concern. This shows that although surveillance in general is considered to be the greatest disadvantage, only a minority of $2.6\% + 2.3\% = 4.9\%$ of our respondents are aware of and opposed to the exchange value and the commodity character of social media.

Just as commodities entail a dual character, namely use value and value, so labour embodied in commodities entails a dual character, namely concrete and abstract labour. Labour contained in commodities has a twofold nature. Concrete labour produces use values, is visible, and is existential for human life. Labour is creating value only as a result of the abstraction from the concrete form of labour; that is, an abstraction of labour occurs mediated by exchange. Marx further differentiates between labour process and valorisation process. The labour process characterizes the qualitative part and creates use value in the process of production, whereas the valorization process characterizes the quantitative part and creates value. This means that for our respondents' answers the perceived social and communicative advantages of social networking platforms such as finding friends and sharing photos entail concrete labour in the labour process and the users produce data profiles being sold to third parties in order to accumulate profit entail abstract labour in the valorization process.

Corporate social media use is the connection of use and exchange value, of concrete and abstract labour, and of a labour and valorization process. Social media platforms simultaneously satisfy user needs and serve profit interests, and are means of communication and means of production (Fisher 2012, 174–177). Human sociality is used for capital accumulation. This dichotomy is reflected in my survey questions about the greatest advantages and disadvantages of social networking sites. It is often claimed that a political economy approach focuses too much on economic structures and overlooks cultural experiences of individuals. On the contrary, cultural studies analyse cultural aspects without taking into account relations and forces of production (Murdock 2000, 2012). Applying Marx's distinction between use and exchange value, concrete and abstract labour, and of a labour and valorization process to commercial social media platforms, takes into consideration that new media entail both creative and social activities and the logic of commodification of personal data resulting in capital accumulation.

The answers about the greatest benefits and risks show that a vast majority of students in the survey perceive social opportunities as great advantages that may be interpreted as concrete labour of creating use value in the labour process of social networking platforms. Only a minority of the respondents are aware of and opposed to the data commodity and the accumulation of profit, which may be interpreted as abstract labour of creating exchange value in the valorization process of social networking sites. Social media platforms present themselves as participatory platforms of sharing and connecting and not as platforms of profit. Facebook says about itself that it is a tool of social relations and creative activities, and avoids speaking about making money.

I have shown in Chapter 1 that technology and media as productive forces are a medium and outcome of capitalist development. Productive forces are an outcome of capitalist movements, because the existing organization of capitalist society and the vital need for constantly raising productivity drives this society towards technological innovations. Media and technology are also the medium of capitalist dynamics, because they are powerful means of raising productivity. Just as media and technology in general, so social networking sites are the media and outcome of capitalist development. The emergence of corporate social software may be seen in the context of the need to find new strategies of capital accumulation under post-Fordist conditions after the dot.com crisis around the turn of the millennium. Social media are thus the outcome of capitalist dynamics. Social networking platforms' business models are based on targeted advertising and may be seen as massive surveillance machinery for producing surplus value and accumulating profit. Web 2.0 is therefore also a medium of capitalist movements.

The leading discourse that "'social media' are new ('web 2.0'), pose new opportunities for participation, will bring about an 'economic democracy', enable new forms of political struggle ('Twitter revolution'), more democracy ('participatory culture'), etc." (Fuchs 2012c, 698) strengthens the ideological agenda of privately owned social networking platform owners. Due to the fact that a large part of social medias' revenue comes from advertising and thus depends on the extensity and intensity of users, it is very important to promote the benefits and to hide profit interests in order to maintain a good image of the service as well as to avoid a reduction of users. The survey results may be seen in this context. The exchange value and commodity character of social media is concealed behind the use value in public discourse, in commercial social media's self-presentation, and obviously in the answers about the greatest concerns and risks in our survey. Social media platforms are "playground and factory" (Scholz

2013). The contemporary Internet is both a social medium and a new space of capital accumulation with ideological tendencies of revealing the first and simultaneously concealing the second. The new media user apparently considers him- or herself as being a social and creative subject, but is treated as an object serving platform owners' capital interests. The following contradiction forms the usage of social media and is partly reflected in our study results: the appearance of social networking sites in terms of being a tool of socializing and networking and the existence of social networking sites in terms of being a massive surveillance machinery of profit accumulation and the total commodification of online social relations and human life. It is often claimed that a critique of political economy, which is rooted in economic theory, focuses more on commodity critique and a critical theory, which is rooted in social theory and philosophy, and more on ideology critique (Fuchs 2012c, 696). Due to the fact that the propagation of ideologies and the availability of commodities are interconnected core elements of capitalist society, a Marxist contribution of media, technology, information, and communication should focus on the role of media in the context of commodification and ideology (Murdock and Golding 1997, 3–5; Fuchs 2012c, 697); or, speaking more generally, in the context of base and superstructure as outlined in Chapter 1. My interpretation of the survey results is an attempt to integrate both basic commodity and superstructural ideology critique. Ideological deceptions concealing the exchange value behind the use value of social media strengthen a further commodification of the online world. Privately owned social software platforms and their interests in data commodity and capital accumulation form ideologies of a participatory culture of sharing and connecting. Hence, corporate social media are characterized by a mutual shaping of ideologies and processes of commodification.

A precondition for the capitalist mode of production is the separation of producers and means of production and the double free worker, which is a result of historical developments. (1) The worker must have labour power at his or her disposal, must be the possessor of his or her person and free the proprietor of his or her own labour capacity and time, and must not fall victim to feudal conditions. (2) The worker must be free of means of production and commodities in order to be forced to offer his or her labour power as commodity on the market.

> For the transformation of money into capital … the owner of money must find the free worker available on the commodity-market; and this worker must be free in the double sense that as a free individual he can dispose of his labour-power as his own commodity, and that, on the other hand, he has no other commodity for sale, i.e. he is rid of them, he is free of all the objects needed for the realization [*Verwirklichung*] of his labour power.
>
> (Marx 1976, 272–273)

Corporate social media's business model requires that users generate data commodities. (1) Users must be free proprietors of their capacities and time in order to fulfil social and communication needs on social software platforms. Besides fulfilling wage labour, people need free time at their disposal to create profiles and share ideas on Facebook, announce personal messages on Twitter, upload or watch videos on YouTube, and write personal entries on Blogger. (2) Users must be free of the commons, resources, and the ownership and control of social net-working sites in order to be forced into expressing experiences and to enter online relations being controlled by capital and producing data commodities as user. In this sense, corporate social media users are double free users.

A negative repercussion of technology in the capitalist mode of production is the redundancy of a human labour force (Marx 1976, 553). A technical innovation in the process of production only takes place if the value of the new technology to the commodity is lower than the value of the former living labour force. This means that capitalists only displace labour power with machinery, if, calculated on a life span, costs can be reduced. It indicates the competitive relationship between human beings and machinery in capitalism. By employing technical innovations the amount of workers will be reduced. This shows the general antagonistic char-acter of capitalism being summarized in the tendency of the rate of profit to fall; that is, the production of surplus value causes a rise in constant capital and a fall in variable capital (c/v rises). New media users are not getting paid in a traditional way as are industrial workers and produce data commodities for free. More users do not result in more costs, but in more profit for corporate social media platforms by reducing variable capital costs. Besides the fact that it seems difficult to dis-place users with technology, the business model of social networking platforms is thus not based on a redundancy of human labour force, but rather on a permanent increase of users and variable capital that is for free. For example, Facebook was initially limited to students of certain US universities when it was launched in 2004. The social networking site is now open to everyone aged 13 years or older and is available in over 70 languages. Facebook had 1.1 billion monthly active users in December 2012 and its annual revenue was US$5.1 billion in 2012 (Secu-rities and Exchange Commission 2013). Taking the development of the amount of human labour power into consideration, one may argue that there is a reversal tendency in the business model of corporate social media in contrast to traditional forms of capital accumulation.

Due to coercive laws of the capitalist process of production, the overall aim of capitalists is to produce as much surplus value as possible in order to accumu-late profit. There are two different possibilities of doing so: the production of absolute surplus value by the extension of the working day and the production of relative surplus value by the intensification of the working day and increasing productivity.

> I call that surplus-value which is produced by the lengthening of the working day, absolute surplus-value. In contrast to this, I call that surplus-value which arises from the curtailment of the necessary labour-time, and from the corresponding alteration in the respective lengths of the two com-ponents of the working day, relative surplus-value.
>
> (Marx 1976, 432)

Social networking services have an interest in that as many users as possible are as active as possible and spend as much time as possible online in order to be able to create as many data commodities as possible resulting in more capital accumulation.

> Capital has one sole driving force, the drive to valorize itself, to create surplus-value, to make its constant part, the means of production, absorb the greatest possible amount of surplus labour. Capital is dead labour which, vampire-like, lives only by sucking living labour, and lives the more, the more labour it sucks.
>
> (Marx 1976, 342)

The extension of online time may be seen as the production of absolute surplus value and the increase of users' productivity may be understood as the production of relative surplus value of social media.

Facebook, for instance, has been very successful in providing its services to individuals everywhere and integrating these services into the daily lives of its users. Many new smart phone providers including Apple, Samsung, Microsoft, Google, and Nokia offer access to Facebook services either through their web-browsers or applications. The applications are developed and provided by Facebook and may be downloaded for free from different stores such as the Apple App Store as "Facebook for iPhone", Google Play (formerly Android Market) as "Facebook for Android", and Windows Mobile Marketplace. The Facebook applications and mobile versions are customized for the use of the social software platform on smart phones and include similar services to the website including extra features such as a real-time locator in order to be able to find nearby places or to share one's current location on Facebook.

There has been a continuous increase in mobile users of Facebook over recent years: 101 million people used Facebook in December 2009, 245 million in December 2010, 432 million in December 2011, and 680 million in December 2012 on a mobile phone every month (Securities and Exchange Commission 2013). Providing such mobile and flexible services may be seen as a very successful strategy to extend users' time of being online, and collecting and selling more data packages and accumulating capital, because it opens up the potential of being connected without spatio-temporal barriers. It is thus no surprise that the CEO of Facebook, Mark Zuckerberg, states:

> I'm … really happy that over 600 million people now share and connect on Facebook every month using mobile devices. People who use our mobile products are more engaged, and we believe we can increase engagement even further as we continue to introduce new products and improve our platform.
>
> (TechCrunch 2012)

Applications such as "Facebook for Android" and "Facebook for iPhone" are very useful tools for the production of absolute surplus value through the extension of online time on social media.

A further strategy to extend online time is Facebook's social plugins such as the Like button, Send button, Comments box, Activity Feed, and Recommendations (other profit-oriented platforms including Twitter and Google+ have similar features). These are features appearing as plugins on websites outside Facebook. When you click, for example, the Like button of an article on the Sun website, it appears on your profile and you are able to share it with your friends and others on Facebook. The plugins are promoted as tools to share experiences off Facebook with friends and others on Facebook. Many popular sites such as the Sun, Nike, Ebay, the BBC, and Al Jazeera have installed Facebook's social plugins.

As long as users are logged in on Facebook, these plugins allow Facebook to monitor visitors across the web, even if those visitors do not click such buttons. When loading a web page having social plugins enabled and the user is logged in on Facebook (it is not necessary that the Facebook site is open in the browser), the user's browser connects to Facebook's servers that record the visited website as well as the visitor's IP address and Facebook ID (Stallman 2012). Facebook's data use policy states in this context:

> We receive data when you visit a site with a social plugin. We keep this data for a maximum of 90 days. After that, we remove your name or any other personally identifying information from the data, or combine it with other people's data in a way that it is no longer associated with you.
>
> (Facebook 2012)

With these tools, Facebook is able to collect a huge amount of data of who visits what and when on sites having enabled such a button. Facebook's social plugins are an extension of being exploited by Facebook and therefore a form of the production of absolute surplus value, because with the help of these tools the corporate social networking site is able to collect, analyse, and sell the personal data of its users, even if they are currently not visiting Facebook.

Privately owned social software platforms collect, analyse, assess, and sell personal data with the help of systematic and automated computer processes. Digital data are packaged together with similar users' data to digital databases. The benefit of digital compared to traditional and analogue data is that they can be automatically collected, assessed, and remixed, and duplicated without destruction of the original data (Fuchs 2011a, 116). Digital data are available in real time, can be distributed at high speed all over the world, are easy and cheap to collect, and are geographically decentralized and temporally continuous (Marx 2002). When, for instance, someone adds the current place of residence and some hobbies on his or her profile of a social networking site, these digital data may be automatically packaged together with several similar users' data commodities being available in real time for third parties, are geographically decentralized, and temporally continuous. The implementation of automated computer processes into social software that generate digital databases for targeted advertising may be interpreted as a form of rising productivity and production of relative surplus value, because it enables more capital accumulation by intensification at a given time period.

Autonomist Marxism has raised the concept of the "common". The germ form (*Keimform*) of capitalism is the commodity and the germ form of communism is the common (Dyer-Whiteford 2007, 81; Hardt and Negri 2009, 273). A commodity is a good produced for exchange and a common is a good produced by collectivities to be shared by everyone. The common is the dialectical sublation of private property and public goods. Murdock (2013, 157) distinguishes in this context between "three moral economies", namely commodities, public goods, and gifts. The idea of the latter is much the same as the concept of the common. By the common Hardt and Negri (2009, viii) mean

> first of all, the common wealth of the material world – the air, the water, the fruits of the soil, and all nature's bounty – which in classic European political texts is often claimed to be the inheritance of humanity as a whole, to be shared together. We consider the common also and more significantly those results of social production that are necessary for social interaction and further production, such as knowledges, languages, codes, information, affects, and so forth.

That is to say, the commons are material/physical and immaterial/intellectual goods that are both incorporated into alternative projects of the multitude and partially produced within the empire. The capitalist logic has a very contradictory relationship to the common, because it needs and opposes it at the same time (Sandoval 2014, 233). Capital rests on the common and cannot survive without it as well as permanently trying to expropriate and commodify the commons. The commons are produced and reproduced by all but are appropriated only by capital in order to achieve profit. Capitalist accumulation and development paradoxically require and even make possible the expansion of the common and simultaneously tend to destroy it (Hardt and Negri 2009, 153). The capitalist logic is based on collective production and productive subjectivities, and depends ever more on the common due to an increased importance of information, communication, knowledge, and creativity for capitalist production. The capitalist command privatizes economic, political, cultural, natural, and technological commons again and again, and strives to transform them into private properties. Hence, current capitalist accumulation expropriates and destroys the commons. But today's network, communication, intellectual, cultural, and creative products are easily reproduced and tend towards being common and thereby question the capitalist logic of private property. Murdock (2013, 162) thus speaks of the "digital commons". The productive forces are organized around informational networks (Fuchs 2008). Information may be duplicated without destruction of the original data and may be distributed all over the world, resulting in a multitude of ownerships, and undermines the capitalist logic of individual private property. Information is hard to control in single places and by single owners, and networks are a negation of individual ownership (Fuchs 2009b, 76; Gorz 2010). Informational products such as communication, affective relationships, and knowledge are able to expand the realm of the social and common. "Contemporary capitalist production by addressing its own needs is opening up the possibility of and creating the bases for a social and economic order grounded in the common" (Hardt and Negri 2009, x). The logic of the common shines through the logic of commodity and as a result contradicts capitalist command. The commons come into friction with capital's hegemony. In this sense, one could say that "not only has the bourgeoisie forged the weapons that bring death to itself; it has also called into existence the men who are to wield those weapons – the digital working class – the creators" (Moglen 2003, 5). The economy of the empire and the economy of the common collide, resulting in social struggles and conflicts. New information technologies appear as both instruments for the circulation of commodities and means for the circulation of struggles (Dyer-Witheford 1999, 121–122). Digital productive forces advance new forms and strategies of capital accumulation, and undercut the commodity character and point towards new forms of cooperation. The productive forces of new technologies and social media are forms of capitalist development and fetters of capitalism. Paraphrasing Marx, one may argue that the digital productive forces have become incompatible with the current relations of production (Fuchs 2009b, 77). "At a certain stage of their development, the material productive forces of society come in conflict with the existing relations of production" (Marx 1951, 329). The productive forces of informational capitalism mature the contradiction and antagonism of the capitalist form of production and simultaneously ripen "the elements for forming a new society and the forces tending towards the overthrow of the old one" (Marx 1976, 635). This means that "the productive forces developing in the womb of bourgeois society create the material conditions for the solution of that antagonism" (Marx 1951, 329).

Alternative and critical social media projects of the multitude that strengthen the logic of the commons include diaspora*, N-1, Occuppii, and TheGlobalSquare. But

> neoliberal capital, confronting the debacle of free market policies, is now turning to a 'Plan B', in which limited versions of commons, pollution trading schemes, community development and open-source and file sharing practices are introduced as subordinate aspects of a capitalist economy, where voluntary cooperation subsidizes: Web 2.0 is a paradigm case.
>
> (Dyer-Whiteford 2009, 1)

Corporate social media platforms of the empire that transform the commons into private properties are, to name but a few, Facebook, Google+, Twitter, and YouTube. If we take a look at the usage of social networking sites in the survey, it must unfortunately be said that the vast majority of the respondents use commercial web 2.0 platforms provided by the empire (96.8 per cent use Facebook, 16.8 per cent use studiVZ, and 11.9 per cent use Xing), and only 0.3 per cent use alternative social media of the multitude (diaspora*). The activities being mentioned as the greatest advantages of social networking sites in our survey are part of the commons and result, as Hardt and Negri (2009, viii) emphasize, out of social production being necessary for social interaction and further production such as knowledge, languages, codes, information, and affects. Social media users are creative subjectivities producing the information, communication, and network commons collectively. Facebook, Google, etc. need and rest on and therefore provide space for the development and expansion of the commons being produced cooperatively. Simultaneously, these platforms oppose the common by expropriating and commodifying it and transform the common into private properties. The antagonistic character between the requirement and need on the one hand, and destruction and elimination on the other hand of the information and communication commons forms profit-oriented social software platforms in contemporary capitalism that is organized around informational networks. Our survey question about the most important opportunities may be seen in the context of the common.

Lukács (1971, 91, originally published in 1923) has already argued that "the fate of the worker becomes the fate of society as a whole". Autonomist Marxism likewise claims that capital tends to subsume the whole society into the production process and the logic of the factory is extended to society (Wright 2002, 37–38). In his article "La fabbrica e la società" (originally published in *Quaderni Rossi*, 1962), Tronti claims that:

> at the highest level of capitalist development, the social relation becomes a *moment* of the relation of production, the whole society becomes an *articulation* of production. In other words, society as a whole lives according to the factory and the factory extends its exclusive domination over society as a whole.
>
> (Tronti quoted in Turchetto 2008, 290)

Capital tends to control society as well as social labour and extends from consumption to reproduction and the organization of leisure. Society functions as a moment of production, where the border between working and spare time becomes increasingly blurred (Gorz 2010, 22) both spatially and temporally.

> The most radical aspect of this socialisation of labour is the blurring of waged and non-waged time. The activities of people not just as workers but as students, consumers, shoppers and viewers are now directly integrated into the production process.
>
> (Dyer-Witheford 1999, 80)

The social factory is therefore a "factory without walls" (Dyer-Witheford 1999, 80). Because capital tends to expropriate elements of labouring communication and cooperation and extends exploitation to networks, the social factory may also be considered as an information and communication factory. Capital automates the entire social factory and the whole of society becomes a wired workplace. It is the pure commodification of human activity. These developments cause a new class recomposition and a widening of the traditional working-class concept including house workers, students, informational workers, the unwaged, retirees, migrants, precarious workers, etc. But the new social class is character-ized by fragmentation and stratification. It is scattered territorially, socially, and culturally, causing new problems of uniting. The oppressed class of the social factory has no central front of struggle. It is a diffuse class in a diffuse factory.

> They [new forms of labour power] are *disorganised*, insofar as they come into being outside the orbit of the traditional workers' movement, towards whose symbols and institutions they are often indifferent or hostile. They are *dispersed*, across an enormous variety of spatially separated and qualita-tively diverse sites. And they are *divided*, in a multitude of ways, but par-ticularly by the lines separating the relatively privileged cadres of "scientific labour" from the super-exploited "social" labour that sustains it – a division frequently reinforced by ethnicity and gender.
>
> (Dyer-Witheford 1999, 96)

One may argue that corporate social media platforms are social factories having extended logics of the factory to the Internet and have subsumed society and social activities into the capitalist process of production. Facebook, Google, etc. have transformed exploitative elements from the workplace to cyberspace. However, this does not mean that exploitative forms of industrial labour no longer exist and are replaced by immaterial labour, as some post-operaist and autonomist Marxists tend to argue (Turchetto 2008). Social media users are part of the social factory that work for free in their spare time by ful-filling social and communicative needs as our respondents indicated in the survey. The platforms may be considered as information and communication factories without walls. It marks the total commodification of social life, human communication, experiences, feelings, and creativity on the Net. The whole of social life is subsumed under capital on the Internet. The users do not share ownerships rights and do not benefit from the profit of these platforms, and are part of the oppressed class in twenty-first-century informational capit-alism. This new social class is spatially and socially fragmented and stratified, and has no political representation or union. Social media users are thus a diffuse class. The survey question about the main concerns and risks may be seen in the context of the social factory.

Although the productive forces of social media are shaped by value creation in capitalist societies, the development of the productive forces indicates opportunities of the commons within different relations of production (see Figure 7.3).

Corporate social media usage is the connection of use and exchange value, of concrete and abstract labour, as well as of a labour and valorization process. This dichotomy is reflected in the survey's questions about the greatest advant-ages and disadvantages of social networking sites. In addition, the commons come into friction with capital's hegemony. The logic of the common shines through beneath the logic of commodity and thereby contradicts capitalist command.

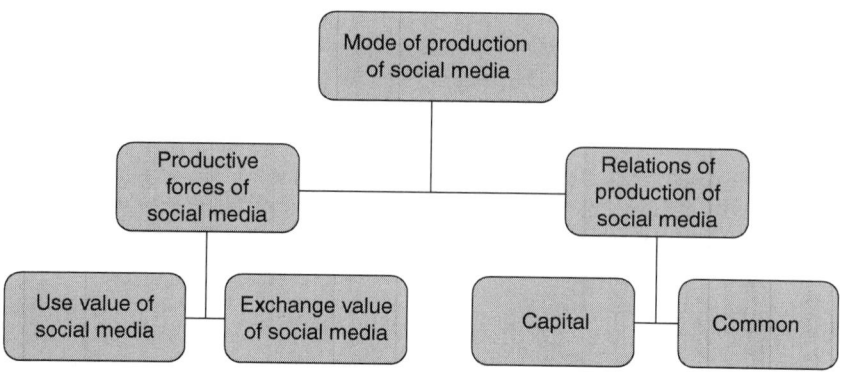

Figure 7.3 Different possibilities of productive forces and relations of production of social media.

Conclusion

This chapter dealt with the dialectics of technological design and assessment and the (dis)advantages of social media in the second section. The following points sum up the most important outcomes:

- The client–server architecture dominating the Internet is designed and constructed as control and surveillance technology, which is embedded in the capitalist relations of production. This technology may increase the risks that people do not know where their data are stored and what is happening to those data. It may strengthen intransparency and uncontrollability of personal data and files. This is reflected in the perceived fears and risks of the survey participants when it comes to the greatest disadvantages of social networking sites.
- The peer-to-peer system and mobile webservers operated with the help of free software could clean up the servers of Facebook, Google, and so on and may undermine the capitalist logic of centralized data storage, surveillance, and the data commodity. Peer-to-peer file sharing allows open access to and free distribution and common ownership of digital knowledge (music, films, software, books, etc.). Such technologies are hard to control and capital's and communities' interests collide, resulting in social struggles and conflicts.
- Our survey shows that only 2.5 per cent of the students list communication in political and interest groups as an important aspect and a beneficial characteristic of social media shows that such platforms are not a priori political and critical places. Although social networking is shaped by individualized communication and corporate interests, it also poses possibilities for group formation and cooperation might being channelled into such

collective political projects, as the Occupy movement, the Indignados movement in Spain, or the Arab Spring showed.
- Corporate social media are ideological platforms, because they give the illusionary impression that everyone now has the opportunity to present oneself to the public and to receive attention, while most people on web 2.0 are marginalized and invisible, and cannot influence political decisions or define cultural values compared to powerful political and economic actors. The material resources of participation are asymmetrical and show the limitations of freedom of speech on new media.

The dialectics of productive forces and relations of production and the (dis) advantages of social media were treated in the third section. The subsequent arguments summarize the main results:

- There has been an intensification and extension of informational commodities being based on knowledge, ideas, communication, relationships, emotional artefacts, cultural content, etc. in the last decades of capitalist production. Labour is not only based on information, but information and communication are now direct forms of labour.
- The productive forces of social media are a system of social media users and facts and factors of the process of social media production that cause and influence online labour. The process of social media production takes place within certain social structures; that is to say, relations of production of social media owners and users.
- The mode of production of social media is based on a dialectical relationship of productive forces and relations of production. The economic structure enables and constrains the development of the productive forces, which form the relations of production.
- Corporate social media use is the connection of use and exchange value, of concrete and abstract labour, and of a labour and valorization process. This dichotomy is reflected in the survey's questions about the greatest advantages and disadvantages of social networking sites.
- Just as with media and technology in general, so social networking sites are media and outcome of capitalist development.
- A precondition for the capitalist mode of production is the double free worker, which is a result of historical developments. A precondition for the capitalist mode of production of social media is the double free user.
- The extension of online time may be seen as the production of absolute surplus value, and the increase of users' productivity may be understood as the production of relative surplus value of social media.
- The antagonistic character between the requirement and need on the one hand and destruction and elimination on the other hand of the information and communication commons forms profit-oriented social software platforms in contemporary capitalism that is organized around informational

networks. The survey question about the most important opportunities may be seen in the context of the common.

- One may argue that corporate social media platforms are social factories having extended logics of the factory to the Internet and have subsumed society and social activities into the capitalist process of production. The survey question about the main concerns and risks may be considered in terms of the social factory.

Note

1 "Mit der Maschine ... erhält die Herrschaft ... nicht nur soziale ... sondern sozusagen technologische Wahrheit."

8   Conclusion

The task of this chapter is to answer the main research question and to discuss the results in more detail. I bring together the arguments presented in the individual chapters and make a final statement about the subject presented.

The display of power and counter-power, domination and spaces of power struggles, and the commons and the commodification of the commons characterize modern society. The Internet and social media are fields of conflict in this power struggle. The media are power structures and sites of power struggles, and are able to support both the expansion and the commodification of the commons. New media are tools for exerting power, domination, and counter-power. Based on a critical and dialectical perspective, it is possible to comprehend these contradictions occurring between emancipatory potentials of new and digital media that imply a logic of the commons and processes of commodification and enclosure that tend to jeopardize the commons and incorporate them into the logic of capital.

Critical and Marx-inspired media and information studies strives for the development of theoretical research methods (epistemology) in order to focus on the analysis of media, information, and communication in the context of domination, asymmetrical power relations, resource control, social struggles, exploitation, and alienation (ontology). Critical media and communication studies wants to overcome social injustices and supports political processes and social transformations towards the "communicative commons" (Murdock 2013, 160) and a commons-based information society (praxiology). The study at hand was structured according to this distinction. Part I discussed the development of theoretical foundations of the relationship between technology and society, productive forces and relations of production, and privacy and surveillance (epistemology). It focused in Part II on empirical results of social media in the context of advantages and disadvantages and emancipation and affirmation (ontology). Part III evaluated the prospects and limitations of the commons and commodification of the commons in the realm of digital media, and argued for the need of a techno-social revolution in terms of achieving a commons-based information society (praxiology). Parts I, II, and III were interconnected and shaped each other mutually. The recommendation to strengthen the idea of the communication and network commons and a real liberation of society was based on an empirical

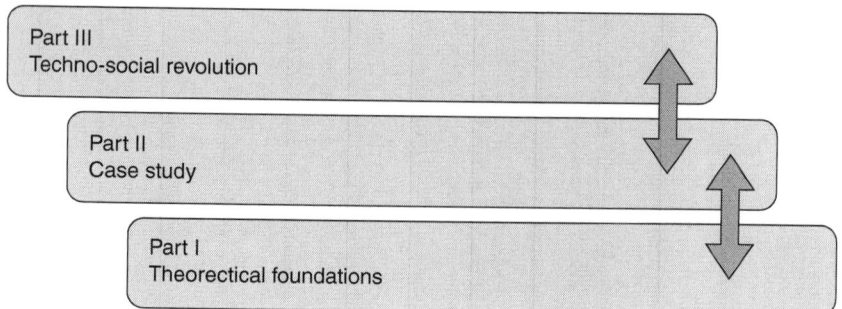

Figure 8.1 Inclusive relationship of Parts I, II, and III of this study.

case study of social media in the context of emancipation and affirmation grounded in the theoretical foundations of media, technology, and society. Part III built upon Part II and Part II built upon Part I (see Figure 8.1).

The overall aim of this work was to study the constraints and emancipatory potentials of new media and to assess to what extent digital and social media can strengthen the idea of the communication and network commons and a commons-based information society. Based on the results of the specific research questions posed in the individual chapters, it is now possible to answer the main research questions:

How do the constraints and emancipatory potentials of new media look like and to what extent can digital and social media strengthen the idea of the communication and network commons and a commons-based information society?

Technological constraints

I argued in Chapter 1 that asymmetrical social relationships of power and domination are already embedded in the conception, construction, maintenance, as well as modification of technics and that the technological design must be rooted in capitalist interests and social forces. Dominating the architecture of the Internet and social media platforms, the client–server computer network may be viewed as empirical evidence for this theoretical consideration. The client–server architecture structures the contemporary online world basically consisting of web servers operated by economically and politically powerful actors such as Google and Facebook, and clients used by individuals including social media users. The physical architecture of the Internet and the corresponding software entail hierarchical and structural forms of control, which enable centralized processing and storage of user data and log files. The dominant client–server technology fits well into the business model of corporate social media platform based on selling personal data. This technology includes the idea of the existence of proprietors of data centres and incorporates the potential of centralized control. It may increase the risks that people do not know where their data are stored and what is happening to those data, and may strengthen intransparency and uncontrollability of personal data and files (Moglen 2010). This is reflected in the perceived fears and risks of the survey participants when it comes to the greatest disadvantages of social networking sites. This example shows that capitalist technology is also, in its foundational form, a technology of power and domination. The repressive elements of technology in capitalist societies are not solely in its applications, but technology may inherently be a means of power and domination. Technology is a form of organization and maintenance of social relations, and a means of control and domination. Technological control is internal to their very structure (Feenberg 2002, 51) and therefore a transformation and redesign of technology is necessary in order to strengthen the idea of the commons and a real liberation of society.

Technological potentials

In contrast, the peer-to-peer system is a computer network where each computer can act as a client or server for other computers sharing access to various digital contents such as audio, video, and data files. Peers are equally privileged participants and are both suppliers and consumers of resources. Moglen (2010) suggests a mobile version for social networking. The best-known realizations of the peer-to-peer technology are file-sharing applications including Vuze and The Pirate Bay. These applications enable the direct exchange of files and data between computers on the Net. File sharing allows open access to and free distribution and common ownership of digital knowledge (music, films, software, books, etc.). Such technologies are hard to control and capital's and communities' interests collide, resulting in social struggles and conflicts. However, the Internet commodity economy also makes use of the peer-to-peer computer network system. This indicates that this technology is not immune to surveillance and commodification. "Everything becomes a commodity" (Gorz 2010, 23). Such a decentralized model could also be subsumed under capital, but with some structures it is more difficult. Overall, this points to the need for class struggle, revolution, and politics beyond technology.

Social potentials

I also claimed in Chapter 1 that technological effects depend on how technologies are used and technology cannot be isolated from its application. I have shown that the effects of the Internet and new media depend on how they are used in society. Social movements such as the Occupy movement and Anonymous and alternative media including Democracy Now! and Indymedia have the potential to establish a "counterpublic sphere" (Negt and Kluge 1993) and question capitalist logics. Or, speaking in terms of autonomist Marxism, the multitude is able to undermine capitalist hegemony in order to strengthen the idea of a commons-based society. The rise of the Internet has brought new opportunities for social movements and alternative media that often suffer from a lack of resources. Social movements are able to publish and spread alternative views and raise critical awareness cost-effectively on a global level. The Internet can support digital grassroots democracy and can give the powerless a say. Real technological potentials of cyberspace could be brought to fruition having "not yet" (Bloch 1986) been realized. The appearance of the World Wide Web and social media also contains potential, and it is important to uncover and reveal that hidden and suppressed potential for a real liberation of human beings. Although social networking is shaped by individualized communication and corporate interests, it also poses possibilities for group formation and cooperation might being channelled into collective political projects (Fuchs 2009b, 83), as the Occupy movement, the Indignados movement in Spain, or the Arab Spring have shown.

Social constraints

However, the multitude is confronted with problems of gaining visibility, and attracting publicity and attention on the Web, which is characterized by capitalist logics, marketing strategies, information overflows, and a loss in cyberspace. Powerful political and economic actors are in contrast very successful in raising visibility and attracting publicity in cyberspace. Due to capitalist structures of the Internet and asymmetrical distributions of material resources between the multitude and the empire on the one hand as well as the logic of one-dimensional thoughts (Marcuse), instrumental rationality (Horkheimer), manipulative culture industry (Adorno and Horkheimer), and global false consciousness of society (Marx) on the other hand, critical social movements and critical (social) media are confronted with marginalization and disappearing attention (on the Internet). The survey result that only 2.5 per cent of the students list communication in political and interest groups as important aspects and beneficial characteristics of social media shows that such platforms are not a priori political and critical places. Corporate social media are ideological platforms, because they provide the illusionary impression that everyone now has the opportunity to present oneself to the public and to receive attention, while most people on web 2.0 are marginalized and invisible, and are unable to influence political decisions and define cultural values compared to powerful political and economic actors, as I have demonstrated throughout this work. "One *believes* that one's contribution matters, that it means something to and within a context broader than oneself. Contributing to the information stream thus has a subjective registration effect detached from any actual impact or efficacy" (Dean 2009, 31). The material resources of participation are asymmetrical and show the limitations of freedom of speech in new media. Structural inequalities and power relations stratify public visibility and participation online (Sandoval and Fuchs 2010, 144). New technologies such as social software are an ideology and an expression of repressive tolerance in capitalist society. This is not caused through technics by itself

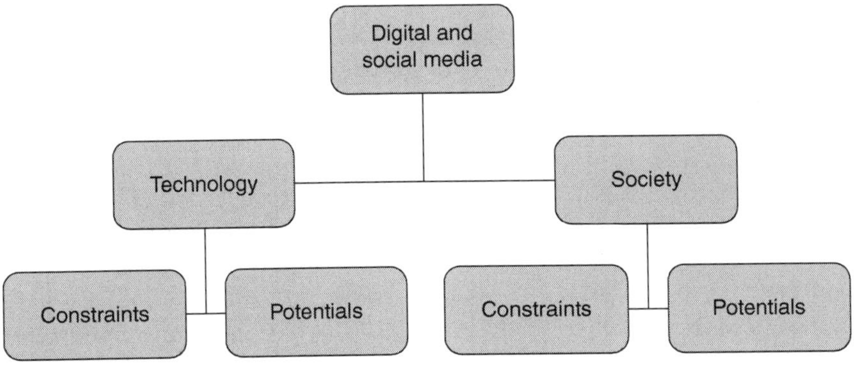

Figure 8.2 Technological and social constraints and potentials of digital and social media.

or by design, but rather results from the application of technology in capitalist society.

Figure 8.2 shows the limitations and emancipatory prospects of new media that are addressed in the main research questions.

In summary, digital and social media incorporate both technological as well as social constraints and potentials.

(Dis)like Facebook? Communication and network commons

The capitalist logic is based on collective production and productive subjectivities, and depends ever more on the common due to the increased importance of information, communication, knowledge, and creativity for capitalist production. The capitalist command again and again privatizes economic, political, cultural, natural, and technological commons and aims to transform them into private property. Hence, current capitalist accumulation expropriates and destroys the commons. But today's network, communication, intellectual, cultural, and creative products are easily reproduced and tend towards being common and thereby question the capitalist logic of private property. Informational products such as communication, affective relationships, and knowledge are able to expand the realm of the social and common. The logic of the common shines through beneath the logic of commodity and thereby contradicts capitalist command. The commons come into friction with capital's hegemony. The economy of the empire and the economy of the common collide, resulting in social struggles and conflicts. Digital productive forces advance new forms and strategies of capital accumulation, and undercut the commodity character and point towards new forms of cooperation. The productive forces of new technologies and social media are forms of capitalist development and fetters of capitalism. Paraphrasing Marx, one may argue that the digital productive forces have become incompatible with the current relations of production (Fuchs 2009b, 77). "At a certain stage of their development, the material productive forces of society come in conflict with the existing relations of production" (Marx 1951, 329). The productive forces of informational capitalism mature the contradiction and antagonism of the capitalist form of production, and simultaneously ripen "the elements for forming a new society and the forces tending towards the overthrow of the old one" (Marx 1976, 635). This means that "the productive forces developing in the womb of bourgeois society create the material conditions for the solution of that antagonism" (Marx 1951, 329).

The activities being mentioned as the greatest advantages of social networking sites in our survey are part of the commons and result, as Hardt and Negri (2009, viii) emphasize, from social production being necessary for social interaction and further production such as knowledge, languages, codes, information, and affects. Social media users are creative subjectivities producing the information and communication commons. Facebook, Google, etc. need and rest upon and therefore provide space for the development and expansion of the commons being produced cooperatively. Simultaneously, these platforms oppose the common by expropriating and commodifying it and transform the common into private properties. The antagonistic character between the requirement and need on the one hand and destruction and elimination on the other hand of the information and communication commons forms profit-oriented social software platforms in contemporary capitalism that is organized around informational networks. Based on a theoretically informed, critical perspective one can like and dislike Facebook simultaneously.

Commons-based information society

In reference to the dialectics of technological design and assessment, it has become clear that both technological and social changes are needed; or, speaking more generally, due to the fact that the productive forces are predetermined by exchange value, besides a change in the relations of production a change in the productive forces is also required in terms of achieving a commons-based information society.

Capitalism is an antagonistic social formation that shapes the ecological, technological, economic, political, and cultural level (Hofkirchner 2009; Fuchs 2011b, 52). An antagonism is a fundamental and aggravated contradiction and social conflict that is immanent to the existing society and cannot be resolved within it. The antagonistic character of contemporary informational capitalism is shown in ecology between ecological destruction and ecological preservation, in technology between technological alienation and human centredness, in economy between total commodification and common good, in polity between totalitarian democracy and basic democracy, and in culture between elitist influence and enclosure and egalitarian participation, openness, and accessibility (see Table 8.1).

Antagonisms such as those between possession and non-possession, decision-making and non-decision-making, and value definition and non-definition are

Table 8.1 Ecological, technological, economic, political and cultural antagonisms in twenty-first-century capitalism

Level	Antagonism
Ecological	Antagonism of ecological destruction and ecological preservation
Technological	Antagonism of technological alienation and human centredness
Economic	Antagonism of total commodification and common good
Political	Antagonism of totalitarian democracy and basic democracy
Cultural	Antagonism of elitist influence and enclosure and egalitarian participation, openness, and accessibility

Based on Hofkirchner (2009).

inherent to capitalist society and indicate economic class relationships and political-cultural social relationships. The challenge of the current century is to sublate (*aufheben*) technology and society in order to overcome the antagonistic characters of the economy, polity, culture, and nature and to point towards a commons-based information society. We need a techno-social revolution (Hofkirchner 2013, 246–247) for transformed productive forces within transformed relations of production and for a different technology in a different society oriented on social needs and ethical dimensions far from bourgeois values.

We must transform new information and communication technologies and begin to intervene in the design and assessment process of technology, instead of turning away from technology as technophobic groups, neo-Luddites, and some reactionary environmentalists suggest (Feenberg 1999, xiv; Dyer-Witheford 1999, 213; Lange 1990, 554). The anti-technological critique often highlights the alienation of human beings from nature caused by modern technology, the importance of "naturalness", and fetishizes traditional forms of exploited labour such as manual and craft labour. Although the technological environment of capitalism causes social and ecological problems and antagonisms, horse and plough are no solution to the alienation and exploitation of modern industrial labour. The nostalgic denial or reduction of technological dynamics to pre-technological and more primitive conditions is reactionary, moralizing, and romanticizing (Feenberg 2002, 188–190). This retreat behind the previous stage of civilization is deterministic, because it reduces social and ecological problems to technological problems and undialectic, because it denies the progressive potential of modern technology. A real liberation of human beings

> presuppose[s] a great increase in productive power, a high degree of its development. And ... this development of productive forces ... is an absolutely necessary practical premise, because without it privation, want is merely made general, and with want the struggle for necessities would begin again, and all the old filthy business [*die ganze alte Scheiße*] would necessarily be restored.
>
> (Marx and Engels 1998, 54)

A real economy in no way means abstinence from consumption and enjoyment, but rather the development of both the capabilities of production as well as the means of consumption (Marx 1997b). It would be dogmatic to deny that certain modern technologies such as radioactivity measuring stations, seismometers, electrocardiograms, the tsunami warning system DART (Deep-ocean Assessment and Reporting of Tsunamis), fire protection systems, and smog and air pollution warning systems (Fuchs 2011a, 129) are able to provide an immense alleviation and protection of human life.

> Not the arrest or reduction of technical progress, but the elimination of those of its features which perpetuate man's subjection to the apparatus and the intensification of the struggle for existence – to work harder in order to get more of the merchandise that has to be sold. In other words, electrification indeed, and all technical devices which alleviate and protect life, all the mechanization which frees human energy and time.
>
> (Marcuse 1969, 90)

We must govern the human metabolism with nature in a rational way and accomplish this with the least expenditure of human energy, because "the realm of freedom really begins only where labour determined by necessity and external expediency ends" (Marx 1991). We must redesign technology and adapt it to the needs of a real liberation of human beings.

My approach is comparable to what Hardt and Negri (2009, 101–118) termed "altermodernity" that moves beyond the opposition between modernity and anti-modernity. Altermodernity differs from modernity insofar as it breaks with modern power relations and it differs from anti-modernity insofar as it also includes progressive elements of modern society. Hardt and Negri accentuate that the concept of altermodernity represents a dialectics between modern society and anti-modern resistance. Altermodernity represents an alternative line within European Enlightenment, is based on workers' movements, and recognizes the importance of the common as a form of life.

> This conception of altermodernity gives us a preliminary way to pose the distinction between socialism and communism: whereas socialism ambivalently straddles modernity and antimodernity, communism must break with both of these by presenting a direct relation to the common to develop the paths of altermodernity.
>
> (Hardt and Negri 2009, 107)

Speaking in terms of dialectical philosophy, a qualitative change and a dialectical sublation (*Aufhebung*) of capitalist technology in general as well as ICT and new media in particular are necessary. That is to say, elimination of regressive elements (destructive productive forces), preservation of progressive elements (constructive productive forces), and elevation of new technological qualities on a higher level. These new emergent qualities are the negation of the negation, cannot be found on the lower level, and are a dynamic process of development.

> Such qualitative change would be transition to a higher stage of civilization if technics were designed and utilized for the pacification of the struggle for existence. In order to indicate the disturbing implications of this statement, I submit that such a new direction of technical progress would be the catastrophe of the established direction, not merely the quantitative evolution of the prevailing (scientific and technological) rationality but rather its catastrophic transformation, the emergence of a new idea of Reason, theoretical and practical.
>
> (Marcuse 1972, 179)

In advanced industrial societies, we do have "the change of turning quantitative technical progress into qualitatively different ways of life" (Marcuse 1969, 19).

The technological forces could reduce necessary labour time to a minimum in order to ensure free disposal over free time and to transform leisure into free time. "For the mature technological society, progressive automation of material and routine production to the point where the traditional ratio of (necessary) working time to free time is reversed – free time becoming 'full-time occupation' at the disposal of the individual" (Marcuse 2001, 42–43). The real technological aim is to eliminate scarcity and to fulfil human needs and ambitions of the "totally developed individual" (Marx 1976, 618). A real economy consists of both the saving of labour time and the development of productive forces.

> The free development of individualities, and hence not the reduction of necessary labour time so as to posit surplus labour, but rather the general reduction of the necessary labour of society to a minimum, which then corresponds to the artistic, scientific etc. development of the individuals in the time set free, and with the means created, for all of them.... For real wealth is the developed productive power of all individuals. The measure of wealth is then not any longer, in any way, labour time, but rather disposable time.... The saving of labour time [is] equal to an increase of free time, i.e. time for the full development of the individual ... being man himself.
>
> (Marx 1997b)

By means of technology we could shift the emphasis away from material production onto human self-realization. The technological progress could serve as the basis for a new way of free development of the human personality and to support the abilities of the socio- and the ecosphere.

> Technological progress would make it possible to decrease the time and energy spent in the production of the necessities of life, and a gradual reduction of scarcity and abolition of competitive pursuits could permit the self to develop from its natural roots. The less time and energy man has to expend

in maintaining his life and that of society, the greater the possibility that he can "individualize" the sphere of his human realization. Beyond the realm of necessity, the essential differences between men could unfold themselves: everyone could think and act by himself, speak his own language, have his own emotions and follow his own passions. No longer chained to competitive efficiency, the self could grow in the realm of satisfaction. Man could come into his own in his passions. The objects of his desires would be the less exchangeable the more they were seized and shaped by his free self.

(Marcuse 1998, 64)

Technology and science would have to be reconstructed in accordance with a new sensibility and new ethical and aesthetical dimensions (Feenberg 2001), where the real material and intellectual needs could be established.

Technique would then tend to become art, and art would tend to form reality: the opposition between imagination and reason, higher and lower faculties, poetic and scientific thought, would be invalidated. Emergence of a new Reality Principle: under which a new sensibility and a desublimated scientific intelligence would combine in the creation of an aesthetic ethos.

(Marcuse 1969, 24)

The technological transformation does not follow an automatic process and is not predetermined, but requires in praxis the human subject and points towards the need for class struggles and revolution.

Bibliography

Abbate, Janet. 1999. *Inventing the Internet*. Cambridge, MA: MIT Press.

Acquisti, Alessandro, and Ralph Gross. 2006. "Imagined Communities: Awareness, Information Sharing, and Privacy on the Facebook". In *Proceedings of 6th Workshop on Privacy Enhancing Technologies*, edited by Phillipe Golle and George Danezis, 36–58. Cambridge: Robinson College.

Adorno, Theodor. 1976a. "Sociology and Empirical Research". In *The Positivist Dispute in German Sociology*, edited by Theodor Adorno, Hans Albert, Ralf Dahrendorf, Jürgen Habermas, Harald Pilot and Karl Popper, 68–86. London: Heinemann Educational Books.

———. 1976b. "Introduction". In *The Positivist Dispute in German Sociology*, edited by Theodor Adorno, Hans Albert, Ralf Dahrendorf, Jürgen Habermas, Harald Pilot and Karl Popper, 1–67. London: Heinemann Educational Books.

Adorno, Theodor, and Max Horkheimer. 2002. *Dialectic of Enlightenment: Philosophical Fragments*. Stanford, CA: Stanford University Press.

Agre, Philip. 1997. "Introduction". In *Technology and Privacy: The New Landscape*, edited by Philip Agre and Marc Rotenberg, 1–28. Cambridge, MA: MIT Press.

Albrechtslund, Anders. 2008. "Online Social Networking as Participatory Surveillance". *First Monday* 13(3). http://firstmonday.org/htbin/cgiwrap/bin/ojs/index.php/fm/article/view/2142/1949 (accessed 25 April 2013).

———. 2012. "Socializing the City: Location Sharing and Online Social Networking". In *Internet and Surveillance: The Challenges of Web 2.0 and Social Media*, edited by Christian Fuchs, Kees Boersma, Anders Albrechtslund and Marisol Sandoval, 187–197. New York: Routledge.

Alexa Internet. 2011. "Top Sites in Austria". www.alexa.com/topsites/countries/AT (accessed 28 February 2011).

———. 2013. www.alexa.com (accessed 24 January 2014).

Allen, Anita. 1988. *Uneasy Access: Privacy for Women in a Free Society*. Totowa: Rowman & Littlefield.

Allmer, Thomas. 2012a. *Towards a Critical Theory of Surveillance in Informational Capitalism*. Frankfurt am Main: Peter Lang.

———. 2012b. "Research Design and Data Analysis, Presentation, and Interpretation". SNS3 Research Paper No. 12. www.allmer.uti.at/wp-content/uploads/2011/11/SNS3-Research-Paper-No.-12-Research-Design-Data-Analysis-Presentation-and-Interpretation-1-1.pdf (accessed 4 August 2014)..

———. 2014. "(Dis)Like Facebook? Dialectical and Critical Perspectives on Social Media". *Javnost – The Public* 21(2): 39–56.

Allmer, Thomas, Christian Fuchs, Verena Kreilinger and Sebastian Sevignani. 2014. "Social Networking Sites in the Surveillance Society: Critical Perspectives and Empirical Findings". In *Media, Surveillance and Identity: Social Perspectives*, edited by André Jansson and Miyase Christensen, 49–70. New York: Peter Lang.

American Management Association and the ePolicy Institute. 2008. "Electronic Monitoring and Surveillance 2007 Survey". http://press.amanet.org/press-releases/177 (accessed 18 December 2012).

Andrejevic, Mark. 2002. "The Work of Being Watched: Interactive Media and the Exploitation of Self-Disclosure". *Critical Studies in Media Communication* 19(2): 230–248.

——. 2007a. "Surveillance in the Digital Enclosure". *The Communication Review* 10(4): 295–317.

——. 2007b. *iSpy: Surveillance and Power in the Interactive Era*. Lawrence: University Press of Kansas.

——. 2010. "Social Network Exploitation". In *A Networked Self: Identity, Community, and Culture on Social Network Sites*, edited by Zizi Papacharissi, 82–101. New York: Routledge.

——. 2011. "Facebook als Neue Produktionsweise". In *Generation Facebook: über das Leben im Social Net*, edited by Oliver Leistert and Theo Röhle, 31–50. Bielefeld: transcript Verlag.

——. 2012. "Exploitation in the Data Mine". In *Internet and Surveillance: The Challenges of Web 2.0 and Social Media*, edited by Christian Fuchs, Kees Boersma, Anders Albrechtslund and Marisol Sandoval, 71–88. New York: Routledge.

Arvidsson, Adam, and Elanor Colleoni. 2012. "Value in Informational Capitalism and on the Internet". *The Information Society* 28(3): 135–150.

Austrian Federal Ministry for Science and Research. 2012. "Uni:Data – Datawarehouse Hochschulbereich des Bundesministeriums für Wissenschaft und Forschung". http://eportal.bmbwk.gv.at/portal/page?_pageid=93,95229&_dad=portal&_schema=PORTAL& (accessed 5 March 2012).

Babbie, Earl. 2010. *The Practice of Social Research*, 12th edn. Belmont: Wadsworth Cengage Learning.

Ball, Kirstie, and Frank Webster, eds. 2003. *The Intensification of Surveillance: Crime, Terrorism and Warfare in the Information Era*. London: Pluto Press.

Batinic, Bernad, Ulf-Dietrich Reips and Michael Bosnjak, eds. 2002. *Online Social Sciences*. Seattle: Hogrefe & Huber.

Baudrillard, Jean. 2007. *Forget Foucault*. Los Angeles, CA: Semiotext(e).

Beer, David. 2008. "Social Network(Ing) Sites … Revisiting the Story So Far: A Response to danah boyd and Nicole Ellison". *Journal of Computer-Mediated Communication* 13(2): 516–529.

Beer, David, and Roger Burrows. 2007. "Sociology and, of and in Web 2.0: Some Initial Considerations". *Sociological Research Online* 12(5). www.socresonline.org.uk/12/5/17.html (accessed 25 April 2013).

Beniger, James. 1986. *The Control Revolution. Technological and Economic Origins of the Information Society*. Cambridge, MA: Harvard University Press.

Benkler, Yochai. 2006. *The Wealth of Networks: How Social Production Transforms Markets and Freedom*. New Haven, CT: Yale University Press.

Bennett, Colin, and Charles Raab. 2006. *The Governance of Privacy: Policy Instruments in Global Perspective*, 2nd edn. Cambridge, MA: MIT Press.

Berg, Bruce. 2001. *Qualitative Research Methods for the Social Sciences*, 4th edn. Boston, MA: Allyn & Bacon.

Bhaskar, Roy. 1998. *The Possibility of Naturalism: A Philosophical Critique of the Contemporary Human Sciences*, 3rd edn. London: Routledge.

——. 2008. *Dialectic: The Pulse of Freedom*. London: Routledge.

Bloch, Ernst. 1986. *The Principle of Hope*. Cambridge, MA: MIT Press.

Bogard, William. 1996. *The Simulation of Surveillance: Hypercontrol in Telematic Societies*. Cambridge: Cambridge University Press.

——. 2006. "Surveillance Assemblages and Lines of Flight". In *Theorizing Surveillance: The Panopticon and Beyond*, edited by David Lyon, 97–122. Cullompton, Devon: Willan Publishing.

——. 2012. "Simulation and Post-Panopticism". In *Routledge Handbook of Surveillance Studies*, edited by Kirstie Ball, Kevin Haggerty and David Lyon, 30–37. London: Routledge.

Böhm, Steffen, Chris Land, and Armin Beverungen. 2012. "The Value of Marx: Free Labour, Rent and 'Primitive' Accumulation in Facebook: Working Paper". www.academia.edu/1571230/The_Value_of_Marx_Free_Labour_Rent_and_Primitive_Accumulation_in_Facebook (accessed 21 April 2013).

Bok, Sissela. 1983. *Secrets: On the Ethics of Concealment and Revelation*. New York: Pantheon Books.

Bourdieu, Pierre. 1977. *Outline of a Theory of Practice*. Cambridge: Cambridge University Press.

boyd, danah. 2007. "The Significance of Social Software". In *Blogtalks Reloaded: Social Software Research and Cases*, edited by Thomas Burg and Jan Schmidt, 15–30. Norderstedt: Books on Demand.

boyd, danah, and Nicole Ellison. 2007. "Social Network Sites: Definition, History, and Scholarship". *Journal of Computer-Mediated Communication* 13(1): 210–230.

boyd, danah, and Eszter Hargittai. 2010. "Facebook Privacy Settings: Who Cares?" *First Monday* 15(8). Accessed April 25, 2013. http://firstmonday.org/htbin/cgiwrap/bin/ojs/index.php/fm/article/view/3086/2589(accessed 25 April 2013).

Brenner, Viktor. 2002. "Generalizability Issues in Internet-Based Survey Research: Implications for the Internet Addiction Controversy". In *Online Social Sciences*, edited by Bernad Batinic, Ulf-Dietrich Reips, and Michael Bosnjak, 93–114. Seattle: Hogrefe & Huber.

Brookshear, Glenn. 2009. *Computer Science: An Overview*, 10th edn. Boston, MA: Addison-Wesley.

Brown, Felicity. 2006. "Rethinking the Role of Surveillance Studies in the Critical Political Economy of Communication". *International Association for Media and Communication Research (IAMCR) Prize in Memory of Dallas W. Smythe, Cairo, 2006*. www.msu.ac.zw/elearning/material/1330622850Curran and Gurevitch.pdf (accessed 25 April 2013).

Bruns, Axel. 2008. *Blogs, Wikipedia, Second Life, and Beyond: From Production to Produsage*. New York: Peter Lang.

Burston, Jonathan, Nick Dyer-Witheford, and Alison Hearn, eds. 2010. "Digital Labour: Workers, Authors, Citizens". *ephemera: theory and politics in organization* 10(3/4). www.ephemerajournal.org/issue/digital-labour-workers-authors-citizens (accessed 16 April 2013).

Camp, Jean. 1999. "Web Security and Privacy: An American Perspective". *The Information Society* 15(4): 249–256.

Campbell, John, and Matt Carlson. 2002. "Panopticon.Com: Online Surveillance and the Commodification of Privacy". *Journal of Broadcasting and Electronic Media* 46(4): 586–606.

Carratu. 2012. www.carratu.com (accessed 11 November 2012).

Castells, Manuel. 2001. *The Internet Galaxy: Reflections on the Internet, Business, and Society*. Oxford: Oxford University Press.

Christofides, Emily, Amy Muise, and Serge Desmarais. 2009. "Information Disclosure and Control on Facebook: Are They Two Sides of the Same Coin or Two Different Processes?" *CyberPsychology and Behavior* 12(3): 341–345.

Clarke, Roger. 1988. "Information Technology and Dataveillance". *Communications of the ACM* 31(5): 498–512.

——. 1998. "Cyberspace Invades Personal Space: Information Privacy on the Internet". *Telecommunication Journal of Australia* 48(2): 61–67.

——. 1999. "Internet Privacy Concerns Confirm the Case for Intervention". *Communications of the ACM* 42(2): 60–67.

Cohen, Nicole. 2008. "The Valorization of Surveillance: Towards a Political Economy of Facebook". *Democratic Communiqué* 22(1): 5–22.

Cohen, Stanley. 1987. *Visions of Social Control: Crime, Punishment and Classification*, 3rd edn. Cambridge: Polity Press.

Comor, Edward. 2010. "Digital Prosumption and Alienation". *ephemera: theory and politics in organization* 10(3/4): 439–454.

COST. 2012. "Memorandum of Understanding for the Implementation of a European Concerted Research Action Designated as COST Action IS1202: Dynamics of Virtual Work". www3.cost.eu/fileadmin/domain_files/ISCH/Action_IS1202/mou/IS1202-e.pdf (accessed 19 April 2013).

Coté, Mark, and Jennifer Pybus. 2007. "Learning to Immaterial Labour 2.0: MySpace and Social Networks". *ephemera: theory and politics in organization* 7(1): 88–106.

——. 2011. "Learning to Immaterial Labour 2.0: Facebook and Social Networks". In *Cognitive Capitalism, Education and Digital Labor*, edited by Michael Peters and Ergin Bulut. New York: Peter Lang.

Couper, Mick. 2000. "Web Surveys: A Review of Issues and Approaches". *Public Opinion Quarterly* 64(4): 464–494.

DataPortability Project. 2013. www.dataportability.org (accessed 26 March 2013).

Dean, Jodi. 2009. *Democracy and Other Neoliberal Fantasies: Communicative Capitalism and Left Politics*. Durham, NC: Duke University Press.

——. 2012. *The Communist Horizon*. London: Verso.

Debatin, Bernhard, Jennette Lovejoy, Ann-Kathrin Horn, and Brittany Hughes. 2009. "Facebook and Online Privacy: Attitudes, Behaviors, and Unintended Consequences". *Journal of Computer-Mediated Communication* 15(1): 83–108.

DeCew, Judith. 1986. "The Scope of Privacy in Law and Ethics". *Law and Philosophy* 5(2): 145–173.

Deleuze, Gilles. 1992. "Postscript on the Societies of Control". *October* (59): 3–7.

Dijck, José van. 2009. "Users Like You? Theorizing Agency in User-Generated Content". *Media, Culture and Society* 31(1): 41–58.

——. 2013. *The Culture of Connectivity: A Critical History of Social Media*. Oxford: Oxford University Press.

DoubleClick. 2012. www.google.com/doubleclick (accessed 14 December 2012).

Dourish, Paul. 2001. *Where the Action Is: The Foundations of Embodied Interaction*. Cambridge, MA: MIT Press.

Dwyer, Catherine, Starr Hiltz, and Katia Passerini. 2007. "Trust and Privacy Concern within Social Networking Sites: A Comparison of Facebook and MySpace". In *Proceedings of the 13th Americas Conference on Information Systems*. Keystone: Association for Information Systems.

Dwyer, Catherine, Starr Hiltz, Marshall Poole, Julia Gussner, Felicitas Hennig, Sebastian Osswald, Sandra Schliesslberger, and Birgit Warth. 2010. "Developing Reliable Measures of Privacy Management within Social Networking Sites". In *Proceedings of the 43rd Hawaii International Conference on System Sciences*, 2968–2977. Los Alamitos: IEEE Computer Society.

Dyer-Witheford, Nick. 1999. *Cyber-Marx: Cycles and Circuits of Struggle in High-Technology Capitalism*. Urbana: University of Illinois Press.

——. 2001. "Empire, Immaterial Labor, the New Combinations, and the Global Worker". *Rethinking Marxism* 13(3–4): 70–80.

——. 2007. "Commonism". *Turbulence* 1: 81–87. http://turbulence.org.uk/wp-content/uploads/2008/07/turbulence_jrnl.pdf (accessed 23 January 2013).

——. 2009. "The Circulation of the Common: Talk for the 'Future of the Commons' Series, University of Minnesota, October 2009". www.fims.uwo.ca/people/faculty/dyerwitheford/Commons2009.pdf (accessed 23 January 2013).

Eagleton, Terry. 1991. *Ideology: An Introduction*. London: Verso.

Ellison, Nicole, Charles Steinfield, and Cliff Lampe. 2007. "The Benefits of Facebook 'Friends:' Social Capital and College Students' Use of Online Social Network Sites". *Journal of Computer-Mediated Communication* 12(4): 1143–1168.

Elmer, Greg. 1997. "Spaces of Surveillance: Indexicality and Solicitation on the Internet". *Critical Studies in Mass Communication* 14(2): 182–191.

——. 2004. *Profiling Machines: Mapping the Personal Information Economy*. Cambridge, MA: MIT Press.

Ess, Charles. 2009. *Digital Media Ethics*. Cambridge: Polity Press.

Etzioni, Amitai. 1999. *The Limits of Privacy*. New York: Basic Books.

Europe-v-Facebook. 2013. www.europe-v-facebook.org (accessed 20 April 2013).

European Commission. 2012. "Proposal for a Regulation of the European Parliament and of the Council on the Protection of Individuals with Regard to the Processing of Personal Data and on the Free Movement of Such Data (General Data Protection Regulation)". http://ec.europa.eu/justice/data-protection/document/review2012/com_2012_11_en.pdf (accessed 26 March 2013).

European Commission's Directorate General for Economic and Financial Affairs. 2013. "Annual Macro-Economic Database (AMECO)". http://ec.europa.eu/economy_finance/db_indicators/ameco (accessed 2 July 2013).

Facebook. 2012. "Info". www.facebook.com/facebook/info (accessed 5 December 2012).

——. 2013. "Prineville Data Centre". www.facebook.com/prinevilleDataCenter (accessed 16 January 2013).

——. 2015. "Luleå Data Center". www.facebook.com/luleaDataCenter (accessed 15 January 2015).

Federal Institute Statistics Austria. 2011. "IKT-Einsatz in Haushalten 2010". www.statistik.at/web_de/statistiken/informationsgesellschaft/ikt-einsatz_in_haushalten/index.html (accessed 27 March 2012).

Feenberg, Andrew. 1999. *Questioning Technology*. London: Routledge.

——. 2001. "Marcuse and the Aestheticization of Technology". In *New Critical Theory: Essays on Liberation*, edited by William Wilkerson and Jeffrey Paris, 135–154. Lanham, MD: Rowman & Littlefield.

——. 2002. *Transforming Technology: A Critical Theory Revisited*. Oxford: Oxford University Press.

——. 2003. "Heidegger und Marcuse: Zerfall und Rettung der Aufklärung". In *Kritische*

Theorie der Technik und der Natur, edited by Gernot Böhme and Alexandra Manzei, 39–53. Munich: Wilhelm Fink Verlag.

——. 2012. "Introduction: Toward a Critical Theory of the Internet". In *(Re)Inventing the Internet: Critical Case Studies*, edited by Andrew Feenberg and Norm Friesen, 3–18. Rotterdam: Sense Publishers.

Fernback, Jan, and Zizi Papacharissi. 2007. "Online Privacy as Legal Safeguard: The Relationship among Consumer, Online Portal, and Privacy Policies". *New Media and Society* 9(5): 715–734.

Field, Andy. 2009. *Discovering Statistics Using SPSS*, 3rd edn. London: Sage.

Fisher, Eran. 2012. "How Less Alienation Creates More Exploitation? Audience Labour on Social Network Sites". *tripleC* 10(2): 171–183. http://triple-c.at/index.php/tripleC/article/view/392/357 (accessed 16 April 2013).

Fiske, John. 1999. *Media Matters: Race and Gender in U.S. Politics*, 3rd edn. Minneapolis: University of Minnesota Press.

Floridi, Luciano. 1999. "Information Ethics: On the Philosophical Foundations of Computer Ethics". *Ethics and Information Technology* 1(1): 37–56.

——. 2005. "The Ontological Interpretation of Informational Privacy". *Ethics and Information Technology* 7(4): 185–200.

Fogel, Joshua, and Elham Nehmad. 2009. "Internet Social Network Communities: Risk Taking, Trust, and Privacy Concerns". *Computers in Human Behavior* 25(1): 153–160.

Forbes. 2013. "Lists". www.forbes.com/lists (accessed 1 June 2013).

Foucault, Michel. 1995. *Discipline and Punish: The Birth of the Prison*, 2nd edn. New York: Vintage Books.

——. 2002. "The Eye of Power: A Conversation with Jean-Pierre Barou and Michelle Perrot". In *CTRL [Space] Rhetorics of Surveillance from Bentham to Big Brother*, edited by Thomas Levin, Ursula Frohne, and Peter Weibel, 94–101. Karlsruhe: ZKM Center for Art and Media.

——. 2003. *"Society Must Be Defended": Lectures at the Collège De France, 1975–76*. New York: Picador.

——. 2007. *Security, Territory, Population: Lectures at the Collège De France, 1977–1978*. New York: Palgrave Macmillan.

Fried, Charles. 1968. "Privacy". *The Yale Law Journal* 77(3): 475–493.

——. 1990. "Privacy: A Rational Context". In *Computers, Ethics, and Society*, edited by David Ermann, Mary Williams, and Claudio Guitierrez, 50–63. New York: Oxford University Press.

Froomkin, Michael. 2000. "The Death of Privacy?" *Stanford Law Review* 52(5): 1461–1543.

Fuchs, Christian. 2002. *Krise und Kritik in der Informationsgesellschaft: Arbeiten über Herbert Marcuse, Kapitalistische Entwicklung und Selbstorganisation: Soziale Selbstorganisation im Informationsgesellschaftlichen Kapitalismus: Teil 2*. Norderstedt: Libri Books on Demand.

——. 2005. *Emanzipation! Technik und Politik bei Herbert Marcuse*. Aachen: Shaker.

——. 2008. *Internet and Society: Social Theory in the Information Age*. New York: Routledge.

——. 2009a. *Social Networking Sites and the Surveillance Society: A Critical Case Study of the Usage of studiVZ, Facebook, and Myspace by Students in Salzburg in the Context of Electronic Surveillance*. Salzburg: Research Group Unified Theory of Information.

——. 2009b. "Information and Communication Technologies and Society: A Contribution to the Critique of the Political Economy of the Internet". *European Journal of Communication* 24(1): 69–87.

——. 2010a. "Social Software and Web 2.0: Their Sociological Foundations and Implications". In *Handbook of Research on Web 2.0, 3.0, and X.0: Technologies, Business, and Social Applications: Volume II*, edited by San Murugesan, 764–789. Hershey: IGI Global.

——. 2010b. "Social Networking Sites and Complex Technology Assessment". *International Journal of E-Politics* 1(3): 19–38.

——. 2010c. "Class, Knowledge and New Media". *Media, Culture and Society* 32(1): 141–150.

——. 2010d. "studiVZ: Social Networking in the Surveillance Society". *Ethics and Information Technology* 12(2): 171–185.

——. 2010e. "Labor in Informational Capitalism and on the Internet". *The Information Society* 26(3): 179–196.

——. 2011a. "How to Define Surveillance". *MATRIZes* 5(1): 109–133.

——. 2011b. *Foundations of Critical Media and Information Studies*. New York: Routledge.

——. 2011c. "An Alternative View of Privacy on Facebook". *Information* 2: 140–165.

——. 2012a. "With or Without Marx? With or Without Capitalism? A Rejoinder to Adam Arvidsson and Eleanor Colleoni". *tripleC* 10(2): 633–645. www.triple-c.at/index.php/tripleC/article/view/434 (accessed 7 February 2013).

——. 2012b. "Critique of the Political Economy of Web 2.0 Surveillance". In *Internet and Surveillance: The Challenge of Web 2.0 and Social Media*, edited by Christian Fuchs, Kees Boersma, Anders Albrechtslund, and Marisol Sandoval, 31–70. New York: Routledge.

——. 2012c. "Dallas Smythe Today – the Audience Commodity, the Digital Labour Debate, Marxist Political Economy and Critical Theory. Prolegomena to a Digital Labour Theory of Value". *tripleC* 10(2): 692–740. http://triple-c.at/index.php/tripleC/article/view/443/414 (accessed 25 April 2013).

——. 2014. *Digital Labour and Karl Marx*. New York: Routledge.

Fuchs, Christian, and Wolfgang Hofkirchner. 2003. *Studienbuch Informatik Und Gesellschaft*. Norderstedt: Libri Books on Demand.

Fuchs, Christian, and Marisol Sandoval, eds. 2013. *Critique, Social Media and the Information Society*. New York: Routledge.

Fuchs, Christian, and Sebastian Sevignani. 2013. "What Is Digital Labour? What Is Digital Work? What's Their Difference? And Why Do These Questions Matter for Understanding Social Media?" *tripleC: Communication, Capitalism and Critique. Open Access Journal for a Global Sustainable Information Society* 11(2): 237–293. http://triple-c.at/index.php/tripleC/article/view/461/468 (accessed 11 June 2013).

Fuchs, Christian, Kees Boersma, Anders Albrechtslund, and Marisol Sandoval. 2012a. "Introduction: Internet and Surveillance". In *Internet and Surveillance: The Challenges of Web 2.0 and Social Media*, edited by Christian Fuchs, Kees Boersma, Anders Albrechtslund, and Marisol Sandoval, 1–28. New York: Routledge.

——, eds. 2012b. *Internet and Surveillance: The Challenges of Web 2.0 and Social Media*. New York: Routledge.

Fuchs, Christian, Wolfgang Hofkirchner, Matthias Schafranek, Celina Raffl, Marisol Sandoval, and Robert Bichler. 2010. "Theoretical Foundations of the Web: Cognition, Communication, and Co-operation: Towards an Understanding of Web 1.0, 2.0, 3.0". *Future Internet* 2(1): 41–59.

Gandy, Oscar. 2012. "Statistical Surveillance: Remote Sensing in the Digital Age". In *Routledge Handbook of Surveillance Studies*, edited by Kirstie Ball, Kevin Haggerty, and David Lyon, 125–132. London: Routledge.

Gandy, Oscar, Jr. 1993. *The Panoptic Sort: A Political Economy of Personal Information.* Boulder, CO: Westview Press.

——. 2003. "Data Mining and Surveillance in the Post-9/11 Environment". In *The Intensification of Surveillance: Crime, Terrorism and Warfare in the Information Era*, edited by Kirstie Ball and Frank Webster, 26–41. London: Pluto Press.

Garfinkel, Simson. 2000. *Database Nation: The Death of Privacy in the 21st Century.* Beijing: O'Reilly Media.

Gavison, Ruth. 1980. "Privacy and the Limits of Law". *Yale Law Journal* 89(3): 421–471.

Gerety, Tom. 1977. "Redefining Privacy". *Harvard Civil Rights–Civil Liberties Law Review* 12(2): 233–296.

Gerstein, Robert. 1970. "Privacy and Self-Incrimination". *Ethics* 80(2): 87–101.

——. 1978. "Intimacy and Privacy". *Ethics* 89(1): 76–81.

Giddens, Anthony. 1981. *A Contemporary Critique of Historical Materialism: Volume 1: Power, Property and the State.* Berkeley: University of California Press.

——. 1985. *The Nation-State and Violence: Volume Two of a Contemporary Critique of Historical Materialism*, 4th edn. Cambridge: Polity Press.

Gill, Stephen. 2003. "Übermacht und Überwachungsmacht im Globalen Kapitalismus". *Das Argument* (249): 21–33.

Gilliom, John. 2001. *Overseers of the Poor: Surveillance, Resistance, and the Limits of Privacy.* Chicago, IL: University of Chicago Press.

Gillmor, Dan. 2006. *We the Media: Grassroots Journalism by the People, for the People.* Sebastopol: O'Reilly Media.

Google. 2007. "Press Center: Google to Acquire DoubleClick: Combination Will Significantly Expand Opportunities for Advertisers, Agencies and Publishers and Improve Users' Online Experience". www.google.com/intl/en/press/pressrel/doubleclick.html (accessed 14 December 2012).

——. 2008. "Press Center: Google Closes Acquisition of DoubleClick". www.google.com/intl/en/press/pressrel/20080311_doubleclick.html (accessed 14 December 2012).

——. 2013. "Zeitgeist 2012: Search Trends: The World". www.google.com/intl/en-GB/zeitgeist/2012/index.html–the-world (accessed 1 February 2013).

Google Official Blog. 2012. "Google+: Communities and Photos". http://googleblog.blogspot.co.at/2012/12/google-communities-and-photos.html (accessed 15 January 2013).

Gordon, Alan. 2002. "SurveyMonkey.com – Web-Based Survey and Evaluation System". *Internet and Higher Education* 5: 83–87.

Gormley, Ken. 1992. "100 Years of Privacy". *Wisconsin Law Review* (5): 1335–1441.

Gorz, André. 2010. *The Immaterial: Knowledge, Value and Capital.* London: Seagull Books.

Gouldner, Alvin. 1976. *The Dialectic of Ideology and Technology: The Origins, Grammar, and Future of Ideology.* New York: Seabury Press.

Graham, Stephen, and David Murakami Wood. 2003. "Digitizing Surveillance: Categorization, Space, Inequality". *Critical Social Policy* 23(2): 227–248.

Gutting, Gary. 1998. "Foucault, Michel (1926–84)". In *Routledge Encyclopedia of Philosophy. Volume 4*, edited by Edward Craig, 708–713. London: Routledge.

Habermas, Jürgen. 1976a. "A Positivistically Bisected Rationalism". In *The Positivist*

Dispute in German Sociology, edited by Theodor Adorno, Hans Albert, Ralf Dahrendorf, Jürgen Habermas, and Harald Pilot, 198–225. London: Heinemann Educational Books.

———. 1976b. "The Analytical Theory of Science and Dialectics". In *The Positivist Dispute in German Sociology*, edited by Theodor Adorno, Hans Albert, Ralf Dahrendorf, Jürgen Habermas, Harald Pilot, and Karl Popper, 131–162. London: Heinemann Educational Books.

Haggerty, Kevin, and Richard Ericson. 2000. "The Surveillant Assemblage". *British Journal of Sociology* 51(4): 605–622.

Hall, Stuart. 1986. "The Problem of Ideology – Marxism without Guarantees". *Journal of Communication Inquiry* 10(2): 28–44.

Hardt, Michael, and Antonio Negri. 2000. *Empire*, 4th edn. Cambridge, MA: Harvard University Press.

———. 2004. *Multitude: War and Democracy in the Age of Empire*. New York: Penguin Books.

———. 2009. *Commonwealth*. Cambridge, MA: Harvard University Press.

Harvey, David. 2003. *The New Imperialism*. Oxford: Oxford University Press.

———. 2012. *Rebel Cities: From the Right to the City to the Urban Revolution*. London: Verso.

Herkommer, Sebastian. 2004. *Metamorphosen der Ideologie*. Hamburg: VSA.

Hewson, Claire, Dianna Laurent, and Carl Vogel. 1996. "Proper Methodologies for Psychological and Sociological Studies Conducted Via the Internet". *Behavior Research Methods, Instruments, and Computers* 28: 186–191.

Hewson, Martin. 1994. "Surveillance and the Global Political Economy". In *The Global Political Economy of Communication: Hegemony, Telecommunication and the Information Economy*, edited by Edward Comor. Basingstoke: Macmillan.

Hinduja, Sameer, and Justin Patchin. 2008. "Personal Information of Adolescents on the Internet: A Quantitative Content Analysis of MySpace". *Journal of Adolescence* 31(1): 125–146.

Hofkirchner, Wolfgang. 2002. *Projekt eine Welt: Kognition – Kommunikation – Kooperation: Versuch über die Selbstorganisation der Informationsgesellschaft*. Münster: LIT Verlag.

———. 2007. "A Critical Social Systems View of the Internet". *Philosophy of the Social Sciences* 37(4): 471–500.

———. 2009. "Einheit durch Vielfalt in der Vernetzten Welt: ICTs und Ihr Beitrag zur Herstellung der Weltgesellschaft". In *Die Philosophie und die Idee einer Weltgesellschaft*, edited by Domenico Losurdo and Stefano Azzarà, 525–550. Millepiani, Pisa: Congresso Internazionale.

———. 2010. *Twenty Questions About a Unified Theory of Information: A Short Exploration into Information from a Complex Systems View*. Litchfield Park: Emergent Publications.

———. 2013. *Emergent Information: A Unified Theory of Information Framework*. New Jersey: World Scientific Publishing.

Holz, Hans Heinz. 2005. *Weltentwurf und Reflexion*. Stuttgart: Metzler.

Horkheimer, Max. 2002. "Traditional and Critical Theory". In *Critical Theory: Selected Essays*, edited by Max Horkheimer, 188–243. New York: Continuum.

Institute of Network Cultures. 2013. "Unlike Us Reader: Social Media Monopolies and Their Alternatives". http://networkcultures.org/wpmu/portal/publication/unlike-us-reader-social-media-monopolies-and-their-alternatives/ (accessed 19 April 2013).

International Labour Organization. 2013. "Global Wage Report 2012/13: Wages and Equitable Growth". www.ilo.org/wcmsp5/groups/public/--dgreports/--dcomm/--publ/documents/publication/wcms_194843.pdf (accessed 2 June 2013).

Introna, Lucas. 1997. "Privacy and the Computer: Why We Need Privacy in the Information Society". *Metaphilosophy* 28(3): 259–275.

Investor. 2014. "Twitter Reports First Quarter 2014 Results". https://investor.twitterinc.com/releasedetail.cfm?ReleaseID=843245 (accessed 9 January 2015).

Jakobsson, Peter, and Fredrik Stiernstedt. 2010. "Pirates of Silicon Valley: State of Exception and Dispossession in Web 2.0". *First Monday* 15(7). http://firstmonday.org/htbin/cgiwrap/bin/ojs/index.php/fm/article/view/2799/2577(accessed 24 April 2013).

Jenkins, Henry. 2006. *Convergence Culture: Where Old and New Media Collide.* New York: New York University Press.

Jin, Dal Yong. 2013. "The Construction of Platform Imperialism in the Globalization Era". *tripleC* 11(1): 145–172. http://triple-c.at/index.php/tripleC/article/view/458/446 (accessed 4 February 2013).

Johns, Mark, Shing-Ling Chen, and Jon Hall, eds. 2004. *Online Social Research.* New York: Peter Lang.

Johnston, Jerome, and Christopher Walton. 1995. "Reducing Response Effects for Sensitive Questions: A Computer-Assisted Self Interview with Audio". *Social Science Computer Review* 13(3): 304–319.

Kang, Hyunjin, and Matthew McAllister. 2011. "Selling You and Your Clicks: Examining the Audience Commodification of Google". *tripleC* 9(2): 141–153. www.triple-c.at/index.php/tripleC/article/view/255/234 (accessed 11 June 2013).

Kaplan, Andreas, and Michael Haenlein. 2010. "Users of the World, Unite! The Challenges and Opportunities of Social Media". *Business Horizons* 53(1): 59–68.

Kennedy, Robert. 2004. "Weblogs, Social Software, and New Interactivity on the Web". *Psychiatric Services* 55(3): 247–249.

Klobas, Jane. 2006. *Wikis: Tools for Information Work and Collaboration.* Oxford: Chandos Publishing.

Kolbitsch, Josef, and Hermann Maurer. 2006. "The Transformation of the Web: How Emerging Communities Shape the Information We Consume". *Journal of Universal Computer Science* 12(2): 187–213.

Kollock, Peter, and Marc Smith. 1999. "Communities in Cyberspace". In *Communities in Cyberspace*, edited by Marc Smith and Peter Kollock, 3–24. London: Routledge.

Koskela, Hille. 2004. "Webcams, TV Shows and Mobile Phones: Empowering Exhibitionism". *Surveillance and Society* 2(2/3): 199–215.

———. 2006. "'The Other Side of Surveillance': Webcams, Power and Agency". In *Theorizing Surveillance: The Panopticon and Beyond*, edited by David Lyon, 163–181. Cullompton, Devon: Willian Publishing.

Krippendorff, Klaus. 2004. *Content Analysis: An Introduction to Its Methodology*, 2nd edn. Thousand Oaks, CA: Sage.

Kroll. 2012. www.kroll.com (accessed 22 November 2012).

Krysmanski, Hans-Jürgen. 1990. "Produktionsverhältnisse". In *Europäische Enzyklopädie zu Philosophie und Wissenschaften. Band 3*, edited by Hans Jörg Sandkühler, 894–906. Hamburg: Felix Meiner.

Kurrer, Karl-Eugen. 1990. "Technik". In *Europäische Enzyklopädie zu Philosophie und Wissenschaften. Band 4*, edited by Hans Jörg Sandkühler, 534–550. Hamburg: Felix Meiner.

Lange, Hellmuth. 1990. "Technikphilosophie". In *Europäische Enzyklopädie zu Philosophie und Wissenschaften. Band 4*, edited by Hans Jörg Sandkühler, 550–560. Hamburg: Felix Meiner.

Laningham, Scott. 2006. "developerWorks Interviews: Tim Berners-Lee: Transcript of a developerWorks Podcast Interview between developerWorks Podcast Editor Scott Laningham and Tim Berners-Lee". www.ibm.com/developerworks/podcast/dwi/cm-int 082206txt.html (accessed 25 April 2013).

Le Monde diplomatique. 2003. *L'Atlas du Monde diplomatique*. Paris: Le Monde diplomatique.

Leisewitz, André. 1990. "Produktivkräfte". In *Europäische Enzyklopädie zu Philosophie und Wissenschaften. Band 3*, edited by Hans Jörg Sandkühler, 914–945. Hamburg: Felix Meiner.

Lessig, Lawrence. 2006. *Code: Version 2.0*. New York: Basic Books.

Lévy, Pierre. 1997. *Collective Intelligence: Mankind's Emerging World in Cyberspace*. Cambridge: Perseus Books.

Lewis, Kevin, Jason Kaufman, and Nicholas Christakis. 2008. "The Taste for Privacy: An Analysis of College Student Privacy Settings in an Online Social Network". *Journal of Computer-Mediated Communication* 14(1): 79–100.

Livingstone, Sonia. 2008. "Taking Risky Opportunities in Youthful Content Creation: Teenagers' Use of Social Networking Sites for Intimacy, Privacy and Self-Expression". *New Media and Society* 10(3): 393–411.

Lovink, Geert, and Miriam Rasch, eds. 2013. *Unlike Us Reader: Social Media Monopolies and Their Alternatives (Institute of Network Cultures Reader #8)*. Amsterdam: Institute of Network Cultures.

Lukács, Georg. 1971. *History and Class Consiousness: Studies in Marxist Dialectics*. London: Merlin Press.

Lyon, David. 1994. *The Electronic Eye: The Rise of Surveillance Society*. Minneapolis: University of Minnesota Press.

——. 1998. "The World Wide Web of Surveillance: The Internet and Off-World Power-Flows". *Information, Communication and Society* 1(1): 91–105.

——. 2001. *Surveillance Society: Monitoring Everyday Life: Issues in Society*. Maidenhead: Open University Press.

——. 2003a. "Surveillance Technology and Surveillance Society". In *Modernity and Technology*, edited by Thomas Misa, Philip Brey, and Andrew Feenberg, 161–184. Cambridge, MA: MIT Press.

——. 2003b. "Cyberspace, Surveillance, and Social Control: The Hidden Face of the Internet in Asia". In *Asia.Com: Asia Encounters the Internet*, edited by K.C. Ho, Randolph Kluver, and Kenneth Yang, 67–82. London: Routledge.

——. 2003c. *Surveillance after September 11*. Cambridge: Polity Press.

——. 2007a. "Resisting Surveillance". In *The Surveillance Studies Reader*, edited by Sean Hier and Joshua Greenberg, 368–377. Maidenhead: Open University Press.

——. 2007b. *Surveillance Studies: An Overview*. Cambridge: Polity Press.

Macpherson, Crawford. 1990. *The Political Theory of Possessive Individualism: Hobbes to Locke*, 13th edn. Oxford: Oxford University Press.

Mandiberg, Michael. 2012. "Introduction". In *The Social Media Reader*, edited by Michael Mandiberg, 1–12. New York: New York University Press.

Marcuse, Herbert. 1955. *Reason and Revolution: Hegel and the Rise of Social Theory*, 2nd edn. London: Routledge & Kegan Paul.

——. 1965. "Repressive Tolerance". In *A Critique of Pure Tolerance*, edited by Robert Paul Wolff, Barrington Moore, Jr., and Herbert Marcuse, 81–117. Boston, MA: Beacon Press.

——. 1969. *An Essay on Liberation*. Boston, MA: Beacon Press.

——. 1972. *One Dimensional Man*. London: Abacus.

——. 1988. "Philosophy and Critical Theory". In *Negations: Essays in Critical Theory*, edited by Herbert Marcuse, 134–158. London: Free Association Books.

——. 1998. "Some Social Implications of Modern Technology (1941)". In *Technology, War and Fascism: Collected Papers of Herbert Marcuse: Volume One*, edited by Douglas Kellner, 39–66. London: Routledge.

——. 2001. "The Problem of Social Change in the Technological Society (1961)". In *Towards a Critical Theory of Society: Collected Papers of Herbert Marcuse: Volume Two*, edited by Douglas Kellner, 35–58. London: Routledge.

Marx, Gary. 1988. *Undercover: Police Surveillance in America*. Berkeley: University of California Press.

——. 2002. "What's New About the 'New Surveillance'? Classifying for Change and Continuity". *Surveillance and Society* 1(1): 8–29.

Marx, Karl. 1951. "Preface to a Contribution to the Critique of Political Economy". In *Karl Marx and Frederick Engels: Selected Works in Two Volumes: Volume 1*, edited by Marx-Engels-Lenin Institute, 327–331. Moscow: Foreign Languages.

——. 1973. *Grundrisse: Foundations of the Critique of Political Economy*. London: Penguin Books.

——. 1976. *Capital: A Critique of Political Economy: Volume One*. London: Penguin Books.

——. 1982. "Zur Kritik der Politischen Ökonomie (Vorarbeiten)". In *Marx/Engels Gesamtausgabe: Abteilung II, Band 3, Teil 6*, edited by Institut Für Marxismus-Leninismus. Berlin: Dietz Verlag.

——. 1986. "Introduction to a Contribution to the Critique of Political Economy". In *Karl Marx and Frederick Engels: Collected Works: Volume 28*, edited by Institute of Marxism-Leninism, 17–48. New York: International Publishers.

——. 1991. *Capital: A Critique of Political Economy: Volume Three*. London: Penguin Books.

——. 1992. *Capital: A Critique of Political Economy: Volume Two*. London: Penguin Books.

——. 1997a. "Draft of an Article on Friedrich List's Book: Das nationale System der Politischen Ökonomie". www.marxists.org/archive/marx/works/1845/03/list.htm (accessed 31 July 2012).

——. 1997b. "Grundrisse: Foundations of the Critique of Political Economy". www.marxists.org/archive/marx/works/1857/grundrisse/index.htm (accessed 26 April 2013).

——. 2000a. "Towards a Critique of Hegel's Philosophy of Right: Introduction". In *Karl Marx: Selected Writings*, 2nd edn, edited by David McLellan, 71–82. New York: Oxford University Press.

——. 2000b. "The Poverty of Philosophy". In *Karl Marx: Selected Writings*, 2nd edn, edited by David McLellan, 212–233. New York: Oxford University Press.

Marx, Karl, and Friedrich Engels. 1998. *The German Ideology*. Amherst: Prometheus Books.

Mathiesen, Thomas. 1997. "The Viewer Society: Michel Foucault's 'Panopticon' Revisited". *Theoretical Criminology* 1(2): 215–234.

McChesney, Robert. 2013. *Digital Disconnect: How Capitalism Is Turning the Internet against Democracy*. New York: The New Press.

McGuigan, Lee, and Vincent Manzerolle (eds). 2013. *The Audience Commodity in a Digital Era: Revisiting a Critical Theory of Commercial Media*. New York: Peter Lang.

Miller, Arthur. 1971. *The Assault on Privacy: Computers, Data Banks, and Dossiers*. Ann Arbor: University of Michigan Press.

Miller, Seumas, and John Weckert. 2000. "Privacy, the Workplace and the Internet". *Journal of Business Ethics* 28(3): 255–265.

Moglen, Eben. 2003. "The dotCommunist Manifesto". http://emoglen.law.columbia.edu/publications/dcm.pdf (accessed 16 January 2013).

———. 2010. "Transcript of Freedom in the Cloud: Software Freedom, Privacy, and Security for Web 2.0 and Cloud Computing: A Speech Given by Eben Moglen at a Meeting of the Internet Society's New York Branch on Februar 5, 2010". www.softwarefreedom.org/events/2010/isoc-ny/FreedomInTheCloud-transcript.html (accessed 16 January 2013).

Moor, James. 1997. "Towards a Theory of Privacy in the Information Age". *Computers and Society* 27(3): 27–32.

Murakami Wood, David. 2003. "Editorial. Foucault and Panopticism Revisited". *Surveillance and Society* 1(3): 234–239.

Murdock, Graham. 2000. "Culture, Communications and Political Economy". In *Mass Media and Society*, edited by James Curran and Michael Gurevitch, 70–92. London: Arnold Hodder.

———. 2012. "Cultural Studies and Cultural Economy". *Study and Exploration* 1(1): 124–126.

———. 2013. "Communication in Common". *International Journal of Communication* 7: 154–172.

Murdock, Graham, and Peter Golding. 1997. "For a Political Economy of Mass Communication". In *The Political Economy of the Media: Volume I*, edited by Graham Murdock and Peter Golding, 3–32. Cheltenham: Edward Elgar.

Murphy, Brian Martin. 2002. "A Critical History of the Internet". In *Critical Perspectives on the Internet*, edited by Greg Elmer, 27–45. Lanham, MD: Rowman & Littlefield.

Murphy, Robert. 1964. "Social Distance and the Veil". *American Anthropologist* 66(6): 1257–1274.

Naughton, John. 2001. *A Brief History of the Future: The Origins of the Internet*, 3rd edn. London: Phoenix.

Negt, Oskar, and Alexander Kluge. 1993. *Public Sphere and Experience: Toward an Analysis of the Bourgeois and Proletarian Public Sphere*. Minneapolis: University of Minnesota Press.

Neocleous, Mark. 2002. "Privacy, Secrecy, Idiocy". *Social Research* 69(1): 85–110.

Nissenbaum, Helen. 2010. *Privacy in Context: Technology, Policy, and the Integrity of Social Life*. Stanford, CA: Stanford Law Books.

Norris, Clive. 2012. "Accounting for the Global Growth of CCTV". In *Routledge Handbook of Surveillance Studies*, edited by Kirstie Ball, Kevin Haggerty, and David Lyon, 251–258. London: Routledge.

Norris, Clive, and Gary Armstrong. 1998. "Introduction: Power and Vision". In *Surveillance, Closed Circuit Television and Social Control*, edited by Clive Norris, Jade Moran, and Gary Armstrong, 3–18. Aldershot: Ashgate.

———. 1999. *The Maximum Surveillance Society: The Rise of CCTV*. Oxford: Berg.

O'Reilly, Tim. 2005a. "What Is Web 2.0: Design Patterns and Business Models for the Next Generation of Software". http://oreilly.com/pub/a/web2/archive/what-is-web-20.html?page= (accessed 25 April 2013).

———. 2005b. "Web 2.0: Compact Definition?". http://radar.oreilly.com/2005/10/web-20-compact-definition.html (accessed 25 April 2013).

O'Reilly, Tim, and John Battelle. 2009. "Web Squared: Web 2.0 Five Years On". www. web2summit.com/web2009/public/schedule/detail/10194 (accessed 25 April 2013).

Ogura, Toshimaru. 2006. "Electronic Government and Surveillance-Oriented Society". In *Theorizing Surveillance: The Panopticon and Beyond*, edited by David Lyon, 270–295. Portland, OR: Willan.

Organisation for Economic Co-Operation and Development (OECD). 2007. *Participative Web and User-Created Content: Web 2.0, Wikis, and Social Networking*. Paris: Organisation for Economic Co-operation and Development.

Orwell, George. 2004. *Nineteen Eighty-Four*. Fairfield: 1st World Library.

PageData. 2013. "Top Pages". http://pagedata.appdata.com (accessed 30 January 2013)..

Parent, William. 1983a. "Privacy, Morality, and the Law". *Philosophy and Public Affairs* 12(4): 269–288.

——. 1983b. "A New Definition of Privacy for the Law". *Law and Philosophy* 2(3): 305–338.

Parenti, Christian. 2003. *The Soft Cage: Surveillance in America: From Slavery to the War on Terror*. New York: Basic Books.

Perrow, Charles. 1999. *Normal Accidents: Living with High Risk Technologies*. Princeton, NJ: Princeton University Press.

Peters, Michael, and Ergin Bulut, eds. 2011. *Cognitive Capitalism, Education and Digital Labor*. New York: Peter Lang.

Petersen, Søren Mørk. 2008. "Loser Generated Content: From Participation to Exploitation". *First Monday* 13(3). http://firstmonday.org/htbin/cgiwrap/bin/ojs/index.php/fm/article/view/2141/1948 (accessed 25 April 2013).

Posner, Richard. 1978. "An Economic Theory of Privacy". *Regulations* (May–June): 19–26.

——. 1981. "The Economics of Privacy". *The American Economic Review* 71(2): 405–409.

Poster, Mark. 1990. *The Mode of Information: Poststructuralism and Social Context*. Cambridge: Polity Press.

Proffitt, Jennifer, Hamid Ekbia, and Stephen McDowell, eds. 2015. "Monetization of User-Generated Content – Marx Revisited". *The Information Society* 31(1).

Prosser, William. 1960. "Privacy". *California Law Review* 48(3): 383–423.

Pryor, Benjamin. 2006. "Foucault, Michel (1926–1984)". In *Encyclopedia of Philosophy. Volume 3*, 2nd edn, edited by Donald Borchert, 698–702. Detroit: Thomson Gale.

Quantcast. 2013. www.quantcast.com (accessed 21 May 2013).

Rachels, James. 1975. "Why Privacy Is Important". *Philosophy and Public Affairs* 4(4): 323–333.

Raffl, Celina, Wolfgang Hofkirchner, Christian Fuchs, and Matthias Schafranek. 2008. "The Web as Techno-Social System: The Emergence of Web 3.0". In *Cybernetics and Systems 2008*, edited by Robert Trappl, 604–609. Vienna: Austrian Society for Cybernetic Studies.

Reiman, Jeffrey. 1976. "Privacy, Intimacy, and Personhood". *Philosophy and Public Affairs* 6(1): 26–44.

Rey, P.J. 2012. "Alienation, Exploitation, and Social Media". *American Behavioral Scientist* 56(4): 399–420.

Robins, Kevin, and Frank Webster. 1999. *Times of Technoculture: From the Information Society to the Virtual Life*. London: Routledge.

Rule, James. 1973. *Private Lives and Public Surveillance: Social Control in the Computer Age*. New York: Schocken Books.

———. 2007. *Privacy in Peril. How We Are Sacrificing a Fundamental Right in Exchange for Security and Convenience*. Oxford: Oxford University Press.

———. 2012. "'Needs' for Surveillance and the Movement to Protect Privacy". In *Routledge Handbook of Surveillance Studies*, edited by Kirstie Ball, Kevin Haggerty, and David Lyon, 64–71. London: Routledge.

Sandoval, Marisol. 2012. "A Critical Empirical Case Study of Consumer Surveillance on Web 2.0". In *Internet and Surveillance: The Challenge of Web 2.0 and Social Media*, edited by Christian Fuchs, Kees Boersma, Anders Albrechtslund, and Marisol Sandoval, 147–169. New York: Routledge.

———. 2014. *From Corporate to Social Media: Critical Perspectives on Corporate Social Responsibility in Media and Communication Industries*. London: Routledge.

Sandoval, Marisol, and Christian Fuchs. 2010. "Towards a Critical Theory of Alternative Media". *Telematics and Informatics* 27(2): 141–150.

Sandoval, Marisol, Christian Fuchs, Jernej Prodnik, Sebastian Sevignani, and Thomas Allmer, eds. 2014. "Special Issue: Philosophers of the World Unite! Theorizing Digital Labour and Virtual Work: Definitions, Forms and Transformations". *tripleC: Communication, Capitalism and Critique. Open Access Journal for a Global Sustainable Information Society* 12(2).

Saveri, Andrea, Howard Rheingold, and Kathi Vian. 2008. "Technologies of Cooperation: A Socio-Technical Framework for Robust 4G". *IEEE Technology and Society Magazine* 27(2): 11–23.

Scanlon, Thomas. 1975. "Thomson on Privacy". *Philosophy and Public Affairs* 4(4): 315–322.

Schmidt, Jan. 2006. "Social Software: Facilitating Information-, Identity- and Relationship Management". In *Blogtalks Reloaded: Social Software – Research and Cases*, edited by Thomas Burg and Jan Schmidt, 31–49. Norderstedt: Books on Demand.

Schmidt, William. 1997. "World-Wide Web Survey Research: Benefits, Potential Problems, and Solutions". *Behavior Research Methods Instruments and Computers* 29(2): 274–279.

Schoeman, Ferdinand. 1984. *Philosophical Dimensions of Privacy: An Anthology*. Cambridge: Cambridge University Press.

———. 1992. *Privacy and Social Freedom*. Cambridge: Cambridge University Press.

Scholz, Trebor. 2008. "Market Ideology and the Myths of Web 2.0". *First Monday* 13(3). http://firstmonday.org/htbin/cgiwrap/bin/ojs/index.php/fm/article/view/2138/1945 (accessed 25 April 2013).

———, ed. 2013. *Digital Labor: The Internet as Playground and Factory*. New York: Routledge.

Searle, Rosalind. 2006. "New Technology: The Potential Impact of Surveillance Techniques in Recruitment Practices". *Personal Review* 35(3): 336–351.

Securities and Exchange Commission. 2012. "Form 10-K: Annual Report of Apple Inc. For the Fiscal Year Ended September 29, 2012". www.sec.gov/Archives/edgar/data/320193/000119312512444068/d411355d10k.htm (accessed 1 June 2013).

———. 2013. "Form 10-K: Annual Report of Facebook Inc. For the Fiscal Year Ended December 31, 2012". www.sec.gov/Archives/edgar/data/1326801/000132680113000003/fb-12312012x10k.htm (accessed 31 December 2012).

Sevignani, Sebastian. 2009. "Ideologie – Kulturindustrie und Hegemonie". Masters thesis, University of Salzburg.

———. 2012. "The Problem of Privacy in Capitalism and the Alternative Social Networking Site Diaspora*". *tripleC* 10(2): 600–617.

Sewell, Graham. 2012. "Organization, Employees and Surveillance". In *Routledge Handbook of Surveillance Studies*, edited by Kirstie Ball, Kevin Haggerty, and David Lyon, 303–312. London: Routledge.

Sewell, Graham, and Barry Wilkinson. 1992. "'Someone to Watch over Me': Surveillance, Discipline and the Just-in-Time Labour Process". *Sociology* 26(2): 271–289.

Shils, Edward. 1966. "Privacy: Its Constitution and Vicissitudes". *Law and Contemporary Problems* 31(2): 281–306.

Shirky, Clay. 2003. "Social Software and the Politics of Groups". http://shirky.com/writings/group_politics.html (accessed 25 April 2013).

———. 2008. *Here Comes Everybody: The Power of Organizing without Organizations.* London: Penguin Books.

Sills, Stephen, and Chunyan Song. 2002. "Innovations in Survey Research: An Application of Web-Based Surveys". *Social Science Computer Review* 20(1): 22–30.

Smythe, Dallas. 2006. "On the Audience Commodity and Its Work". In *Media and Cultural Studies: Keyworks*, 2nd edn, edited by Meenakshi Gigi Durham and Douglas Kellner, 230–256. Oxford: Blackwell.

Solove, Daniel. 2002. "Conceptualizing Privacy". *California Law Review* 90(4): 1087–1155.

———. 2004. *The Digital Person: Technology and Privacy in the Information Age.* New York: New York University Press.

———. 2006. "A Taxonomy of Privacy". *University of Pennsylvania Law Review* 154(3): 477–564.

Spinello, Richard. 2003. *Cyberethics: Morality and Law in Cyberspace*, 2nd edn. Sudbury: Jones & Bartlett.

Stalder, Felix, and Christine Mayer. 2009. "The Second Index: Search Engines, Personalization and Surveillance". In *Deep Search: The Politics of Search Beyond Google*, edited by Konrad Becker and Felix Stalder, 98–116. Innsbruck: Studienverlag.

Stalin, Joseph. 2000. "Marxism and Problems of Linguistics". www.marxists.org/reference/archive/stalin/works/1950/jun/20.htm (accessed 24 April 2012).

Stallman, Richard. 2012. "Facebook". http://stallman.org/facebook.html (accessed 2 February 2013).

Statistical Office of the European Union. 2012. "Eurostat". http://epp.eurostat.ec.europa.eu/portal/page/portal/eurostat/home (accessed 28 March 2012).

Tapscott, Don, and Anthony Williams. 2006. *Wikinomics: How Mass Collaboration Changes Everything.* New York: Portfolio.

Tavani, Herman. 2007. "Philosophical Theories of Privacy: Implications for an Adequate Online Privacy Policy". *Metaphilosophy* 38(1): 1–22.

———. 2008. "Informational Privacy: Concepts, Theories, and Controversies". In *The Handbook of Information and Computer Ethics*, edited by Kenneth Himma and Herman Tavani, 131–164. Hoboken: Wiley.

———. 2011. *Ethics and Technology: Controversies, Questions, and Strategies for Ethical Computing*, 3rd edn. Hoboken: John Wiley & Sons.

TechCrunch. 2012. "Facebook Announces Monthly Active Users Were at 1.01 Billion as of September 30th, an Increase of 26% Year-over-Year". http://techcrunch.com/2012/10/23/facebook-announces-monthly-active-users-were-at-1-01-billion-as-of-september-30th/ (accessed 20 April 2013).

Terranova, Tiziana. 2004. *Network Culture: Politics for the Information Age.* London: Pluto Press.

The Information Society. 2013. "CFP: Monetization of User-Generated Content – Marx Revisited". www.indiana.edu/~tisj/cfp_marx_revisited.pdf (accessed 21 April 2013).

The Washington Post. 2013. "U.S., British Intelligence Mining Data from Nine U.S. Internet Companies in Broad Secret Program". www.washingtonpost.com/investigations/us-intelligence-mining-data-from-nine-us-internet-companies-in-broad-secret-program/2013/06/06/3a0c0da8-cebf-11e2-8845-d970ccb04497_story.html (accessed 16 July 2013).

TNS Opinion & Social. 2011. Special Eurobarometer Report on Attitudes on Data Protection and Electronic Identity in the European Union: Conducted by TNS Opinion & Social at the Request of Directorate-General Justice, Information Society & Media and Joint Research Centre of the European Commission. Brussels.

TorrentFreak. 2012. "Pirate Bay Censorship Backfires as New Proxies Bloom". http://torrentfreak.com/pirate-bay-censorship-backfires-as-new-proxies-bloom-121222(accessed 27 March 2013).

tripleC. 2013. "Announcements". http://triple-c.at/index.php/tripleC/announcement (accessed 21 May 2013).

Turchetto, Maria. 2008. "From 'Mass Worker' to 'Empire': The Disconcerting Trajectory of Italian Operaismo". In *Critical Companion to Contemporary Marxism: Historical Materialism Book Series: Volume 16*, edited by Jacques Bidet and Stathis Kouvelakis, 285–308. Leiden: Brill.

Turow, Joseph. 2005. "Audience Construction and Culture Production: Marketing Surveillance in the Digital Age". *The ANNALS of the American Academy of Political and Social Science* 597(1): 103–121.

———. 2006. "Cracking the Consumer Code: Advertising, Anxiety and Surveillance in the Digital Age". In *The New Politics of Surveillance and Visibility*, edited by Kevin Hagerty and Richard Ericson, 279–307. Toronto: University of Toronto Press.

Tuten, Tracy, David Urban, and Michael Bosnjak. 2002. "Internet Surveys and Data Quality: A Review". In *Online Social Sciences*, edited by Bernad Batinic, Ulf-Dietrich Reips, and Michael Bosnjak, 7–26. Seattle: Hogrefe & Huber.

UNESCO Institute for Statistics. 2012. "ISCED: International Standard Classification of Education". www.uis.unesco.org/Education/Pages/international-standard-classification-of-education.aspx (accessed 12 April 2012).

Unibrennt. 2013. www.unibrennt.at (accessed 22 April 2013).

Warren, Samuel, and Louis Brandeis. 1890. "The Right to Privacy" *Harvard Law Review* 4(5): 193–220.

Webster, Frank, and Kevin Robins. 1993. "'I'll Be Watching You': Comment on Sewell and Wilkinson". *Sociology* 27(2): 243–252.

Westin, Alan. 1967. *Privacy and Freedom*. New York: Atheneum.

———. 2003. "Social and Political Dimensions of Privacy". *Journal of Social Issues* 59(2): 431–453.

Wikimedia Commons. 2013a. "P2P-Network". http://commons.wikimedia.org/wiki/File:P2P-network.svg (accessed 15 July 2013).

———. 2013b. "Server-Based-Network". http://commons.wikimedia.org/wiki/File:Server-based-network.svg (accessed 15 July 2013).

Williams, Raymond. 2005a. "Base and Superstructure in Marxist Cultural Theory". In *Culture and Materialism: Selected Essays*, edited by Raymond Williams, 31–49. London: Verso.

———. 2005b. "Means of Communication as Means of Production". In *Culture and Materialism: Selected Essays*, edited by Raymond Williams, 55–66. London: Verso.

Winseck, Dwayne. 2003. "Netscapes of Power: Convergence, Network Design, Walled Gardens, and Other Strategies of Control in the Information Age". In *Surveillance as*

Social Sorting: Privacy, Risk, and Digital Discrimination, edited by David Lyon, 176–198. London: Routledge.

Wright, Steve. 2002. *Storming Heaven: Class Composition and Struggle in Italian Autonomist Marxism*. London: Pluto Press.

YouTube. 2013. "Charts". www.youtube.com/charts/videos_views?t=a (accessed 30 January 2013).

Zhang, Yin. 2000. "Using the Internet for Survey Research: A Case Study". *Journal of the American Society for Information Science* 51(1): 57–68.

Zuboff, Shoshana. 1988. *In the Age of the Smart Machine: The Future of Work and Power*. Oxford: Heinemann Professional Publishing.

¡Democracia real YA! 2013. "Manifesto (English)". www.democraciarealya.es/manifiesto-comun/manifesto-english/ (accessed 21 June 2013).

μTorrent. 2013. www.utorrent.com/ (accessed 26 March 2013).

Index

Page numbers in *italics* denote tables, those in **bold** denote figures.